Dear Customer:

Inside the World of Baristas, Upselling, and the Rules of Serving a Special Cup of Coffee

By

Sean William Brown

TABLE OF CONTENTS

Dedication:

Dear barista, greeter, super glue, coffee server, waiter, waitress, retail worker, sales person, food service worker, bartender, customer service specialist or anyone who ever has to wait on or work for an asshole or a bitch:

<u>This is for you.</u>

PROLOGUE

I have changed literally thousands of garbage bags in my life. I found it slightly amusing when I couldn't peel the top of the garbage bag open. Maybe my hands were too dry or too oily, maybe I just wasn't paying attention until I realized I had been trying to get the bag open for too long. Sometimes a particularly troublesome bag would lead me to imagine I was in a competition to be the best garbage bag opener in the world, or in a race to open the bag because a gun was held to my head. But it would open and I wouldn't think about a garbage bag being troublesome for a very long time.

Now I'm on the clock to not only change the garbage, but to clean the Mix-Ins station. It's not so fucking funny now when I can't get the fucking garbage bag open because people are coming into Caribou and I'm supposed to be on the register and clean the dining room area. It is almost bringing me to tears. That gun to my head wouldn't be so bad now because then at least I wouldn't have to face another rush. Kirsten shoots me a look: *What the fuck are you doing over there?*

I get the bag open as the door chimes again. I want to scream *Yes! I did it! Celebrate with me!* I hear the door chime in my sleep now and feel the panic. My heart races and I feel tense and anxious. I'm always anxious. I was never an anxious person before working at Caribou Coffee. I

I get the garbage out of the can and am now putting the new bag in the can, debating whether I have time to double bag it. I don't. That will come back to haunt me when I change the garbage again and coffee leaks through the bag and drips all over the floor. Then I have to get the mop and the bucket. It will delay another task or customer in some way. This is my life.

The door chimes again.

I race back to the register as Kirsten already has the drinks made and I have to get them into the register and take payment. Somehow Kirsten can remember what each customer orders without using our computer screen. I'm not quite there yet. Or even close, and it is embarrassing.

There aren't that many things to know at Caribou or any coffee shop, but you have to work fast and repetition makes you great. Combine that with basically being on stage, and it is double frustrating. The customers are watching me work and know if I am decent. A coffee shop is one of the few places where customers watch the process. And anything we as Americans watch, we think we know. And therefore we have unrealistic expectations. Which creates pressure for me and makes it an even less desirable job. Being a complete idiot doesn't help matters.

Customers tell me their drink orders with the register in front of me and I still can't remember their orders or how to ring them! I used to be smart, or did I just think I was smart? I can't remember and I laugh inside at the correct way to describe my former smartness in this chaos. Kirsten makes four drinks without looking at the drink screen. As soon as the order leaves the customer's lips it's locked in her head. And each drink is customized. You coffee house lovers might be saying to yourself, "Duh!" But I had no idea. I had never thought about how specific each drink can be.

"Okay what was this one?" I ask the customer.

"A large, moosed, mocha with milk chocolate less chocolate." The customer says way too quick. Oh boy. Okay…a mocha…large…milk chocolate. Relieved, I find the buttons.

"Now what else?"

The customer sighs. "Moosed."

"What?" *What the fuck does Moosed mean?* I scan the register for a picture of moose.

"That means an extra shot of espresso!" Kirsten says reading my mind. *Why don't we fucking just say extra shot of espresso?*

Kirsten can read my mind.

"It's to have fun, Ben! Woo-hoo!" Yes. Fun. We are having fun.

"It was less chocolate, too." I'm about to hit the less chocolate button because it's less chocolate.

"The less chocolate button is the more chocolate button, Ben!" Right. Got it locked and loaded.

I do not have it locked and loaded. I knew I would screw up at Caribou, but after a few days my new mantra was not to screw up twice on the same thing. I have failed at that too. I screw up the same things over and over again. I remember not remembering what 'moosed' means, but I in no way remember that it means an extra shot of espresso. I remember not remembering where the triple berry muffin is located.

Actually, I remember three customers that ordered it and what they were wearing and the day of the week and the weather that day, but I for the life of me can never find the triple berry muffin button.

I feel bad upsetting the customers for being slow, but I shouldn't. Not only do they know I'm struggling, but they don't care. They want their coffee. And they want it now.

I stare at the register and it might as well be in German. Focus! After a few days at the register I should have it down by now. The Caribou register builds the drinks in a certain order, but not alphabetically. Some drinks are on the screen, but if you build them wrong on the register the price can come up wrong for some dumb fucking reason I will never figure out. Mocha with milk chocolate, shot of caramel, whipped cream, Snickers, and caramel drizzle will result in a higher price than just tapping the Turtle Mocha button. And god help you if the price is different than what the customer is expecting.

"It's usually different, but whatever, I guess."

"Uh. It is?"

"Yeah. You must not be very good at math." That really doesn't have anything to do with it, but I realize my error.

"Let me try something here," I say, slowly realizing I built the drink wrong way. (If you really didn't care, why did you tell me?) I delete it out and start over.

"I think you miss hit a button. That price isn't right," another customer notifies me, and I cringe. I cringe a lot. The problem with that is that Kirsten has already started preparing that drink. I have now deleted it. Sometimes the shop is too busy and too loud for her to hear the drinks, so she now has to rely on the screen. And me.

"Hey, what the heck, Ben?!" Kirsten stops. The whole store seems to stop and stare at me. Waiting to see if I fucked up again.

"Ah…Just hold on a sec." I scramble trying to find the right fucking button. Worse, sometimes I have completely entered in the wrong drink. And Kirsten has already started making it. Now when I delete it out and re-build the correct drink I hear the longest, loudest sigh from the end of the bar. Often Kirsten will hear the drink, see I did not enter it correctly, and slam a pitcher of milk down to get my attention. This is really helpful. I flinch too. I was not a flincher before I worked at Caribou Coffee. I imagine having to watching a video of myself and it would be torture.

The memo option on the register allows me to type in, slowly, anything to the barista from the register. Sometimes I can't find a flavor shot or some weird extra/add-on the customer wants, so I have to memo it in. Light ice or half a Splenda or add ice to a hot drink are examples. I can think of a hundred television shows or movies where an actor ordered a very complicated drink at a coffee shop. And I laughed! Funny stuff. The problem is if there isn't a button for the request, I have to memo it in. And that takes time. And backs up the line. Requests like four ice cubes, half a packet of anything, light foam, light froth, whole milk with a bit of soy, cinnamon but on the bottom of the cup. Also, when you have an idiot like me I memo in requests that do have a button. And the customer isn't charged properly.

"Why did you memo in almond?" Kirsten screams from the bar. "You're costing me money, Ben!"

I wince. I am doing it in the name of speed of service. I read a book about two prisoners separated by a wall and they would play chess, without a board or pieces, in their minds. They both had to visualize the board, the pieces, and the moves over days and days. But I can't fucking remember where to find the triple berry muffin button! It's not just the register, but also so much more. It's figuring out the drink, with someone in a hurry staring at me in a full coffee shop, plus knowing I have to refill the bakery, plus knowing the coffee is getting low, and then hearing the bell chime as a large group comes in. And no, I can't find the almond flavor button. I did very well on both the ACT and SAT, by the way.

Customers do not help by ordering in the reverse sequence of how I need to build the drink on the register. They will order a large, skim milk, with extra caramel, no whip...but they haven't told me if it's a mocha, a latte, or a Caramel Highrise. Then they say Caramel Highrise and it's the inevitable, "Okay. So a large Caramel Highrise with what kind of milk?" Serenity now!

"Oh and make that iced." Fuck! Fuck! Fuck! The iced option is the second button I needed to press. I delete it, restart, and Kirsten keeps sighing and the line keeps growing.

I had no clue the service industry would be so intense. I am not used to the pace, and until a few days ago, I didn't know the difference between a mocha and a latte. You may not know what a "rush" is because I sure didn't. For whatever reason, stoplights, TV shows, traffic or weather patterns, no one really knows, it gets fucking busy in the service industry at odd times for no reason.

We all know the mornings are going to be busy at a coffee shop. But for no apparent reason at 1:10 p.m. on a Tuesday everyone fucking decides to get a drink at Caribou and 20 people show up at the same time. That's a fucking rush. A rush will usually run its course and you will have another slow period where you can remake coffee, fill up supplies, clean, and basically get ready for that next rush. But sometimes, on the worst of worst days of my life, the rush never ends. And help isn't coming. You have to make people wait. And people don't like to wait.

"Hey, Kev!" Kirsten yells out to a regular from behind the bar.

"I'll have a medium latte, with skim and a half a shot of almond. An oatmeal with half strawberries and half almonds. And a Star Trib."

He walks away without paying.

"Sir!" He comes back.

"A medium latte with which flavor?"

He gives me a look that I think is meant to say don't you know who I am, but I'm just trying to get his drink because I'm worried about telling him I don't think we even have strawberries for the oatmeal.

"He does half a shot of almond, Ben! And I know how to make his oatmeal, just put it in as very berry." Where the fuck is the oatmeal button?

The guy shakes his head in a 'why is this happening to me god' way. Is god punishing him or me, I wonder? Kirsten would later tell me "Kevin is so rich that rules don't apply to him."

"Is that why he orders and walks off?"

"Yeah, his head is thinking about different things." *I think he's an asshole and I hate him!*

As I finally get Kevin's order together, his friend joins him. Butting ahead of the growing line.

"Get whatever you want, man." Kevin says to his buddy.

"Just a small coffee." I'm relieved because I know where that button is.

"Are you sure, man? That's it? Get whatever you want."

"You know maybe I will get a hot tea. I'll have a large, uh, what kind of teas do you have?"

"Uh…" I have no fucking idea. Luckily I remember they are in cans on the wall behind me. I do my best Vanna White.

"I'll have a large cinnamon roobios." I stand staring at the register for too long finding the cinnamon roobios button. Every second seems like five minutes. I start sweating. It sucks dying under pressure. Their stares and the growing line are not helping me.

Now, you would think hot teas are easy to make and they are, in the big scheme of things. I foul things up pretty quick, by not putting a coffee clutch, or sleeve, on the cup. I grab two packets of the tea and hold them with my finger as I begin to fill the cup up with 200-degree hot water. My hand can take only so much heat with no clutch. And without a clutch to hold the end of the tea bag the string falls into the water when I pull my finger off for a millisecond because it's so fucking hot.

The bell keeps chiming. Kevin and his buddy are staring me and my hand is red and fucking hurting. On top of all this I ruined the second easiest drink to make besides fucking coffee! I get my wits about me. I grab another large cup, put the clutch on, grab two more bags of tea, tuck it properly, and as I'm pouring the 200 degree water, I vow to never forget a clutch.

As I'm finishing up the order, trying to find the fucking correct tea on the screen, Kevin says something poignant to his friend.

"I couldn't do what they do." His friend nods in agreement.

Oh, you could do this job. Anyone can do this job. If you HAD to.

CHAPTER 1
WHAT FEEDS YOUR SOUL?

Dear customer who orders "expresso":
It is pronounced espresso. I'm not being a dick. I didn't know either until I
started working for Caribou Coffee.

I walk into the Caribou coffee shop as it started to snow outside. I was
expecting a quiet interview with Caribou managers excited someone actually
showed up to the job fair. In actuality I was in a sea of craziness.

"Are you here for the job fair?" Three frantic Human Resources women
stare up at me wild-eyed from a folding table overflowing with paperwork.
The whole store is overflowing with people, jackets, boots, scarves, and an
unemployed vibe. The waiting applicants stare at me like Hitchcock's The
Birds.

"Did you have an appointment?" the lead Human Resources woman
asks me.

"Yes. I'm Ben Thompson."

They look relieved. "More people have showed up than registered. Get
something to drink on us. Just tell them you are here for the job fair. We
will find you when it's your turn. Try to grab a place to sit."

There's no place to sit. Every chair, sofa, ledge, and table is filled with
either glum looking applicants, or Caribou managers interviewing desperate
hopefuls. As I observe and eavesdrop on conversations and interviews, I
can't believe how many people are at this job fair! I had run job fairs myself
and never had this kind of turn out. I was envious. People wanted to work
at Caribou apparently. I try to find the Craigslist ad on my phone,
wondering how many people they were hiring. I wasn't actively looking for
a new job, but I cruised Craigslist, Monster and Career Builder most every

hour. So, actually, I guess you could say I was looking. The Craigslist ad said two store manager openings for the northwest area of the city.

I got my free hot chocolate and instantly thought about leaving. The place was chaos. If they didn't call my name in a few minutes I was out of there.

"Ben Thompson!" I feel the stares from other applicants in the room as I walked to the HR table. My first official Caribou interview was in the corner of the store, knee to knee, on two folding chairs with a HR flunky named Roxanne. I already knew what this interview was. Root out the underqualified and crazy.

"So I see you're with Wal-Mart as a manager. Why do you want to leave Wal-Mart?"

"Because it's Wal-Mart."

She laughs knowingly.

"Wal-Mart is the best place I have ever worked and the worst." I can see she gets what I mean.

"How many hours a week do you work?"

"Anywhere from 55 to 80."

She nods. From here Roxanne brings me to a table with other applicants waiting for the second interview. It is awkward. I think about making chit-chat, and start to wonder if this is part of a secret interview process. Are they watching how we interact? The other five at the table aren't saying a word to each other. I decide to keep silent too. I text my fiancé Gisele I've passed the first round. "You will do great!" She texts back.

Roxanne eventually retrieves me and brings me to a back corner high-top table. "Larry will be here as soon as he's done with another interview." As I sit at the table, other applicants enter the shop. It becomes obvious it was picked because of the huge dining room. I watch the chaos ensue. I haven't been to many Caribous, but I can tell this is big.

As the customers walk in the look on their face is priceless. *What the fuck?* The HR people are quick to surmise if the people are applicants or customers.

Larry arrives wearing an Old Navy sweater, jeans and dress shoes, and he looks exactly like a short Bradley Cooper. Larry tells me about his "Caribou journey" and about how he loves the working for the company. Larry is the district manager of the downtown market and tells me a seemingly rehearsed speech about the challenges of the weekday business crowd.

I realize then that Caribou managers love to talk. I keep asking him questions and he really doesn't interview me. He talks about Caribou. This is completely different than my Wal-Mart interviews, where hiring managers have a list of questions they don't deviate from. I don't think they could comprehend being asked a question. Until it was question time!

"We've only got a short time today and I have to ask you some questions." Larry flips open an interview guide and I'm not worried. I have interview questions down pat with genuine inflections, staged laughs, and little embarrassments about how I learned something. My answers are all set. I am the interview king! I love being interviewed because it's a chance to talk about myself and show off. The interview trend is generally behavior-based answers meant for showing an example of a past behavior. Wal-Mart specifically wanted two-minute answers to each question and they had to comply with SMART, an acronym for situation with metrics, actions, results, and tie-in.

However, the Caribou interview guide was unlike anything I had ever seen.

"What is the food that feeds your soul?" Larry stared at me with the Bradley Cooper smile and glint, his Bradley Cooper canine teeth grinning.

Did he know this was going to throw me off? Did he know I had never been asked this before? Was he enjoying this? Does he think he got me? For the first time in years–maybe ever–I am caught off-guard by an interview question. So I answered honestly with no time for editing or preparation.

"The food that feeds my soul? Interesting. Well I guess my family is what feeds my soul–my fiancé Gisele and my one-year-old son Matt. I would do anything for them and they give me the energy to do everything. Sometimes I don't know why they are so confident in me." I laugh a little. Larry nods and smiles and jots notes.

"What would be the headline of your life right now?"

Ahh…. I think in my head. The only thing worse than a bad answer is no answer.

"Right now, the headline would be, 'My little boy is a biter.' And I don't know what to do about it. I could use some advice." Larry laughs. I've got him. He sets down the pad.

"Are you getting married soon?"

"We don't have a date yet, but someday."

Larry tells me he recently married and peppers me with questions about having a newborn. Eventually he moves on.

"We are doing a round robin interview format and then all of us will share notes tomorrow." He shakes my hand firmly as he leaves. "Great to meet you!"

Roxanne comes back and says I will meet with District Manager Pat when he is done with his other interviews. Roxanne brings me to a different table and it seems this is my competition. Three women and two men are chatting amicably, led by one woman who explains she has been a store manager at Starbucks for 10 years and needs a change. They all wear suits and have briefcases or fancy bags. They ask where I work and I tell them Wal-Mart. Telling strangers you work for Wal-Mart is a dangerous business because people have passionate feelings about Wal-Mart. Usually the passionate people are passionate about hating Wal-Mart. However, none of my co-applicants say anything rude or awkward and I feel like they dismiss me as competition for the job.

As I wait for my interview with Pat I listen to other interviews taking place. I listen to one applicant blank on the "food that feeds your soul" question. Another applicant says the headline of her life is that she is being interviewed right now. I try to answer other questions in my head in case Pat asks me them. "How do you eat an Oreo cookie?" "If you were a superhero who would you be?" "If you could be any tree what tree would you be?" These are the craziest questions!

Roxanne saunters up to our table looking at her clipboard. My fellow applicants and I wait expectedly and I pray it's my name so I don't have to sit at this awkward table in this chaotic environment anymore.

"Ben. Pat is ready for you." I stand up slowly and nod to the table. *So long chumps.*

Pat is in his fifties with sandy-gray hair. He is wearing a North Face vest over a checkered shirt and tan Dockers with black dress shoes. We immediately hit it off. Pat reminds me of my Uncle Don, which means smart, laid back, West Coast articulate, semi-hippie but really hard working. I get Pat talking and he loves to talk. He tells me about how he loves talking coffee with customers and loves hopping behind the counter and making drinks. Pat asks me how I handle upset customers at Wal-Mart. I tell him it is real easy–I make them happy. Pat says a great stress in his life is Caribou employees not re-making drinks that weren't made correctly.

"If they don't want whip, don't spoon off the whip. Re-make the drink." I nod knowingly. I have no idea what he is talking about. Whipped cream on coffee is something I can't wrap my head around at that moment.

"If you could hire anyone in the world, who you know or don't know, who would it be and why?" Pat does not use an interview guide nor writes down any notes. I don't know if this is a Caribou question or a Pat question.

"I would hire my mentor at Wal-Mart. She was really hard working, but had a good time too. She made work productive and fun."

"I like asking that question. There's not a right answer, I just like to see what people say. Some say President Obama, some say their mom, some can't come up with anything."

"The interview questions are different, that's for sure."

"A lot of the questions are kind of silly and really we are just looking for personality. That's it." I file that bit of information away. Pat talks and I listen until Roxanne starts hovering.

"Well, after this cattle call of interviews the other managers and I share our notes. If you are selected for the next phase, one of us will call you this week." Pat explains as he shakes my hand.

Nothing ventured, nothing gained I think as I head home. Gisele and I laugh together as I tell her about the crazy Caribou interview questions.

At 10 a.m. the next morning Pat calls and wants me to do an in-store visit. "This allows you really see what the job is and ask a manager things you might not be comfortable asking me. If you are still interested?"

I arrive at the Caribou at 10 a.m. for my in-store visit and it's quiet at the shop. I think about Wal-Mart at 10 a.m. and it's packed full of shoppers. I could get used to this! The store manager, Anne, is nice and shows me around the operation. She says I can't make a drink, but I can watch. She makes us hot apple blasts and we sample scones. She has three other girls working, so I help unload the bakery order into a large freezer.

"This is nothing," I tell her. "I have to unload entire frozen trucks by myself at Wal-Mart, on the worst of worst days." I could get used to this, I think again.

Anne says something that Pat and Larry mentioned in the interview process, that Caribou managers are expected to "be on the floor" 40% of the time.

"What does that mean?"

"That means you have to be the barista, greeter, or super glue on the schedule."

I have no idea what that means, but I nod. "I'm not one to sit in the office at Wal-Mart, so it shouldn't be a problem." I specifically remember the smile Anne gave at that moment. She didn't tell me what was ahead. I have later interpreted that smile as saying, "I wonder if he'll make it?" crossed with "He has no fucking idea."

Pat arrives as Anne is showing me the employee wall, which has a picture of each employee, their interests, their hobbies and something they decorated. "This creates community and the place that I want to be for employees and customers." I have 250 people that work for me at Wal-Mart and I barely know most of their names and have not met some others.

Pat and I sit and he talks. It's relaxing, it's really fun, and I think this will be a great place to work. Pat talks about opportunity and how Caribou is rapidly going into new markets and opening stores. The sky is the limit for people who want responsibility. Pat explains he is going on vacation for a week, so he will put together an offer this week.

I leave thinking maybe I should give my notice to Wal-Mart today. I decide to wait until I receive an actual offer from Caribou.

I never heard from Pat again.

When I didn't hear from Pat that first week I cut him some slack. He was going on vacation, probably got busy, and I slipped through the cracks. We've all been there in pre-vacation preparation. Then I didn't hear from him for two weeks. Then three weeks. Then a month. Gisele wanted me to call or e-mail him, but I didn't want to be the guy who didn't get a job and then kept calling back. If they didn't want me, they didn't want me. I forget about Caribou.

One day, about a month later, my phone rang from a number I didn't recognize and I let it go to voicemail.

"Hi Ben. My name is Caroline and I am in Human Resources for Caribou Coffee. I know you interviewed with Pat. I want to apologize to you, as Pat is no longer with the company and we are following up with a lot of his loose ends. Again, I'm really sorry I haven't gotten a hold of you earlier." *They like me, they really like me!*

I call back and Caroline sets up an interview with another district manager, Christian. Caroline is apologetic. They seem like an unorganized mess.

But maybe they could be my unorganized mess.

I meet Christian in an inner city Caribou, but the type of inner city that is trendy with the beatniks and yuppies and soccer moms.

I arrive early and I pick him out in the shop in the classic Caribou casual dress code. He is wearing a purple polo shirt, expensive looking jeans, and brown dress shoes. At the job fair none of the Caribou people wore business clothes. I watch him interact with an employee of the store and wait until he is finished. When I introduce myself he doesn't stand up but he does shake my hand. He is quiet. Reserved. But he asks me many of the same questions Larry and Pat did and I get him laughing. The headline of my life? "My baby is a biter! Please post comments on how to stop this!" I'm not saying I dominated the interview because I had already heard the crazy Caribou interview questions before, but I think it has definitely helped.

Christian has three kids and is married. He has graying brown hair and isn't wearing earrings but his ears are pierced with three holes each. He has left a little patch of beard below his bottom lip, a soul patch. He is a hipster and comes off as an aging rebel, but one who has a successful day job. Christian and I talk for over an hour and he asks questions about Wal-Mart and my other various jobs.

"Why do you want to leave Wal-Mart?"

I had worked for Wal-Mart for too long as a manager. I started looking for a new company with a good reputation and nothing really more than that.

I wanted my new company to pass the "family gathering litmus test." Meaning at family gatherings, my new company would spur good and wholesome comments, not Wal-Mart-is-ruining-the-world comments. Caribou would pass the family gathering litmus test. It's the second largest coffee chain in the world and everyone likes it because it isn't Starbucks. The employees are nice and the shop has a cabin-like atmosphere. It's cozy with couches and a fireplace.

Later, Christian told me he had hired me because of one answer. Christian asked me how competitive I was in a scale of one to 10. I said a nine. "I'm competitor but within reason."

"Within reason?"

"Yeah. Some Wal-Mart managers would buy merchandise at their own store and return to other stores on their way home to make sales. There is a line for me."

"Wow."

"But my family is competitive. We compete in ping-pong, putt-putt golf. Actually, my fiancé Gisele was kind of shocked by my family's trash-talking Scrabble games."

Christian told me later, "That's why I hired you. The trash-talking Scrabble games."

Looking back on the whole interview process now, I realize I was always at a Caribou either at night or around 11 a.m., which are two of the quietest times at Caribou. I accepted the job without knowing really what I would be doing. I had no clue what it took to work in a coffee shop, much less what it took to run a coffee shop. I have never figured out if this was planned ignorance on Caribou's part. At the very least, I now know why Christian looks for competitors. The job is so fucking difficult the weak wilt under the immense daily pressure.

CHAPTER 2
COFFEE TALK

Dear customer who orders a Grande Salted Caramel Mocha Frappuccino:
   I have no fucking clue what that is or what to say to you when you order it. Oh it's from Starbucks? I still have no fucking clue what it is. You might as well be talking to me in Chinese.

My first day at Caribou is so relaxing and enjoyable I know I made a great career decision. Christian and I meet at the Lake store, which for 12 weeks will be my training store. Christian, once again wearing a designer tee shirt and jeans, introduces me to my training manager, Kirsten. She brings little cups of different coffees, we sample a new breakfast sandwich that Caribou is excited about, and she makes me a hot chocolate! Does this get any better?! We talk a little coffee, a lot about our families, and more about coffee, which I know absolutely nothing about. Christian says it will take about five months to pick up the nuances of coffee, and to taste everything I can.

   Christian is relaxed but stylish, professional but interested, and goal-oriented. He is exactly who I would imagine running Caribou coffee, which is the opposite of who I would imagine working for Starbucks–an uptight, yuppie, number-cruncher. Kirsten and Christian talk about their kids and the differences in school systems. Christian has three kids and lives in the city. Kirsten describes where she lives as near an incredibly rich area near a prestigious lake community, but kind of out in the country. I guess she lives in the rich part. I'm nervous to say her name because I forget is it is Kirsten or Kiersten or Kristen.

   Kirsten appears to be in her late 30's, with brown hair, and has kind of the natural look going. She wears a long brown skirt and blue top (each Caribou employee must wear blue or brown shirts) and no make-up. She is quiet, curt, and lets Christian do most of the talking. I can tell she respects and admires Christian, but still complains to him about things he has no control over. Kirsten would like to close at 9 p.m. instead of 11 p.m., but

Christian shrugs and says he has done all he can. He asked and was told no by his boss.

We spend 70 percent of the time talking about family and personal interests and about 30 percent of the time on coffee, operations and upcoming Caribou promotions, and Kirsten's employees. This is what I signed up for!

"Try to pick a little something to say about each coffee." Christian explains calmly, as we do a "coffee talk" on a Sumatra, the name of a coffee. A "coffee talk" is performed every day by Caribou employees on every shift. Every employee tastes the coffee of the day, and talks about taste, smell, origins, and likes/dislikes to better connect with customers.

"Don't be afraid to tell a customer a coffee is not for you. We don't need to love everything we sell and it builds credibility." Christian explains and Kirsten nods.

To encourage beverage knowledge, and to add to the benefits of working at Caribou, employees can have one free specialty drink each shift and all of the free coffee they want. "This effectively increases their average hourly rate of pay and it encourages them to try everything so they can speak to our product with customers." Plus, each employee can take home a half-pound of any coffee beans each week. Gisele is quite excited about all the free coffee I will be getting!

Caribou's training plan is day one on bar, or being the barista, day two as the greeter, and day three as the super glue. All three days are with a buddy so questions can be answered and you are not thrown right in. Caribou wants a great training environment to retain employees and maintain product quality. Caribou prides itself on good training and has invested a lot of money into training books and computer courses. Christian and Kirsten walk through my 12-week training course and it seems like an old corporate training program. Which is what I know. I could write these corporate training programs!

"Every week we will meet and go over your week and what's ahead. Just take it week to week. What would a regular employee be expected to know in the first week?" Christian asks Kirsten.

"How to make a latte, a mocha, and ring at the register."

"That seems reasonable," Christian adds. I nod. This all does seem reasonable.

I never looked at the training plan again.

I sit at the table with Christian and Kirsten chitchatting about coffee and it is all so relaxing. It is everything I thought it would be for that one moment.

I was tired of beating my head against the wall at Wal-Mart and thinking that I was overworked. I had no fucking clue how easy I had it, or anyone who works at Wal-Mart has it. The Caribou honeymoon ended on my real first day.

CHAPTER 3
A REALLY, REALLY BIG MISTAKE

*Dear customer who wants half a Splenda, half a sugar, half a raw sugar, and
half a brown sugar packet in your latte,*
What the hell is wrong with you?

The next day I arrive at 5:30 a.m. expecting to read manuals or watch
training videos. Nope. Kirsten shows me how put the super automatic
espresso machine back together after the nightly cleaning. There are three
espresso nozzles and Kirsten has the whole machine put back together
before I can get even one nozzle lined up. She grabs it out of my hand and
screws it in.

We make tea extracts. I don't know if it's because it is 5:45 a.m. or I'm
an idiot, but I have no idea how to make the tea extract or what the tea
extract is for? I couldn't wrap my head around half of the stuff we were
doing. I find out later you mix the tea extract with water for different iced
teas. We don't have much time for questions because the store opens at 6
a.m. and Kirsten isn't in the mood for questions. Each task is shown quickly
and without much explanation. I'll pick it up later, I decide. I follow Kirsten
around, trying to soak something (anything) in.

Nash is on with us as the greeter, or cashier, but he is busy with his own
routine. A couple of times we start talking about personal stuff, because that
is what normal people do at work when someone new is hired. Kirsten
clears her throat when she notices and Nash quickly wanders off to another
task.

We check cooler mix amounts and stocked sandwiches. Which really
amounts to Kirsten checking and stocking and me asking, "What is a cooler
mix for?" and "I didn't know we sold sandwiches?" At 6 a.m. we unlock the
doors. The people don't quite pour in, but there is a line of four people

waiting. In no time at all, the line reaches to the door and I am in the middle of my first morning at a coffee shop.

"Grab the skim and pour it to the medium line and froth to 100." I suddenly blank and can't remember if the top of the skim milk carton is pink or light blue. I stare.

"Never quit moving, Ben!" Kirsten screams. "Pink top!" She can read my mind.

"Put whip on that with about 10 chocolate chips, put whip on that and three circles of caramel." I grab the whipped cream like a normal person.

"No! Like this!" Kirsten holds the can upside down and introverted. I try it and shoot whipped cream too fast and mocha splashes everywhere. Kirsten quickly fills it up with more hot milk and applies the whip carefully. *Okay, Okay, I got it now.* I hold the canister like Kirsten and…shoot whipped cream out too fast and spill the mocha everywhere. *Fuck me!*

"Put a Chicken Apple Sausage Day Breaker in the oven." *A what? We have chicken and apples in a sandwich?* I open the fridge and every sandwich looks the same. The sandwiches are wrapped in different colors but I don't know what the colors mean, so it doesn't help much. But I find it! I want to scream and celebrate! Then I can't rip it open. The thing is wrapped so fucking perfectly I can't get my finger in an edge. I finally rip the thing open and throw it onto a pan and shove it into the oven. The customers are watching, knowing I'm the new guy and knowing Kirsten is also watching the new guy. I get the sandwich in and wait.

"Never quit moving, Ben!" I would do something but I don't know what to do as I watch the oven timer count down. I'm not lazy, I just don't know what to do to be a help in 20 seconds or less. The customers stare at me. *You poor bastard,* I can hear them think. I wouldn't mind if she yelled at me to do specific task, not just yelling to keep moving.

The sandwich is done and I have to get it into a bag with dripping hot cheese, folded and looking nice, using a spatula.

"That's for here!" Kirsten yells. I take it out of the bag and put it onto the plate. It looks like shit all squished and wrecked from the bag.

The woman customer looks at it like, *What the fuck?*

"Ahh…I'll make you another one." This was a really sweet, customer-servicey thing for me to do, and a huge mistake. Because the sandwich and drink orders keep coming. And coming. Kirsten gives me a look which I interpret as I *know you were trying to do right, but you fucked up in the first place putting the sandwich in the bag and now we are in the fucking weeds!* Later, Kirsten explains when we get backed up customers become upset and may "peel off," or leaves the store in a huff without buying anything. "That's bad," Kirsten says gravely. I begin to expect customers to peel off, hoping in a way, because we are not keeping up. The customers never peel off, and the line is out the door. *Why are these people waiting in line?* I scream in my head. *Leave! Just go to your homes!*

The sandwich is ready and I learn my first hard lesson of my Caribou career. Shit is hot. The oven is hot, the water is hot, the coffee is hot, the machines get hot. You make a mistake around something hot and you remember it. The oven beeps, the sandwich is done. I slid the metal plate under the sandwich and try to shimmy it on the plate. It gets stuck with hot cheese. I don't want to touch the sandwich with my bare hand and Kirsten had said it takes too long to put on a plastic glove every time. Right at the moment I'm thinking about putting on a plastic glove, the sandwich slides and hits my hand, I jerk it away but it still catches a bunch of hot cheese right out of the oven. I do everything I can to not throw the sandwich in the air so I can wipe the hot cheese off my hand. *Fuck that cheese is hot!* My face is flushed, I'm sweating, and my hand is now red. I hand the women her sandwich, and she's been watching the whole thing. '*I'm actually very normal,*' *I want to tell her.*

I go back to the bar and shoot the whipped cream out too fast and overflow the drink. *Fuck. I have used a whipped cream can millions of times! How can I be so bad at this?* The whipped cream is made in store, so it's different and the canister isn't like Reddi Whip. Kirsten grabs the can again and deftly tops the drink, while pouring another drink with her right hand. While she is making two different drinks with two different hands, she yells out the drinks with the customer names at the top of her lungs.

I once heard on NPR about a study showing that people subconsciously decide in the first two hours of a new job if they are simply going to stay. *I don't know.*

When I start some new jobs, I think I will be good at it once I get it down. This job though, I'm not so sure I will ever get it down.

Kirsten expects me to know what's in a latte, what's in a mocha, and the subtle differences. I told her I have only ever ordered the Campfire Mocha for my fiancé and I hated the taste of it. I envisioned a manual that showed the ingredients to each drink for us beginners. *Does everyone just get thrown in like this?* A customer then orders Campfire Mocha and I am pleasantly surprised to learn a mocha has caffeine and chocolate. That makes sense. Kirsten slams the milk carton down to wake me from my daydream.

The pace of a coffee shop is not something I thought about before I worked at Caribou, during my interview, or really until the morning rush started. It's a lot busier than I ever thought it would be and that is the understatement of the universe. Kirsten yells at me to grab this or do that, but I stand there like a fool not comprehending what she wants. It looked so calm and fun. It looked relaxed. It is anything but calm or relaxed.

I hear the customer order a vanilla latte and I watch the drink pop onto our screen at the bar. And then the drink looks like it's in Chinese to me. The drink screen separates each drink in order and changes color as the drink has been on the screen too long. It's a touch screen, so the barista will tap the drink off when it's completed. "The home office keeps track of the times too," Kirsten tells me, but I notice she taps the drinks off on her time instead of right after she makes the drink. Sometimes one drink will stay on the screen for hours. The drink screen is easy enough to understand, but it I have to get used to the abbreviations. I have to keep looking at the screen to confirm I have the right ingredients.

Medium, vanilla, latte, with 2% milk. I look at the screen again. Medium, got it. Except the cups are not organized small, medium, large. They go small, large, medium and it confuses me. Suddenly I cannot figure out the difference between a medium and large?! Which makes me feel pathetic. I have the medium cup and I look back to the screen again for the reassurance and I see I need to add vanilla flavoring. I check down at the flavor shot combinations Kirsten wrote with paint pen right below all the bottles of flavor shots and see it's 3-4-5 for the hot drinks. I begin to squirt the vanilla but notice there are two bottles for vanilla. I look back to the screen for more reassurance and notice the other bottle is sugarfree vanilla. I don't need that. The first shot of vanilla in the morning must have some crust because it shoots out sideways and hits Nash in the face some four feet away.

"Dude!"

"Sorry." I finish squirting the vanilla in the cup, but lose track of the count when a customer asks where is there a breakfast place around here. On a vanilla count of four, I'm pretty sure I pumped nine shots in the cup. Then added two more shots just make sure it looked like I knew what I was doing. I nodded, as telling myself, to someone looking on, that I knew those were the last two pumps.

I check back to the screen for reassurance and see I need 2% milk. I bend down to the refrigerators at my knees and....forgot which milk I need. I peek back up and see I need 2% and grab the jug. Kirsten has been observing me make the most popular drink in the world in record-setting slow speed and throws me out of the way and does it herself. I pick up a wet rag and keep cleaning the same spot. I guess just trying to make a drink impresses only me. I am really just going through the motions trying to look a lot smarter than I am. I couldn't make an accurate drink if you had a gun to my head. Even though it looks relatively simple, it's not when you are behind that bar. I watch Kirsten work the morning rush and I try to stay out of her way, but also look like I'm doing something. It's a really great learning environment.

Nash is on the "greeter spot" and the morning is constantly busy. I haven't read any training materials yet and I'm overloaded. Nonetheless, Nash gives me a quick low-down on the greeter spot that sounds more complicated than the barista. Nash is early 20's, obviously lifts weights, and I feel like outside of Caribou we would get along and be friends. But in this moment we are two cogs in the morning coffee shop machine and there is no time to get to know each other. And in the big scheme of things, as Kirsten explains later, each new employee has just three shifts with a training buddy. Then they are live on the schedule. Meaning I will be live on the schedule so I better fucking start paying attention.

"We have to brew coffee every hour, or before if it runs out. Always check this gauge." Nash points to a gauge that is so old the lines are worn off.

"How do I tell how full it is?" I ask, as I'm squinting at the gauge.

"Yeah the gauges are old so just keep track in your head."

"Right." I'll just keep track of that in my head. Nothing can go wrong with that!

"So we have light, dark, and decaf. The coffee is laid out here." Nash pulls open a huge drawer filled with coffee beans in white pouches.

"How do we know which is light or dark?"

"You'll pick it up."

"We don't label it?"

"Nope. Takes too much time." Nash grabs one of the pouches with coffee and dumps it into the grinder.

"So you have to make sure if you have a light or dark roast, and if it's a half or full batch. And if it's a different coffee we have to change the sign."

I start tuning him out with information overload. He finishes grinding the coffee, which was really loud, but he just keeps talking. I hope he didn't cover anything important when the grinder was going.

Nash deftly dumps old coffee grounds in a round filter into the garbage, washes out the metal filter and puts in a new filter lining, which I initially thought was a white pouch like an idiot coffee virgin. He adds a new filter, expertly dropping the edges under spokes.

"I always put the filter in when it's a little wet so it sticks. You have to get it under the edges there or it will fold in when it's brewing. Then you have to remake it."

"That sounds bad."

"If it folds down, grounds can get in the coffee and customers don't like it."

"So then we scoop the grounds off?"

"Dump it out and remake it. You can't get the grounds out."

"That would take awhile and it's wasting the coffee."

"Kirsten doesn't like waste." He says to me earnestly. Nash takes a 3-foot coffee urn to the small sink and flips it up and sticks the end of the faucet in the top. He swishes it around for a while.

"You have to rinse it three times, but never use soap or it'll screw up the coffee taste."

"No soap, got it."

Nash sets the coffee urn under the brewer.

I try cleaning the next urn but it's not done quite as deftly. I spill water out the top, which is too hot and splashes on my hand. I drop the urn in the sink and it makes a clatter. I blush, but pick it up and clean the urn with ice cold water instead. Cleaning with cold water is fine, right? Then I dump more water on the floor when I flip the urn upright. I realize then a lot of things look easy in a coffee shop, but it takes a lot of repetition to even do the easy things. The problem is similar to a golf swing. You hit a great drive, but then you don't use your driver for 20 minutes. I need repetition to learn a lot of the deft moves, but those moves aren't needed very often. The coffee urns only need to be cleaned once an hour.

"Remember half and full batches brew different amounts of water. So if you run a half on full the coffee will be watery. And if you do it the other way it will be too dark." He flips a side switch on and off and on again. I have no fucking clue what he is talking about.

"Got it." I nod.

Nash begins to explain the bakery case first in, first out system, but it's like a scene in a movie where a character is mouthing words, but the voice-over of my thoughts has started. I survey my settings, as Nash chatters on.

Kirsten's Caribou is next to the most popular lake in the city. Huge mansions and prestigious apartment complexes circle the lake, but less than five blocks from the store is low-income housing. And straight west on a highway are the rich and sprawling suburbs. This Caribou attracts regulars from poor and rich areas and people from all over the city who are visiting the lake or events at the lake. It can be busy at any hour of the day or at any moment. It sits between a Chipotle and Noodles and Company, so it has almost perfect real estate positioning. The store also can be seen from the sidewalk when walking the lake, and the only real competition from the area is a Jamba Juice in Whole Foods, but Caribou is closer to the lake. There is a also a fancy coffee shop and bakery across the street too, but it doesn't seem to affect our business. The store's location can lead to the perfect storm of consistent business.

Again Kirsten shows me how to froth milk to 100 degrees. I hold the milk pitcher with the steam wand just under the surface of the milk.

"That's how you get that nice frothing sound," Kirsten tells me and she seems to be happy with my progress. Right on cue the pitcher flows over with milk because I filled it too full. Kirsten shakes her head as I re-do the whole process. *Son of a bitch!*

I pour the milk into a latte but I have poured too little milk this time because it has spilled over. I serve it without taking time to froth more milk. I try to spoon in more froth and foam to make it look filled up. I don't know a thing about coffee, but I know too much foam in any drink is bad. And this is too much foam. The customer takes one sip and turns around.

"This isn't even filled up." *Fucking eh.*

"Fill the cup to the top, Ben," Kirsten says her stern voice. A voice I have grown sick of hearing after a few working hours with Kirsten.

It's not that I'm trying to cheat the customer, it's just that I don't know how to accurately guesstimate how much milk to pour, so I under-guess. I start filling the pitchers to froth again and Kirsten says, "We don't want to waste milk." *Well,* I think, *I'd rather waste a little milk than piss off a bunch of customers. This sucks!* I barely know how to make these drinks and now I'm making them in a huge rush! Where is quality control?

"Is there a spot you fill to, so you know it's enough milk?" I ask Kirsten.

"You just start to know. You know what I mean." *Is that in the manual?*

We are finally relieved by Beck and Carlee for the day and are off the floor. I have never been so happy to see co-workers in my entire life. I want to jump up and down when I see them walk into the shop. Yes! I'm almost fucking done! Hug me and rejoice! But I play it cool.

Kirsten shows me how to count down registers and count the safe, and where supplies are located. I look at a wall of cups. "How do I know which ones are smalls, mediums, or larges?" They aren't labeled.

"You'll learn by feel soon enough."

"Uh okay. But until then do you put large, medium, and then small on the wall?"

"No." And she returns to the computer.

I don't pay too much attention. I am wiped out from the day. Fuck that was brutal. I had no clue it would be so crazy.

Kirsten apologizes to me for being crabby and rude. She explains she had a really bad experience with her last trainee, Vicky. *Well, life moves on.* I'm not in a contemplative mood though. I'm exhausted.

"When you train someone, it is a relationship for 12 weeks. I'm just not ready for another relationship yet. So, sorry."

Okay thanks, I guess.

"Vicky just zapped my whole energy system." Kirsten looks like she is going to cry. Nash bounds in with his register and cup of tips. Kirsten and I don't get tips because we are management.

"Are you coming back tomorrow?" Beck asks me on my way out. Beck meant, am I on the schedule for tomorrow, but I took it to mean was I literally returning to this job. I stared at her.

"10 o'clock I guess."

Filled with self-doubt, embarrassment and shame, I head home for day.

CHAPTER 4
THERE IS NO ONE ELSE

Dear customer who whispers, "He must be new" to their friend,
    Yes I'm fucking new! Do you think there is a farm team of coffee shop workers practicing every day to make the jump to the coffee shop big leagues? There isn't! I'm what you've fucking got today! I obviously don't know where the fucking button for the bag of chips is! I'm not fucking stupid. You don't need to whisper to your friend I'm new because everyone fucking standing in line knows I'm fucking new!

On my third day of employment at Caribou Coffee the plan was to work with Kirsten at the register for the whole shift. The Caribou training program schedules observation time with your trainer and encourages lots and lots of questions. When I felt comfortable I could take over the register with Kirsten nearby for more questions and followup. Antonio was scheduled to be on bar. And Antonio, that son of a fucking bitch, never showed up. I don't even know Antonio but I want to kill him. At least beat him up a lot.

"Uh, what do we do now? Can Beck or Nash stay late?" I try not to sound frantic.

"They can't stay today," Kirsten replies while putting on her light blue apron, different than the brown apron I wear, which was given to her by the Caribou vice president for being a great store manager.

"Call someone else in?" My heart is racing. I'm not ready to work a Saturday afternoon at Caribou. *It's my third fucking day. And I haven't even been fucking paying attention!*

"There is no one else," Kirsten replies curtly.

"What do you mean there is no one else?"

"Everyone else is close to 40 hours and I'm not fully staffed. There is no else to call, Ben!"

"What about from another store?"

"I would never ask another store for help. The register isn't hard; you'll pick it up quick. You worked a little with Nash yesterday, didn't you?"

Good, good. Don't panic. I'm having a good time.

"Sorry I can't stay today. I have to go to my other job," Beck says. "I'm really sorry."

It's 10 a.m. on a Saturday at Caribou Coffee. It's my second day working the floor. Can I quit? Should I call Christian? What are my options? Am I on the Truman Show? The hardest day of my life begins. *This fucking sucks.*

"Good luck man," Nash says as he orders his shift drink. Which is a ridiculously complicated two shots of raspberry, two shots of sugarfree raspberry skim latte. Nash hands me his employee discount card and tries to talk me through the screen without looking at it. It is three buttons to push and none say employee discount. The line starts to back up as my first customer, Nash, is fucking helping me! This is a bad sign.

Kirsten and I have an unspoken agreement I will trudge through on the register, try to handle the bakery, and try to keep up with making coffee. I don't know when the coffee is going empty and I don't know how to decipher light from dark. Honestly, I didn't worry about anything except for taking the customers' orders and trying to find everything on the register. I learn everything from Kirsten yelling from the bar or from the customers. Neither are very nurturing.

The basics of Caribou selling at the greeter position are all in the name of making a customer's order bigger, Kirsten explains in her abrupt, stilting and condescending way.

"When they say a drink, we ask, will that be a large? The most profitable drink is a large," she says sternly. "Never say 'what size!' Always ask, 'Will that be a large today'?"

"Okay." I nod.

"Got it? We want to sell larges."

"We want to sell larges." I repeat like a robot. I understand that Kirsten is enforcing my selling behaviors right from the get-go. I understand that and in any other training situation it would be commendable, but the problem I have is that I don't have the simple operations of the register down. A customer orders a drink and I literally cannot find the initial button to start the drink creating process. The seconds creep by as I stare at the register.

One of my first customers order a medium mocha. I offer a large for 30 cents more, but she says, "Oh no thanks." I am about to swipe her credit card when she says, "Okay you talked me into it. I'll take a large." Great! I have no idea how to erase the drink and make it a large. I imagine her telling her husband later he sounded so competent on the upsell, but he couldn't figure out how to make it a large? He must have been a real idiot honey, her husband will reply.

I want to upsell more but the customer gives a loud audible sigh when I stare at the register for a few seconds finding the drink and then offer to make it a large for 30 cents more.

"We never ask 'Anything else?' Always ask, 'would you like a cookie or sandwich or some sort of add on?'" Kirsten wants to me to mention a bakery item, but not say 'bakery item.' I did that once and her head almost exploded. She wants me to mention a specific item from the bakery. Between customers Kirsten quickly explains that Caribou wants us to start out each transaction offering a hot breakfast sandwich.

"Good morning. Would you like to try a Chicken Apple Sausage Day Breaker today?" Most of the customers are confused, just as I was, wondering what the hell is in this sandwich.

"A what?"

"A chicken apple…a breakfast sandwich." *I'm Ron Burgundy?* I quit offering the breakfast sandwiches, not because I sound like an idiot and it confuses the customers, but because the sandwich buttons on the register are just abbreviations and initials. If they do decide to get a breakfast sandwich it takes me several long and frustrating seconds, sometimes into the minutes, to decipher TAPS, TBM, BM,BBM, RLT, MNRO. I have no fucking clue which one is which. So I guess! Kirsten makes a bacon mini, but the customer wanted a turkey bacon mini. Kirsten speaks loud and clear when the customer says he got the wrong sandwich. "That's the sandwich that was on my screen, but I will make you the correct one." *My face flushes hot. I live under the bus.*

The greeter basics are harder to do than you might think. Not asking 'anything else' is a hard one for me. A few times Kirsten yells out "Ben!" McDonalds and Burger King ask it every order. Not at Caribou. Kirsten pulls me aside and says not to ask anything else! *Really? You are yelling at me on my second fucking day in front of all these customers when it's your fucking fault I'm here in the first place?* But I focus at the end of each customer interaction and break the cycle.

People would simply stare at me not knowing what to make of the guy at Caribou who said, "Anything, er, brownie?" All I could think of was a brownie! At 10:30 a.m.!

"No." Each time a customer says no it stings because they turned me down. But it was awesome because then I don't have to find anything else on the register.

I then focus on just one bakery item to sell. Blueberry muffins. I was confusing myself trying to match the customer's drink with a bakery item that would go nicely. Caribou had a beautiful chart that paired the flavors.

Looking at the chart at this point in my Caribou career made me dizzy and I want to sit down. Blueberry goes with everything, at least to me. I sold a few, which was awesome, and Kirsten gave me a nod, like good job. She doesn't normally open up like that, and I laugh. But then I couldn't stop myself from offering blueberry muffins.

"Blueberry muffin with that today?"

"Yeah that sounds good!" The guy answered. We bonded a little! A blueberry muffin does go with everything. I went to grab one from the bakery case and remembered I sold my last one. Fuck!

"Ah, we're out of those actually." I envision the guy later telling his wife about the dumbass guy at Caribou offering items they were out of. "Why would they do that?" He would ask her incredulously. She would hmph-hmph while reading a book on the couch. He would grab her shoulders and shake her and scream, "Why would he offer something they were out of?!" My shitty service may be leading to domestic violence.

The bakery case seems like an easy enough premise. Customer orders something, I grab the item with a tongs and put it on a plate or bag. Easy peasy right? We have all seen it done literally thousands of times and any idiot can do it, right?

I am 6'3" and I have normal size hands for someone 6'3", which means they are bigger than average hands. This doesn't affect me much in life, but the bakery is low to the ground, the racks are close together, and the one-size-fits-all plastic gloves don't fit me. The gloves would make it easy to grab a piece of bakery. The first and only time I try to put the glove on it barely fits over my fingers, so I give it a yank and it explodes down and tears around my fingers. Now I can't get the glove off and my left hand is sweating trying to get the glove off my right hand, which makes it even harder and the whole time five customers are watching me. *What if I can't get this fucking glove off?!* Kirsten comes over and rings while I get the glove off. I start laughing thinking if someone caught that on their phone it would go viral pretty quick.

I throw the box of gloves aside and grab the tongs. My new bakery weapon of choice and I hold them up to the light. *You will be an extension of my own body!* The problem is I didn't realize bakery items are so fucking delicate. The muffins hold up okay, but trying to get a cinnamon bread, lemon poppyseed bread or cookie into a bakery bag without breaking it in half is almost impossible. I get a hold of one cookie and it breaks in half. I grab the next one and it breaks in thirds. There is only one cookie left. Fuck! The customer is watching too! I grab the cookie delicately, but firmly. I pull it slowly towards the small bakery bag, but I get too excited when it's inches from the bag and press the tongs too hard. The cookie breaks in half.

"I can take a broken cookie. I don't mind." The sweetest customer in the world tells me.

"Thank you." It is the most honest thank you of my entire life.

Another sanitary option is to grab a piece of bakery with the bakery tissue. I'm one step from just grabbing the bakery with my bare hands, which will probably get me fired and Caribou in trouble for health code violations. I'm running out of options though!

The bakery tissues work for me. I grab the pieces of bakery delicately, but firmly, pick up the bakery item and put it into the bag. I get into a groove until I get a cranky old woman who has fun making me miserable.

She has her own tumbler and orders a macchiato, but wants it made like Starbucks. I have no idea what this means, but apparently Caribou macchiatos are different than Starbucks. I thought Kirsten would know what that meant, so I write a memo. She also wants piece of banana bread. We are out of banana bread.

"You are always out of the banana bread. Maybe you should order more!" *It's my third day, lady, I want to scream*! And it's really not an ordering problem either, but a thawing problem. Kirsten had me pull five bakery items of each and another five are thawing. This is usually enough, unless a large group or a family orders all of one particular item. Then it's three hours to thaw more. If we pull too much bakery and don't sell it, then it's waste. And Kirsten doesn't like waste. I don't think the woman wants to hear this though and to be honest I barely get the concept of the whole thing at this point in my Caribou career.

"I'll look into that."

"Oh give me that last croissant."

I ring up the macchiato and croissant and am about to swipe her credit card.

"Did you get my discount?" Discount, discount? "My own mug. You always forget my sustainability discount." Even though it is my third day the lady is right, I do always forget the .10 cents off for customers with their own mugs. It's like nine buttons in to find the fucking discount button! I find it and take her money.

I grab the bakery tissue, grab the bakery bag, go to grab the croissant...

"Ben! What is this Starbucks memo?"

"She wants her macchiato like a Starbucks macchiato."

"I don't know how Starbucks makes their macchiato?" This conversation is taking place in front of a busy coffee shop by the way. This is how Kirsten has decided to handle this.

"We don't know how Strarbucks make their macchiatos." I say to the woman in a monotone voice even though she heard Kirsten.

"Oh just make it how you make it, I guess!"

And then I grab the croissant, stand up to put it in the bag, and the tissue paper and the overly dry croissant create a slippery little scene. I drop the croissant on the floor. My first thought is can I pick it up without anyone noticing? It's the last croissant! I peek at the lady and she is not paying attention. But I can't.

"Uh, now you're really going to be mad. I'm sorry I dropped your croissant. And it was the last one."

She's not happy. "I can get you anything you want from the bakery?" I emphasize 'anything' as if I will have sex with her if she doesn't make a big deal out of this. No, I mean she could have something more expensive in the bakery if she wanted.

"Nope. Refund my money. In fact I don't want anything! Just give me my money back."

Kirsten takes her sweet old time finishing what she is doing and comes over and does the refund. The woman holds the receipt up in the air to the line of people.

"Didn't get anything today!" She waves her receipt to the line. I sigh. We trudge on.

This would be a good time for a break, but for six straight hours I do not get any breaks, snacks or downtimes beyond a few seconds when there is a customer lull. And then those few moments are precious time to stock up on cups and clutches, make and fill the coffee, fill the soda fridge, fill the milk, clean the mix-ins station, fill the bakery, and clean up the neverending coffee spills.

When I do well, or at least decent at something, Kirsten adds a new layer or wrinkle to what I'm doing. "We always get names so whoever is on bar can create a moment and call out their name. Plus, people forget their drinks and the names help a lot when it's busy."

"People forget their drinks? Really?" I'm surprised. I've never forgotten what I ordered at McDonalds.

"You wait and see, Ben." She smirks.

I find a nice little challenge in moving a customer from a medium to a large or adding on a cookie. "Christian is going to love you!" Kirsten exclaims. "That's what he and corporate want!" Kirsten tells me I do great with upselling to larges, that I'm a natural at selling. But to get to know the drinks better, I start asking too many questions for Kirsten.

"Don't ask what kind of milk they want," she explains. "If they don't say anything it's two percent. It slows us down if we ask everyone!"

Later, "Ben! Don't ever ask what kind of chocolate they want. The standard is milk chocolate. We don't have time to ask that! Some store managers would get really mad at you for that." *It's a good thing you don't overreact to stuff.*

The problem, I've discovered, with not asking what kind of milk or chocolate a customer wants is it comes back to fuck with me. Because the one person I don't ask about the kind of milk tells me at the end of the order they want soy. Or skim. Or whole milk, whatever the fuck that is! Fuck! Now I have to re-enter the drink on the register and I hear Kirsten slam down her milk pitcher and re-make the drink.

"Sorry," the customer will say.

"No, that's okay," I say. Sigh. The same goes for chocolate. After entering in the drink I get the, "Oh. Can I get dark chocolate?" AHHHHHHH!

My least favorite question is asking the customer their name. "Why do you want my name?" I'm a pervert and I am going to start stalking you! I know everything about you now because I know your name.

"We put names on the drinks for easy ordering." She looks confused. Her boyfriend orders next.

"And your name?"

"Can't you just put her name on the whole order?" Are you so fucking important you can't be bothered with giving me your fucking name? What is your name?! What is your fucking name?! Is your name your social security number and therefore it's a problem? The customer is not always right because the customers are dumbasses. I try to avoid asking names, but Kirsten is a stickler for it.

"Caribou wants us to asks names to create a friendly first name atmosphere, Ben!" Kirsten wants names because yelling "Jason!" gets a reaction. Yelling iced vanilla soy latte can get no reply. People forget their drink, or don't pay attention, but they hear their name if it's yelled. I dread asking for people's names and that's even with easy names. The Lake store is a cultural melting pot, with Hispanic names, Asian names, European names, African names, everything under the rainbow. I have to guess at the spelling and I have to do it in about a half a second. And the register isn't like a perfect keyboard, so I have to hunt and peck. All of which leads to misspelled names and then mispronounced names. Anytime Kirsten mispronounces a name, whether her fault or mine, she will quickly throw me under the bus to the customer.

"You should see how he spelled it!" She laughs and shakes her head. I want to yell "Fuck you!" sometimes, but that wouldn't help. It would just feel good and be hilarious later. But if I don't ask for the name, Kirsten just yells out "Names, Ben!"

"I'll have a vanilla latte, large, two large dark roasts, one blueberry muffin and one turkey sausage mini." I stare down at the register and repeat the order in my head. I get fixated on the blueberry muffin and find the button, but realize we are out. So delete that and punch in the two coffees. Did he say light or dark? Fuck it they are the same price. And then....I blank.

"What did you want again?" This happens a lot more than I like to admit or tell any of my friends or family. The person who they know as a bookworm, a Jeopardy/trivia, and stats geek, a person who can name every Minnesota Twin stat from that last 15 years, and where every, yes every, NBA basketball player went to college, cannot remember a simple drink order after literally five seconds.

I get better though. I get the coffee down. Almost.

"Medium dark with a lot of room."

"Room? Room. Room?" I repeat it loudly and look to Kirsten for a definition of this coffee term. She's busy.

"Room for milk." He says. Okay. I fill the coffee up and leave about two inches of room from the top. He comes back a minute later and says this is too much room. Can I fill it up more? Sure.

Another customer asks for room and I leave about a half-inch.

"This isn't enough room. Can you pour some out?" All of these people coming back ruin my concentration with the customer I'm with. And slow the line down.

There is a bell on the front door to alert us to customers and I want to beat that bell with a baseball bat.

"Large dark and double cup." I look for the double cup button. Nothing.

"Double cup?"

"Yeah...double cup..."

"You want a large split up into two cups."

The guy sighs. "No, double cupped." He repeats louder. Again I hope Kirsten is listening and will save me but no.

I grab two cups and look at him and then slide them together.

"Yes."

"So two cups together so it's not so hot on your hand." Was that so hard to fucking tell me! I get better. I hit three drinks in a row and get in a flow. I upsell. Then a customer orders a specific drink and the whole store comes to a crashing halt as I cannot find the fucking button.

That we are even maintaining business with me at the register on my second days is a quite an accomplishment to me. In the down seconds I think about quitting. This is rough. I'm not cut out for this job. Kirsten is fucking busting her ass. So am I. Even if I knew how to do everything it seems like this still sucks.

The customers are killing me with their annoyingness.

"Give me a large red eye with dark."

"A red eye....red eye." I search the screen and don't see a red eye button. "What is a red eye?"

The guys holds his hands up and laughs. "It's a...red eye. You know, a red eye." The guy laughs to the other customers around him, like, 'can you fucking believe this? It's a red eye but he doesn't know what a red eye, is the dumbfuck who works at a coffee shop.'

I yell to Kirsten, "What's a red eye?"

"I don't know!"

Well now I don't feel bad. If she doesn't know there is no way I should know! She's been doing this for like 10 years. That she yelled I don't know to me on my second day while with a customer in front of me is something at any other time in my life I would have pushed back, at the minimum, or most likely freaked out on Kirsten. But at Caribou I just nod.

"Oh wait does he mean coffee with a shot of espresso?"

The guy nods. "We call that a Depth Charge," I say.

"So a large coffee with a shot of espresso."

"Yes that's right." You couldn't fucking explain that to me you jackass!

At about hour 4.5 I encounter a minor emergency. I have to go pee.

I try not to think about it. I concentrate on the customers and registers and don't think about it. It's not going away. I then start trying to time a chance to dart to the back of the store. Waiting for just a mini-lull. None comes. Then I imagine the horrible scenario of me wetting my pants. On the job. I remember the last time I wet my pants when I was about eight years old. I was on the phone with my grandma in Seattle and I didn't want to be rude and tell her to hold on.

I finish up with a customer and I haven't heard the bell chime. I dart off.

"I have to go to the bathroom quick." Kirsten doesn't say okay or fine. "Hurry," is all she says.

I don't make any eye contact with customers in the dining room. I didn't realize until now that the dining room is packed and full of dishes, empty cups, garbage, and that is my responsibility to clean up.

I finally reach the men's room and...it's locked. No! I jump up and down on one foot and think about going back to the register. I see Kirsten is ringing up one customer, but not a huge line. Caribou has a men's and women's bathroom, designed for one customer at a time, with a lock only from the inside. I start to head back when a woman exits the women's bathroom. Fuck it! I go in and lock the door and let loose. I think back to my OSHA training at Wal-Mart and know hands should be washed for 20 seconds in hot water. Ha! I get those employees must wash hands signs now too. But I don't have 20 seconds! I squirt soap on my hands at least and wash them off in cold water. I don't have time to wait for the hot water to kick in. When I get back the line is to the door. Kirsten is stressed out.

The next time I won't wash my hands. And pray to god I don't have a bowel movement while at work.

At four o'clock a women suddenly steps behind me and I realize she is wearing a Caribou shirt.

"I can take over." It's Carlee, here to relive us along with Stephen. I almost drop to my knees in tears I'm so thankful.

"Wow that went by quick." I say out loud. Bluffing no one. It did not go by quick and was the worst six hours of my life.

And eventually, much, much, much later, I would realize, it was the greatest six hours of my life too.

CHAPTER 5
IT'S SUPPOSED TO BE THIS AWFUL

Dear customer who comments how they've always wanted to work in a coffee shop,
There are 13 people behind you in line on a busy morning and I am busting my ass. The barista has 10 drinks on her screen and she is busting her ass. Am I making this look that fucking easy? Because I am frantically doing this job and I would literally do anything to switch places with you in a second so I would not have to do this fucking endless job anymore.

With Kirsten's staffing problems she has no other choice to put me live on the schedule. Even though some employees could use extra hours, calling another store for help is not even an option for Kirsten. I have not read a manual or a playbook, I haven't watched any training videos, and I have never partnered for a shift with another employee. I learn literally everything by doing or watching or guessing. Every day I think about coming in early or staying late and just shadowing someone, but after my shift I say fuck it and run out of the store as quick as I can. Before my shift I say fuck it, I'm not going in early.

At the end of my first week at Caribou, Christian arrives for our first weekly touch base. And I have to say I am impressed he showed up on the day he scheduled. It's a small thing, but I wouldn't even plan on going to meetings at Wal-Mart because they were consistently cancelled at the last minute.

"How is it going?" Christian asks. I think about telling him how I was thrown in on my first day, and second day even worse, about how I haven't had really any basic training but I'm on the schedule, about how I hate the job and the customers and the pace. I think about crying to him and knocking over the table and walking out and quitting.

"It's going okay. I need to get better. At everything." Christian nods. "Your first five weeks here should be incredibly frustrating."

I must look surprised.

"Learning this business, much less from someone who has no service industry experience, there are going to be some bumps and bruises along the way."

"Yeah, it's been tough."

"Every week should get a little better. But then you are going to be learning more and more things, and it will get even worse." If Christian has one skill as a manager, it's making me feel like things are going to be okay. I try to stretch out our meeting just so I don't have to go back on the floor. It's really juvenile and reminds me of 8th grade history class when I would rewind the video we were watching when Mr. Bourne left the room. He wondered why it took six days to watch a movie? I did it then for good-natured fun, but now I stretch out our meetings out of sheer fear.

Kirsten has taught me "management" things like counting the safe, bringing the daily deposit to the bank, and doing the weekly supply order. These tasks actually have nothing to do with management and are jobs that Kirsten doesn't want to do. A Caribou manager is expected to work anywhere from 40 hours to 47 hours. To cover the schedule, Kirsten is currently working roughly 60 hours a week. That's not sitting behind a desk 60 hours a week, but working the bar, a brutal daily grind of 60 hours a week. She is often a mess, tearing up, crying, snapping, and then mood swinging back to super happy if one of her favorite customers comes in.

I don't know if Kirsten hates me, likes me, or cares at all about me in any way personally or professionally. I wouldn't be shocked if one day she said this job isn't for you. You are fired. I really don't care what she thinks about me personally, but it could be a lot more fun to go to work if Kirsten wasn't so rude.

I leave the store empty every day just wanting to get home to my family to get recharged. I have 12 weeks here to train. I will get what I need and get out.

"It sounds like your meeting with Christian went good?"

"Yeah. Fine I think." It dawns on me Kirsten might have been worried I told Ben about all the craziness and my lack of training. Maybe by not squealing I have passed a Kirsten test of some sort?

I have never been a clock-watcher at any job in my entire life. I have never wished it was time to go home, or looked at the clock every 10 minutes, and I have never commiserated to anyone near me the day is going so slow! The majority of my career I've enjoyed my job and the time has flown by. The worst job I ever had previously was at a grocery store in high school. I arrived at 5 a.m. to stock produce, fill the salad bar, and every employee was old and weird. It really wasn't that bad, but I hated it. I hated it so much when I was off work and I saw a clock my mind would instantly calculate how long until I had to go back. My mind does that again for only the second time in my work life. Damn it, I think, as I catch the time on my cell phone, I have to go back in less than 12 hours. Here at Caribou when it's time to go home is the best time of the day and maybe some of the top moments of my life. When the employee scheduled to relieve me walks in that door I literally have to stop myself from yelling a scream of joy.

"It is so great to see you!" I try to say even keel.

I sit in my car and contemplate my life twice a day, every day. Once when I arrive at Caribou. I stare at the store just fucking praying it will be slow today. And I stare at the store when I am leaving and think about how I can't wait to get away from this cursed place and be with my family. Like the black shadow of a demon clinging to me, I start worrying about the next rush. I stare at myself in the rear-view mirror, hating my black polo shirt. Caribou requires black shirts or brown shirts, so my second day Gisele went to Marshalls and bought three of each. I rotate three pairs of jeans and the only person happy about this arraignment is Gisele.

"The laundry is so easy without you having to wear dress clothes!" She almost sings. I used to give Wal-Mart managers crap when they wore basically the same thing every day. Now I find myself doing. Those managers hated Wal-Mart.

I vividly remember Kirsten calling Antonio and yelling at his voicemail. I vividly remember thinking she was really rough and I would never talk to someone like that, whether personally or work related. Kirsten hissed venom and yelled that he left us out to dry. "Ben is new and doesn't know anything! You left us all out to dry!" I shrugged and thought this is how it works here. And thank you for pointing out I don't know anything. I vividly remember Beck walking into the back room moments later and Kirsten telling her she left a message for Antonio. Beck said she already called and chewed him out. He deserved a double chewing out, they shrugged. Beck was kind of Kirsten's second in command. Beck helped out Kirsten because she cared, but she could be really abrasive sometimes. I didn't know what to think about Beck yet.

I thought about those phone calls to Antonio as I was standing in front of the store at 5:30 a.m., alone and shivering. Antonio was late. Did we ever get a hold of him to see if he was coming back? Did anyone talk to him in person? Is he in a hospital, in jail, or dead? I did not have keys to the store nor an alarm code. The plan was for Antonio and me to open the store and Kirsten would arrive at 8 a.m. She said she was going out the night before so would be in a little late. I could not imagine doing this job hung over. I can barely do it well rested and focused.

I was getting really nervous and thinking about calling Kirsten. It was 5:35 and the store opened at 6 a.m. An old Plymouth K-car shot around the corner and bottomed out on the parking lot driveway. It slammed to a stop right in front of the store. Two girls were in the front and the back door opened and a tall white kid with dreadlocks hopped out and was surrounded by a plume of smoke. The radio was booming and the girls were laughing.

The guy who I assumed was Antonio walked up and threw a set of keys high in the air. I caught them with my right hand.

"I quit." He turned around and got back into the car. It sped off and bottomed on the way out of the parking lot.

I just stood there. I should have thrown the keys right back at him and said, 'No, I quit.' That would have been cool. I called Kirsten. It went to voicemail. I called back again. Voicemail. I called back again. Voice mail. "Antonio just quit and gave me his keys. So uh, yeah, call me back." Moments later she called back.

"Okay I'll get ready, but you'll have to open the store. I'll call Beck to come in too."

"I thought I couldn't be in the store by myself?"

"We have to open at 6!" She screamed.

"Okay, okay!"

"My alarm code is 8901. You have 45 seconds to disarm it."

"And then..."

"And then start opening the store, Ben!"

"Okay, okay."

She calmed herself. "Do your best, Ben. I'll call Beck and I will get there as quick as I can."

I'm having a good time.

I unlocked the door and began to hear a beeping inside the store. 45 seconds!

I had opened the store exactly three times. And to be honest I wasn't paying attention the first time and the second two times I only paid attention to the stuff I would be accountable for.

The first key item I realized I didn't know about opening, was where the lights are. It was fucking dark. I used my cell phone to follow the beeping noise and found the alarm panel. I entered Kirsten's code and....it kept beeping. I knew I was getting close to 45 seconds. I entered it again just to make sure I had it right. Nothing. I started to panic a little, envisioning the alarm going off and the police and fire department arriving.

I entered the code again and decided to try the pound sign. It worked! The alarm stopped. *The pound sign would have been good information, Kirsten!*

The lights, the lights. I knew I was wasting precious time looking for the fucking lights. I envisioned coming in with Kirsten. What did she do? Where did she go?

"Fuck this sucks!" I screamed out loud. *Breathe. Grandma.* I laugh to myself at a "Happy Gilmore" reference to myself in a time of panic.

I looked behind the doors between the front of the house and the stockroom and found the fucking light switch. Let there be light! I was so happy.

Reality quickly jarred me. Now what the fuck do I do? I stared at the tidied up, put together Caribou. I knew Kirsten always started with the espresso machine, building it back together, but I wouldn't know where to start with that. I was overwhelmed, under trained, and the store opened in 16 minutes.

Okay, okay. Do what you know how to do and fuck the rest! I know how to make coffee! I got the coffee going, the roast of the day signs up, the chairs off the tables. I fumbled my way into the safe and got a register drawer out. I knew the safe should be counted but I had no idea how. I can at least sell a cup of coffee. The espresso machine stared at me, mocking me. I remember vaguely Kirsten putting it together. I didn't know how to put it together nor how to make any drinks on it if I did get it put together. I shuddered thinking about the people coming at 6 a.m. with me alone. This could get ugly.

I ignored the espresso machine and got the bakery out in recorded fucking time. The bakery items go on long plates and I usually waste about four minutes wiping them off because the water from the night before hasn't dissipated yet. It annoys Kirsten, but I think putting bakery items on water is gross and it gives me a stomachache. I envision grabbing a brownie and finding it covered in mold.

But today? Fuck it! I got the extra bakery and sandwiches items out and put away. I put away all the dishes and then remembered to turn the back office computer on, so the register would work accurately. I am a genius!

Except for the fact that I didn't know how to make a drink or turn on the super automatic espresso machine. The easiest espresso machine in the world is foiled by my incompetence. I picture the engineers building the machine, "A monkey could run this thing!" Not me.

I looked into the parking lot and saw the cars waiting. Fuck. I would tell them the espresso machine is broken and we only have coffee or tea today. Hot tea that is, as I didn't know how to make the iced teas yet. I barely remembered something about making tea extract but not really. And there was a five-gallon bucket full of...something on the counter.

I started to sweat when the door burst open and Beck ran in. Thank God!

"The espresso machine!" I blurted out. Beck got things pulled together and by 6:00 a.m. we were ok. Kirsten arrived awhile later.

I heard Beck tell her I didn't start the espresso machine. "I don't think he knows how."

"I don't," I yelled from the other side of the store.

"You did good Ben," Kirsten told me earnestly.

We never mentioned it to Christian. In fact I don't mention it to anyone. I have quit complaining to Gisele and my family about the job. I put on a good face. I think my hair is turning gray.

CHAPTER 6
THAT'S NOT A LINE

Dear customers who pay in all coin change,
You are not doing me any favors by paying in change! It's taking forever to count out, at least have it fucking ready. Why do you have all this change in the first place? "Coffee shops are a great place to get rid of change! They are?! Is that some old adage? Because it fucking sucks! Get a debit/credit card like the rest of the fucking world. I have to get rid of all this change, you say? Go to a fucking bank! There is a special place in hell reserved for those who pay in all change.

I leave to drop off the daily bank deposit and Kirsten says to hurry right back. She heard there is a big event at the lake from a customer. *I want to say how the fuck can you not know about these events?* Kirsten schedules the same amount of people no matter what is going around the most popular lake in the city. A marathon, a car show, a dance, nothing changes her scheduling. She does that because she has only so many people to work right now. As I drive to the bank I notice they are closing down streets. *Shit.* This is going to be busy.

I get back from the bank and the line is out the door.

"Do exactly what I say or we won't get through this," Kirsten growls.

We do a two-person bar and Rachel and Beck are on registers. I should note this is my "administration time" when I am supposed to be reading drink manuals, operations whatnots, and core Caribou principles. It's loud and fast and I have no idea what I'm doing. Kirsten sets up the drinks and I call them out. It's pure hell. I think about quitting any moment I am not thinking about what to do next. 'If I hadn't forgot to water the money tree I could quit,' I laugh to myself. *This job is turning me into my grandpa with these lame folksy jokes.* I forget to put the cover on the blender. *Fuck.* Cooler mix sprays onto the wall. *Double fuck.* The one towel I find is so wet and full of espresso beans it creates a worse smear on the wall then the cooler mix was. *Double fuck again!* Kirsten allots only four towels a day because Kirsten doesn't like to pay for extra towel cleaning.

We get through the rush and in the lull start fill up supplies for the next rush. 'What am I doing here,' I think, and 'Why do people do this for a living?' This is awful. I'm not sure what I hate most about this job. The never-ending tasks, the constant cleaning, the re-doing of the same tasks, the endless customers, the rude customers, or Kirsten's personality and her general lack of getting ahead of the business? It's hard to decide. Almost each minute I re-rank what I hate most about the job. For some reason, it's really soothing to re-rank what I hate about the job.

I realize that Kirsten doesn't really want me training in her store but needs me to fill shifts. Kirsten has people to work mornings, and nights, but not many to fill in the mid shifts. Mind you, I didn't say good people. And if anyone calls out, or sick, she personally has to cover the shift. At Caribou there must be two people in the store at all times. If only one shows up the store has to close. And that isn't good for anyone. But we obviously have already broken that rule. Caribou store managers should only be working 47 hours or else they get overtime. But overtime is a huge drain on payroll, and gets Christian in trouble, so store managers will work off the clock in times of dire need, because they don't want to ask for help or close the store. The unwritten rule is if you close the store you are fired. Plus, many stores have lease agreements and by not staying open in posted business hours it violates lease agreements. That's not good for anyone.

Kirsten is a training store manager, so she is salaried. So it doesn't matter how many hours she works—except to her well-being. Kirsten is so understaffed that if anyone requests off days for school or general life stuff it makes for lean times. And the worst part is she literally has no one to overlap. So on the busy Friday, Saturday or Sundays Kirsten has only two people to work when it needs four. Or at least three. And this is with me working there because I don't know shit. But without me she would be fucked because she would have to work a lot of hours.

There is nothing more frustrating than wanting to be good at something and just not knowing how to be good at it. There is a Human Resources industry built on effectively training people so they don't quit. Every person has a realistic idea of how they should complete their job to be satisfied at the end of the day. I have too much pride to quit (and I need the money and health insurance) and I have too much pride to complain that I haven't been trained properly. I think about doing both all day, though.

I am not a genius and that is abundantly clear. At this point in my Caribou career, I cannot be expected to remember every customer's name. And that is a problem with regulars who expect--downright demand--that I remember their names. Some Caribou employees are great at remembering drinks or names or both. I can barely get through the day. It's awkward when I recognize the customer's face and I remember what they drink, but I have to ask their name. Again and again.

"It's Phillip. I'm here most days," he says with a pissed-off attitude. I want to pull Phillip aside and apologize. Apologize that I am doing the best I can and I am certainly not enjoying having to ask for his name. He seems upset and thinks either I know his name but ask for it to piss him off, or else I am too stupid to remember it. I would like to tell him it's neither and I'm doing the best I can. I don't have time for that, though. So I silently call him a dick.

My most embarrassing moments are when Kirsten knows the customer and has their drink made because she sees them in the store before they have ordered. She places the drink on the counter and I have to fumble through the register for a fucking drink that is already made while Kirsten and the customer chitchat, my face reddening because it's something complicated.

"What is this drink again," I chime in between their laughing and catching up.

"It's a half café, soy, caramel high rise." Kirsten says in about one-quarter of a second. I wait a moment.

"Uh, half café what again?" I ask, wincing. She sighs.

Sometimes I guess and the total comes out wrong. Kirsten comes back to the register and deftly hits a few buttons. This of course is followed by a "he'll learn" or worse, "hopefully he'll learn soon" comment between her and the customer.

I screw up in so many comical ways I laugh at the thought of someone watching me in a movie. This would be a hilarious comedy. But it's my life and it's actually not so funny.

Everything I took for granted in my life is challenged in this environment. I can never remember how light and dark roast are labeled or I forget to set the timers to remind me to make more coffee. I forget to put the top on the blender and it flies all over the wall. I don't put a coffee top on snug enough and it spills out all over the counter. Or I'm pouring coffee and talking to the customer and it overflows. Or I upsell a muffin and forget to give it to them. High comedy.

I watch Kirsten because I want to be as good as her. Christian obviously respects her because he sends all the trainees to her. Sometimes I wonder why, though, especially when she loses it.

A customer ordered a large Americano, which is espresso and water, but the customer wanted it with just a little water. The water for the Americano is my responsibility to get and put on the bar for Kirsten. Naturally, I usually forget. This time I remember.

"Only a little water," the customer says again as I'm filling it up. I usually end up putting too much water in or too little water for Kirsten's taste. Which gets fun sighs and eye rolls when she's dumping it out or filling it up more.

"Water for the Americano," I yell out as I set it on the bar.

"Thanks, Ben!" She is happy I remembered.

"She only wanted a little water," I say before Kirsten has a nervous breakdown because I didn't put enough water in the cup.

Kirsten makes the Americano and then the woman tells her she'd like some warm milk in it. Kirsten gave her a smart look with her hand on her hip. Uh-oh.

"Next time we will charge for milk." The woman storms off obviously offended. I have no idea what is going on, so in the next lull I ask Kirsten.

"The woman got a latte but ordered an Americano because it's cheaper." Kirsten can wear her emotions on her sleeve and has little tolerance for customers or employees who are yanking her chain. It can be really awkward. I watch a computer training video which explains no matter what a customer requests, we do. If they think a drink is in any way wrong we offer to re-make it with a smile. If a customer wants something we don't make, we still try to make it. Kirsten doesn't quite agree with that. She is so confident in her skills and experience she will argue with the customers. If a customer sips a drink and makes a face or a comment that it could be a little off, Kirsten is quick to respond.

"I made it perfect, but I can re-make if that's something you think you need." That is my favorite Kirsten quote. Nash and I repeat it to each other when Kirsten is out of earshot and laugh when we need a good laugh. Customers give confused looks and shrug. I'm confused by Kirsten's behavior because she should have realized years ago you can't argue with stupid. Anyone in a customer service job learns it very quickly.

The days begin to fly by, but the actual day goes by terribly slow. Which I know doesn't make much sense.

I walk into the store one day and it's a madhouse. "We've been swamped!" Beck tells me. I dive in right away and apparently am not doing what Kirsten wants. But she hasn't said anything. She wants me to read her mind.

"You need to start doing what I want because I'm about to get really mad. " Her nose is about an inch from my nose.

"Just tell me what you want me to do."

"If I have to tell you what to do then it's too late," she snaps. I think about quitting at that moment. I envision throwing down my towel in a classic movie you-can-take-this-job-and-shove-it moment.

I pick up the pace a little but basically tend to her needs instead of Beck's needs. We also have a run on sandwiches so I stand there and make sandwiches. Which sucks.

This all sucks, I decide. Even with three people it's still barely manageable. How the hell do we do it with two people most days? Kirsten flies around the bar with a frantic, wild look, but every move has a purpose. She kicks the fridge door shut, throws a towel on the counter, pours the hot milk over the towel into a cup, serves the drink, and cleans the counter with the ready towel. Without looking you wouldn't notice, but what would take me seven movements took her two.

On the floor Kirsten is a, for lack of a better word, bitch. Off the floor she is a different, so I try to treat her as two different people. Off the floor I try to pretend we are friends and I don't even know her on-the-floor personality. On the floor Kirsten runs into me when I am getting hot water for a tea and doesn't say sorry. On the floor Kirsten sighs and shakes her head and embarrasses me in front of customers with her expectations of what should I know and what I should do. Off the floor Kirsten realizes she is in a bad spot as store manager.

I have learned, (in small doses), that Kirsten was formerly a waitress at a fancy restaurant. She is somewhat recently divorced and has three kids. She has worked at Caribou for almost nine years. I ask her if it has been too long at one spot?

"Sometimes."

She is rough and abrupt and hard to read and then overly easy to read. She spares no one's feelings when she wants something done her way, which is most often the Caribou way.

"I've been told I'm condescending." I don't tell her I noticed that. "I'm trying to be more positive. I'm not doing very well at it." She is very close with many of the customers who tell her intimate things about their life. Kirsten seems like a bartender hearing about the boozy drinker's day, only we are a coffee shop and it's in much quicker doses. She cries too much. She talks about "problems" she has to me and speaks a like a hippie with energy and Zen and good flow thoughts. She is complicated. And yet overly simple.

"I need to take back control of the store," Kirsten tells me. "It's just so hard, you can't understand."

"Tell me."

"I had this great team for awhile, it was so much fun and everyone was super, super good. Then Vicki came along and everyone left." Vicki was Kirsten's last store manager trainee.

"Because of Vicki?"

"No, but her negative energy didn't help things. People leave because people leave," Kirsten shrugs. "Colton graduated and got a real job, Beth got a real job, Sarah was promoted to another store, Danielle got promoted to another store. So it looks good for me and Christian likes it when they get promoted, but it sucks for me. I didn't have much turnover for awhile. And now…." Her eyes tear up. I notice that Kirsten's eyes tear up a lot when she is feeling overwhelmed. Which is almost every day.

"I've really lost the store to Beck. I've let her take over everything and I need to take it back." Beck is a whole reality show just by herself. She wants opportunity to advance and helps out with the day-to-day operations. Beck wants to be a store manager and will help out whenever she can. The problem with Beck is she's not exactly a people person per se. She can be almost evil.

Kirsten is fucked. Because as Christian puts it, she didn't "feed the monster."

"We are in a service industry, but we don't tell people that. You need to constantly be hiring, because the minute you stop and think you are all hired up, the bottom falls out."

The bottom falling out means a manager doesn't have enough people to cover the hours. Or enough people to adequately cover the store hours, or enough decent people. You are forced to cover the hours with people who don't care about speed of service, upselling, not upsetting customers, or really anything except getting a paycheck. You may recognize these people when you walk into your local McDonalds or Subway. Lifeless, droll people going through the motions of selling and serving. The opposite of what Caribou wants, but a few bad hires and then good people leave, and you are now leaning on the bad people to fill hours.

"The first thing you do when you start at a store is what? Start hiring. And never stop," Christian tells me every time I see him.

Kirsten runs the bar five days out of the week by herself, which is brutal on her. She leaves the greeter spot for whoever is scheduled with her, as Kirsten doesn't trust the bar to anyone else. But it is busy and Kirsten is so good at the bar she does the work of two people. Which in awkward moments, she says out loud.

"You almost ran out of coffee! I'm doing the work of three people with the bar and sandwiches and watching your coffee." *Thanks for that. That makes me feel good.*

It's her own fault though as she schedules the same way each day, not forecasting for local events that may bring in more customers. She doesn't think about holidays or good weather or promotions that may bring in customers. It leads to days that the store is over run with customers and not enough employees. Kirsten thinks that is the norm.

"The line is out the door, maybe we should schedule more or hire more?" Maybe she just hasn't thought of it?

"That's not a line. One time at my old store we completely stopped serving drinks because we got so backed up. That was a line." Is she arguing for my point or against my point? The time I'm supposed to spend doing computer base training I spend covering shifts at the greeter spot.

Even though Kirsten is moody and sometimes a terrible boss and trainer, what sticks out to me is how much she loves Caribou. She loves everything about Caribou. She will still complain about certain things, but that is the norm with any company. She loves the culture, she loves the home office, and she has pictures of herself up in the stockroom with different executives. She talks about how Christian respects her and the people in the company respect her. It's amazing really. I've never worked for a company where I genuinely felt the love for the company and its goals. Caribou strives to be the community place I love. I ask the other employees why they work at Caribou, everyone answers that its the people they work with or because they love Caribou.

Kirsten was saved by Caribou from the horrible world of waitressing. Many Caribou store mangers are former waitresses or bartenders or restaurant managers, and Caribou saved them. They can give up the world of dickhead managers, not getting paid on time, and constant sexual harassment, long hours and drunk customers.

"It was a pretty crazy environment, but I was really strong, you know." She flexes her arms. She really loves Caribou. At Caribou, the corporate environment is friendly, positive Zen-type hippie stuff, and the hours may be crazy but still are better than any bar or restaurant. And she gets paid regularly and receives health insurance, without her boss or customers grabbing her ass as she walks by.

Kirsten explains that "reflection time" is a new Caribou program. Basically, for one hour a week you get out of the store, put away laptops and cell phones, and reflect on the past week and the week ahead. It is time to get centered and grounded.

"Do you ever do it?" I ask her. It sounds really different and maybe a little beneficial. I can't imagine Wal-Mart encouraging anyone to take time to reflect.

"God no! We don't have time for that here, Ben!"

I have been at Caribou for three weeks, but I continually re-live my first day. Over and over again. I never feel like I'm getting better.

CHAPTER 7
DAYDREAMING DUMBASS

Dear customer who needs a receipt,
   Welcome to 2012. The banks will keep track of your finances electronically so I don't have to hit nine extra buttons to give you a receipt for $1.68. What the fuck do you need a receipt for anyways? Are you fucking expensing this fucking cup of coffee you cheap fucking bastard? Not to mention why don't you kill some more trees! I have a little baby so lets leave the earth in decent shape!

Each morning, each day, each shift, I focus on learning new things and trying to do things I should already know. I watch Nash and Kirsten and Stephen and try to get faster and better at everything I do. The first mornings were rough because I didn't know the difference between the blueberry and triple berry muffins, or the scones, and I didn't know where in the case they went. There was a diagram of where each bakery piece should go and it looked like Japanese to me. I really used to think I was smart. It was a lot more confusing than I ever thought it could be. And I'm a man who has bought a lot of bakery items. Finally, stuff starts to sink in and I'm at least not running around like a fool. Well, at least not as much as I was.

   In the mornings I start brewing the coffee, which starts with grinding the coffee laid out yesterday. All I have to do is figure out which is dark and light and which is a half batch. Then I make sure the brewer is on half batch and start brewing. The first batches are easy too because you can tell which are light, dark, half, and full batches. It gets harder as the day goes on because the drawer becomes messy and unorganized. And, I get dumber as the day goes on.

   From there I bring in the newspapers and pull some frozen bakery for when we run out. We always run out of bakery and I ask Kirsten, why don't I just pull it all right now?

"No! Caribou Coffee policy says not until we are running low. Less waste." True, but it leads to less sales, too. And Caribou didn't plan their system with the idea of two people working when there should be four people working. If we have a run on something in the bakery, it's my job to get to the bakery freezer and pull more. Sometimes I realize the bakery is running low, but could not possibly leave the register to go into the freezer. There is rarely enough time to do it. Some days I upsell a blueberry muffin and then realize the entire bakery case is empty. The customers come so fast and so steady, I eventually break out of my daze and realize everything is a mess around me. And empty. Kirsten will run off from the bar and grab the bakery tins. She slams them down behind me.

I have to label which bakery was pulled from the freezer today and which was left over from last night because bakery can only be out for one day. If it's not sold it's donated to the foodshelf. The first day I didn't label anything and I could tell Stephen wanted to yell at me, but Kirsten didn't tell me. If she did, it was in a stream of telling me a million things, and it went in this one ear and out the other.

I'm usually feeling good about the open until the customers show up. The coffee is brewed at exactly 6 a.m., the bakery out and labeled, the newspapers in, but I forgot to put 2% milk and heavy cream in pitchers out on the mix-ins table. Kirsten's first big sigh of the day, as a customer asks for cream with a shocked face, looking like he is going to have a nervous breakdown. Then I get an order and I realize I forgot to brew the decaf coffee.

"Decaf in the morning," I ask innocently. The customer stares at me. I have to quickly grind the decaf into a filter and do a pourover.

"It'll be a few minutes."

"I can make you a decaf Americano if you'd like," Kirsten yells over. I don't know why we are acting like this guy needs his coffee stat? It's decaf! He nods and Kirsten makes him a decaf Americano. Or a hot cup of water for $2.64, I want to say. I didn't think anyone really drank decaf at Caribou. What's the point?

The greeter position's responsibilities are to ring up each customer, tend to the bakery, keep the mix-ins table clean and stocked, keep the soda and juice fridge stocked, and handle all things coffee and tea. The tea part is easy. The coffee thing is easy, too, unless you are a daydreamer like me who simply forgets to monitor the coffee. A smart coffee seller watches the gauge on the urn to see how much coffee is left, and when it gets to a certain point starts brewing more. Or keeps track of how many larges or mediums they have sold and then start brewing more. The goal is to never run out of coffee and keep a customer waiting.

Daydreaming is my first problem. In the moment, when Kirsten and customers are staring at me as we wait for coffee to brew, I question whether I can do this job. It takes 35 seconds to grind the coffee and pour it into the filter. Kirsten butts in and does the whole thing about four seconds.

The second problem is the pace of the job. It isn't like you grab the coffee from the drawer, pour it into the grinder, grind it into the bag, dump the bag in a filter, put the filter brewer, and click the brewer to drain into a big empty urn. You do all of that, but in 10-second bursts between customers. As I pour a coffee I grind beans. As I wait for a customer to get their change, I wash an urn. As I am grabbing the bakery I drop off the dishes. Hundreds of little tasks broken up into even smaller tasks. I am constantly going over the list of tasks in my head because the one time you lose focus you fuck up.

Between these times, a customer comes in and gets in line. I quickly dump the beans into the grinder. But all of a sudden he orders five drinks and a rush ensues. I have now forgotten I already put beans in the grinder, so I grab another bag of beans and now I'm fucked because I combined the two. So then I have to throw away those beans, earning a eye roll from Kirsten, and take more beans that have been laid out to grind, which means I have to eventually go in back and get a bag of beans from the stockroom and re-lay out so we don't run out.

And then there are those Fridays, Saturdays and Sundays when the rush never stops. I feel bad making a long line of people wait while I quickly make coffee, but it has to be done. If we had three people, the third person or the "Super Glue" would do those chores and it would make life a million times easier. But no Super Glue is coming and the line gets so long I no longer have to hear the door chime because the door never closes.

I zone out and completely forget to re-fill the bakery or make coffee or tend to the tables. I start thinking about a book I read, or a certain customer reminds me of someone in a movie and my brain wanders. Or I think about Matt and Gisele and how I can't wait to be home with them. Meanwhile, I go to pour a cup of dark roast and it's bone dry. I hope the customer doesn't notice. I then go to pour a light roast and it's bone dry. Worse, Kirsten will go to pour a cup of coffee to help me out in a rush and everything is bone dry. FUCK!

"Do you have any bakery left?" I look at the bakery case and it's empty except for two chocolate chip cookies. Kirsten looks and slams the milk pitcher down. I wince.

"Don't worry man, you'll get it down," Nash says. "When I started I didn't know how to do anything either. It's all practice."

"It's my third week here. I feel like I should have this stuff down by now."

"Don't be too hard on yourself. It's not easy."

I would like to say Nash is my first friend at Caribou and he is consoling and encouraging through rough times. But he is and he isn't. It's too busy to chitchat much and in the mornings when Nash works, it's fucking busy.

"Do you like this job?" I ask Nash.

"It's the service industry. So I like the customers and hate the customers. It works with my schedule and the tips are nice in the morning." Nash has sandy blond hair and a scrunched face. In the back cooler he keeps protein shakes and healthy smoothies, and during lulls he runs back and chugs them down. He wears medium Caribou shirts to accentuate his muscles, which are already huge. I'm not sure if he really respects Kirsten or is in love with her. Or if he just needs someone on his ass all the time.

Nash tells me he went through rehab for drinking. "The restaurant I worked for let me drink while I did the dishes. It got bad." Now he works early mornings, lifts weights constantly and is going to a community college and hoping to get accepted to the university. He doesn't mind the job, just the customers who are jerks.

"Our old shift supervisor, Brad, would get tons of numbers here."

"Really?"

"He'd start chitchatting on the bar and seal the deal by the time they got their drink." I can barely hear myself think when I am in this coffee shop. Much less have an agenda with customers.

"I hope I get there someday. Not getting girl's numbers, but just being able to do the bar."

"Kirsten doesn't have much patience, but you're doing better than most trainees."

"Oh yeah?" I blush. "Have there been some bad ones?"

"Kirsten has had to yell at a few and I'm sure you heard about Vicki."

Stephen chimes in and agrees that Kirsten has no patience. "She is really good at what she does and expects everyone to know how to do it and do it her way."

Stephen is from Mississippi and moved here to go to seminary school. He is thin and neat, but wears the same black shirt every day. He has thinning brown hair and may be addicted to the licorice rope Caribou sells. We bond over "The Game of Thrones" books we are both reading. Stephen only works in the afternoon, so he doesn't deal with the morning rush.

"Those morning rushes are killer, man. You'll pick it all up soon enough." I'm just not used to this pace. Who is? I have been in thousands of bars and restaurants and fast food joints and never recognized the pace. The fucking pace is a killer. It just grinds me down. I have no time to breathe. Every day while I am working I fantasize about being off and sitting on the other side of the store. Sipping my drink and watching other people work. But I scurry out as quickly as I can when I'm off. As do all of the

other employees. I don't want to spend one more second in hell. I don't tell
Nash or Stephen these thoughts. I don't tell anyone.

"One trainee just started crying when the line got too long. Another guy
we called Twitch would just panic when he was on the bar. He couldn't
remember the drinks and would just get so flustered if even three people
were in line." Nash tells me horror stories of people who obviously felt the
way I feel, but couldn't keep it inside.

"I've seen a lot come and go and I haven't even worked here that long.
People work a shift and never show up again. Kirsten can be pretty hard on
people, but we don't have a lot of room for errors."

I can tell Nash respects Kirsten and wants to do right by her. He
respects her authority. Sometimes I don't get why he works here. Or why
anyone would work here if they had a choice.

"Some of them have been just awful. One was Westin."

Kirsten has told me a little bit about Westin and how she didn't think he
was fit to be a store manager. Kirsten is a training manager and is working
on a system of checklists to determined if a new manager is Caribou
material. Kirsten has mentioned she has had too many managers in training
who were horrible, but she still had to train them. As she tells me this I can't
help but wonder what she has told Christian about my performance. I know
I suck at this job.

"Yeah. Brad and Kirsten were yelling at him every day that he was slow.
He couldn't figure out how to run the oven. The oven! He just didn't go fast
enough. Probably didn't help everyone was yelling at him."

"But he's still with the Caribou?"

"Yeah they promoted him to store manager." He shrugs. I take solace
in Nash's comments. He doesn't think I'm doing that bad and it sounds like
Caribou doesn't fire people no matter how bad they suck. How can they not
realize I'm drowning, though?

I definitely want to talk to Nash and Stephen and the other employees
more, and bond, and get their stories about why they work at Caribou. But
it never happens because we are so fucking busy. Even at night there is
always stuff to do and the store is too big to talk while we are working. The
fucking coffee shop is always busy. Morning regulars, mid afternoon, rush,
and the night regulars create different little coffee shop worlds. When I
watch TV shows now I start yelling at the TV about 'where is the rush?
Where are the customers?' If you have time to make these jokes and
conversations you don't have it so bad!

"Two Broke Girls is the most unrealistic show I have ever seen!" I yell.
Gisele tells me to shut up.

CHAPTER 8
BEING OWNED

Dear customer who orders "the usual,"

Ha! You are hilarious if you think I remember your face or your drink! I must be making this look easy because I can barely remember how to ring up a vanilla latte and I do that 80 times a day! The usual! Are you the guy who says "It's me" on the phone after two dates with a girl? Do you ask a co-worker for a ride to the airport? Because that's what is going on here, you are level jumping our relationship. Most of all you are making me feel like a dick and slowing down the line.

My cousin Aliza complained she couldn't get a summer job at any Caribou. Before I worked at Caribou I would say, "Yeah, why won't those bastards hire you?" Our family openly mocked Caribou because why wouldn't they want a smart college girl for the summer? It didn't make any sense.

Now I know why. Because she is a student and she'll be leaving at the end of the summer. Not only would she be leaving when she was all trained up, but she would be hurting the store because her time on the floor and hours could be used for someone else getting trained. It takes time and payroll to train people. You are shooting for them to stay six months to a year and half. Anything more than that and Caribou considers itself extremely lucky. And if they are good, they could be promoted if they want and if they are smart, they will graduate and leave. Christian explains store manager Billy's hiring philosophy, "Hire people who are smart enough to do the job, but have no outside interests."

In Kirsten's defense, it's hard to hire people in any industry, in any field, in any part of the country, but what makes hiring harder is that Kirsten's Caribou is next to a Chipotle, Noodles and Company, Jamba Juice, Barnes and Noble, Whole Foods, and numerous Mom and Pop stores. Not to mention, within about a three-mile radius the city contains many more Starbucks, and two more Caribous, plus three local coffee houses. It's ridiculously hard to hire and find people who haven't already been hired by someone else.

Obviously, any interview process is not a science. Kirsten does an interview and decides: Do they seem hard working? Would you like to spend a day working with them? How long will they want to work for Caribou? Many people want to work in a coffee shop because it looks fun and cool. It's not. So you look for people with food experience or someone who is used to the pace. So work history is semi-important. Regular people like me are not used to the pace. So then the decision is, can this useless person with no rush experience pick it up and contribute?

The position of a coffee server starts at $7.50 and if they have good experience the store manager can pay up to $8. Nash makes about $30 dollars in tips in the mornings. Kirsten and other store managers don't get a cut of the tips, but the other employees normally have to split their tips.

When Kirsten is not there, one team member acts as the shift supervisor that's really the same thing as being a regular team member, but they must count the money in the safe, which is $400, and have an alarm code to the building. And if a customer gets pissed they have to deal with it. A lot of team members, like Nash, don't want to be shift supervisor because for only a dollar an hour more you get a lot of extra hassle and work.

"I'm not cut out to deal with the customer complaints. I don't know why. Something about it bothers me, and I would probably end up yelling at someone and getting fired--for a dollar extra an hour," Nash explains.

Kirsten did not feed the monster, so her day-to-day life is very stressful. She constantly worries about the store just being covered. "It's no way to live," she tells me with tears in her eyes.

Kirsten and I scour the on-line application system and set up a bunch of interviews. There aren't a lot of great applicants, and the good ones already have interviews set up at other Caribous. Or they are overqualified and ask for $15 an hour for a part-time job at a coffee shop. There is no way they will stick around. Some are engineers, some are teachers, some are people who have tons of experience but not in anything related to what we do. They might be great, but if you pick an applicant and they quit it's a waste of time and energy. Kirsten also breaks every hiring law with comments like, "They seem like they might be kind of old," or "We don't want to hire too many boys." She remains, or tries to remain, diligent in hiring more people.

"We have to start checking this first thing in the morning every day, so we get a shot at the best applicants." *Right, first thing in the morning. I'll put that on my list.*

One day Kirsten and I interviewed three people and I thought two of them were decent. One I didn't like was named Ansair and he and Kirsten started arguing during the interview. That wasn't going to work. That would have been a fun reality show!

The second girl, Heidi, I thought was okay. She had worked for Subway and talked about horrible rushes when a high school football team bus would pull in. She had a good sense of humor and was looking for something in the area because she lived close. Kirsten didn't like her because she thought she was "faking." *What?* It's Kirsten's store so I don't really care, but we need the people. If someone takes the energy and time to fake, then what really do we care? The third girl Kirsten didn't like either but she couldn't explain why. "I don't know if she has the right energy?" Again, I have no idea what this means. Jenna just moved to the city from a small town in North Dakota and she has Starbucks experience. "That can be a bad thing," Kirsten explains. "Sometimes you have to re-teach them out of bad habits."

We give Jenna a shot. Her first day we do orientation and it goes great. The second day she buddies with Kirsten at the bar and she does great. Way better then me! I'm happy because maybe we can start scheduling more people on the weekends! My life will get exponentially better!

And then she doesn't show up her fourth day. And I realize the problem might not be hiring, but the team. The problem might be Beck. Kirsten and I were off and Jenna worked with Nash and Beck. I asked Beck how it went.

"Good. Real good. She was doing well and she said 'see you tomorrow.' She was excited about being done with training so she'd get tips."

"Any reason why she wouldn't show up?"

"None that I can think of. Did she know she was scheduled today?"

I ask Kirsten if she's going to call Jenna and she shrugs. "If she doesn't want to be here, she doesn't want to be here." I call Jenna and leave her a message and I never hear back.

I ask Nash how it went with Jenna yesterday. Nash gives me "the look." The look that says, 'I don't want to say anything, but I want you to know it went bad without saying anything so it doesn't make my life shitty, but you need to know so maybe you can do something about it.' He motions to Beck and grimaces. The problem might not be with the hiring, but with the trainers and the team. I casually ask Beck if new trainees often quit.

"Oh it always happens to me!" She laughs. "One guy, Chad, said he would take the garbage out. I thought, 'oh good, he's actually going to do something.' He never came back!" I fake laugh with her, but she catches on. "Oh, he wasn't mad at me, just the company." *Yes, so many employees hate Caribou.*

"Another guy was supposed to be with me in the morning. He pulled up, looked me right in the eye, and then drove off!" She laughs.

"Wow. What did you do?"

"I called the store manager at that store and he came in."

"Why do you think he quit like that?"

"He was just really upset at the company. And have you heard about Twitch? I thought he was stealing so I started yelling at him and he just quit."

"What was he stealing?"

"It turned out he wasn't stealing, but just made a mistake at the register."

"Oh, I see."

"He would get really nervous when I worked with him, so he wasn't really cut out for it, you know?" Sure. All these people really upset at a company that people are so passionate about loving?

My weekly touch-base with Christian coincides with Kirsten's store manager touch-base and it allows me to observe a store manager touch-base. Every six weeks Christian meets with each store manager and rates each employee, sets hiring goals, and goes over sales numbers.

Before our meeting Kirsten tells me, "Do some of the essential training. Enough for Christian to think you are doing all the training." I don't know why I don't say something, like 'I should probably know all of that stuff before I am on the floor?' One day I cruise through about 10 videos, hardly paying attention, running out to the floor to help. My lasting image from training is a voiceover saying, "after watching fundamental equipment care, you're now ready to handle all equipment maintenance." *Fuck I probably should have been paying attention!*

Do I have Stockholm Syndrome in some weird way? Kirsten confides in me that we are skipping my training so I can help on the floor, and I don't say anything.

When Christian arrives we do a coffee talk and chitchat for awhile about family stuff and then Christian pulls out a store roster. Kirsten starts giving each employee a letter grade and she encourages me to chime in if I have any input. I stop her after one grade.

"You're giving Beck a C?" I ask a little incredulously.

"Do you disagree with that?" Christian asks.

"Um, ah, yeah. Are we talking about the same Beck?"

"What do you mean?" Kirsten asks.

Working with Beck is like permanently working in a "Saturday Night Live" skit. Neither is funny, but it's kind of like a train wreck. It's fun to watch. Beck has red hair and wears it in pigtails. She has freckles and big old-fashioned metal braces. Her smile is a metal, sometimes evil, glow. Beck looks like she is 16 but is actually 27 years old.

The first time Beck freaked out at me was when I was putting the extra clutches away in a basket besides the coffee urns.

"What are you doing?!" She had run across the backside of the bar. "The Caribou logo should face the doors!" Her face was red and she was sweating. I've never been as concerned about anything in my life as Beck was about which way the clutches were facing.

"Is that the company policy or something?"

"No, no." She was composing herself. "I just like them that way, so they are organized properly."

"Right." *'A little OCD?,' I want to ask her.* Beck had regained control and it was an interesting process to watch.

"Does it affect productivity?" I asked her.

"No."

"Is it a rule or something?"

"No. I just…I just like it that way. "

"Okay."

"I just want you to be trained the right way." She said with a smile full of metal. Beck had been one of the most helpful people at Caribou. She knew, literally, everything. She was great on the bar, was great with customers, and ran the store in terms of getting supplies filled and ready for the next day. At one point I asked Kirsten why Beck wasn't more than a shift supervisor, as she seemed really good. Kirsten ignored me.

The next time Beck lost it was because I almost put a dish with crumbs on it in the sink. The nerve of me!

"Stop! Stop! Stop! I hate crumbs in the dishwater! I just hate it!" I found myself staring at the plate with a few crumbs. Am I missing something? Beck grabbed the dish from me and wiped it off, then put it in the sink.

"I just hate crumbs in the dishwater."

I mention it to Kirsten later. "Yeah, Beck is weird about her dishwater. But at least she does dishes." True, I guess.

One afternoon, Beck asked Stephen to make her shift drink. Beck wanted an iced vanilla latte. Stephen, who has made probably thousands of iced vanilla lattes, started his process of squirting the vanilla, adding the milk, and starting the espresso shots, and that's when Beck lost it.

"Do I look like I want burnt plastic in my drink?!" Beck grabbed the cup of the machine and told Stephen to put ice in first. She told him this from about an inch away from his face with spittle shooting from her braces. Stephen started to add ice without saying a word.

"Isn't that the process for making it, though?" I asked.

Beck turned on me with a crazy look in her eye. Then reigned it in.

"I prefer to have the espresso added after it's iced. Less of a chance the hot espresso will melt the cup." After this incident, I realized everyone hated

Beck. Including Kirsten, who also knew everyone hated working with Beck. The problem? Beck owns Kirsten.

As I learn more and more about running a coffee shop, I learn more and more about how destructive a shift supervisor and co-worker Beck is. Kirsten's store will never run correctly with Beck empowered to be herself.

Beck does everything a good manager should not do. She likes things done her way, which is not according to Caribou policy. And then loses her shit on whichever employee does something she doesn't like.

Beck assigns blame, almost systematically. As soon as I walk into the store she gives me a list of things that weren't done, or done correctly, and who was to blame.

"The safe was $1 off. Stephen miscounted last night." This in no way effects anything we do. "The cooler mix wasn't done so we might run out tomorrow. Medora didn't make enough." This can be fixed in four hours by making some right now. "We are low on quarters. Kirsten didn't get enough again at the bank yesterday." Again, we can find quarters in about 10 minutes. Beck's worst management attribute is telling everyone the sky is falling over every little thing. She relishes the sky falling. It's exhausting not worrying about what she worries about. And then on the other hand, Beck cares about the store and the customers, and I can see why Kirsten trusted her. But the more and more I learned about the operations of Caribou, I realize Beck screws up like everyone else once in awhile, but she will not admit or accept it.

Beck forgot to order more quarters and blamed it on someone else. It's not a big deal that she forgot, but now she is blaming someone else. One day I realize the closing shift forgot to make the iced coffee. It was Beck, but later she blamed Liz.

Some of the regular customers, love–just love–Beck. Some people only come on the days Beck works because she makes them the best latte! Beck is our own little Eddie Haskell. Beck is awesome at selling, can do the bar in the morning rush, and she loves Caribou and wants to become a store manager. A growth candidate to boot! She will help any other store if they need help and she takes ownership!

When Kirsten is gone, Beck will make sure everything is up and running, but Beck's interpersonal skills keep things going badly for Kirsten. Kirsten knows Beck is ruining things, but she needs Beck to keep the store from going down in flames. One day Beck comes in after Stephen and I had the place looking great after a huge rush. Sensing our success, Beck said she could get the place put back together even if it was busy tonight. Stephen, the seminary student, said, "What the fuck is she talking about?"

"So what would you do if you ran the store?" Christian asks me.

"Easy. I would fire Beck. No other choice." Christian nods gravely and Kirsten looks off and tears up. "She is horrible for the store." Kirsten looks away and starts crying. "It would be hard to account for the hours at first. But after a while it would be a lot better."

But Beck owns us. And we all know it. Beck runs off good employees, so we keep hiring hoping people stick, in the meantime depending on Beck. It's a fun, sick cycle and I feel for Kirsten having to live through it. It's going to be a huge effort to get out from under Beck's thumb.

Christian and Kirsten have talked to Beck about her behavior, but she doesn't see it. "Worse, she wants to be a store manager, but will not be a part of the process. The normal course is assistant manager in training, assistant manager, then store manager in training and then store manager. Beck just wants to go right to the top."

Kirsten has wiped her tears away. "I'm really impressed you have sensed what we saw, so quickly." *It wasn't that hard.*

"Or we could just promote her! That's really the easiest way to get rid of someone. Ship her off to another district," I offer. Christian doesn't laugh, though. "It gets more complicated," he says, shaking his head. Christian explains the new vice president of operations trained a few weeks ago at the Lake store for two days. All Caribou executives spend time at a store. This would be Christian's boss's boss. And guess who the new VP loved? That's right, she worked with and loved Beck.

"When she was done with training, her parting comment was, 'We've got to keep that Beck,'" Christian laughs a little and then looks like he is going to cry.

My God, Beck does own us.

CHAPTER 9
IS THIS THE ONE WITH CHOCOLATE?

Dear customer that deeeeeeeestroys the mix-ins table,
   What the fuck does your house look like? How can you spill so much sugar in literally five seconds? How can you spill so much cream? How can you grab for one napkin and pull out 40? How can you not throw the wrappers in the garbage, but just leave them on the table? That's what I don't understand! Did you not see the garbage right next to you? It's fucking hard to miss! So you must have opened the Splenda packets and just left them on the table for someone else to throw away. You make me we want to punch you! Even if you are in a hurry, it would take literally a half a second and then I wouldn't have to spend 10 minutes cleaning up. Because that's time away from getting people their caffeine quickly.

After almost a month at Caribou, I make a lot fewer mistakes and even Kirsten notices. "Good job, Ben! You didn't forget that much stuff today." I'm not cut out for this work and I think she notices that too. She asks me if I am culturally aligned with Caribou. I don't know what to say. I think so? Sometimes I think it's not that I have gotten better at the job, it's just that I cover up my mistakes better.

   I do a little task like get the filter out. Then while pouring the next coffee, I empty it. I am doing little pieces of little jobs every second I can. But then my mind starts daydreaming about being a movie producer or something. And I forget what step I was on. Then all of a sudden I have filled the grinder with two batches of coffee. Shit. A few weeks ago I would start the whole process from the beginning. Now? I guesstimate. Or I mix up the dark and light batches. I guess again. Hoping no one notices. And no one ever does.

   I mix up the coffee a lot. Kirsten has color-coded everything blue and green so you know which one is light and dark. But I forget if green means light or dark roast. I used to ask Kirsten which color meant what again, but now I just mix them and don't worry about it. And I don't have to listen to Kirsten sigh as much, which is nice. I have messed up the coffee so badly I'm surprised no one has complained. I'm surprised no one has noticed.

On another long Saturday, Kirsten tells me yet again that if she wasn't there I would have run out of coffee. There was a line out the door so I never quit ringing people up. Faster than you can believe, the coffee has run out. She has to realize we could run these weekend days better, right? The endless line creeps out the door, and the bakery case is empty. We get no lull, and I just keep going. I forget about basic needs like having to go to the bathroom, eat, or drink water. I have never had a 15-minute break or a lunch break. I've never had a break besides counting down my drawer or quickly running off to the bathroom. Gisele makes me these beautiful huge lunches, but I tell her not to bother. I have no time to eat at Caribou.

"If people are hungry they just grab something," Kirsten tells me and I don't know if she is being funny or serious. My throat is dry. I'm crabby. The worst part is the time doesn't go by fast. You would think being insanely busy, I would look up at the clock and three hours would have gone by like a snap of my fingers. Nope. Time does not fly if you are not having fun.

I make myself avoid looking at the clock constantly and dive into the work. As a treat, I occasionally allow myself to look at the clock. Then my spirit is crushed as only 35 minutes has passed. Not the whole shift as I was wishing.

I drink coffee in the morning now with lots of cream just for the caffeine buzz, but I also have a small coffee bladder. Eventually I have to go to the bathroom. In a mini-lull, I run back to the bathroom and pray the men's room is empty. I have a small amount of time to get in and get out. I do the whole thing in less than nine seconds. You don't want to know how. The door keeps chiming. If the bathrooms are full I have to go back to work and wait for the next lull. Usually our longest shifts are six hours. It sucks.

I think about quitting hourly. Doesn't everyone here? Am I a quitter? No, I'm not going to quit. It's just fun to think about to get me through the day. Thinking about quitting is almost a euphoric feeling that I think about a lot while I'm working. I imagine a big show of quitting and throwing down my towel! Or just never showing up again! Or meeting with Christian and saying I need a new place to train. It is no way to live.

The endless rush and busy work, the constant chatter and annoyances of customers. Everything is constant. It seems like the day will never end and then I start thinking about having to come back the next day. It's just me and one other person again tomorrow. Worse than being in the middle of a huge rush with just Kirsten and me, is that I have to come back tomorrow and do the whole thing over again. Do you understand being in a hellish rush and I'm already starting to sweat about the same thing tomorrow?

Nothing is getting better tomorrow. There is no help on the horizon. *This is the job, I sigh.*

I think about crying or hitting someone or quitting. I think about getting through a rush and then working even harder to get cleaned up for the next rush. No matter how good things are going there are other rushes right around the corner. Unmanageable rushes. Soul crushing rushes that four people might be able to handle comfortably but, two people cannot handle. My days turn into a dreary existence.

Like seeing the sun through the clouds, I notice my parents walk in with Matt. There is no one behind them, a lull that I should be frantically filling and cleaning, but I am able to hold my son for a few moments. My baby. He gives me energy. I remember why I'm here. Kirsten comments how cute he is, and as I give him back to my Mom he wants to come back to me. Holding my little boy gets me through the day.

That is why we are all here. My coworkers all have a Matt in their life. The day goes by a little easier after having him in my arms. I have to keep going for my family. It gets me through the days. It could always be worse, I think. I could be shoveling shit or tarring roofs or doing horrific job in a mine. It's easy to think of much worse jobs. The real question I think about at night is not so easy to answer. Is Wal-Mart a worse place to work then Caribou? Hmm…I tell myself I'm not ready to answer yet. I have to give Caribou more time before deciding.

One day Kirsten tells me we will do the final touchbase as teammate certification. "Uh, okay. All I've done is work the floor as greeter." She doesn't care. I am in no way ready.

I take a test on the computer with 50 multiple-choice questions. I have never heard a lot of the questions, but it's multiple choice so I get an 84 percent. Kirsten tells me Caribou has changed some of their policies, so about five of the answers have changed since when the test was written. That makes me feel better. Unless they were the ones I got right? *I'm sure that not knowing the current policies and procedure will not backfire.*

Then Kirsten brings me out to the bar. "I have a list of drinks you should be able to make. Then I weigh them and taste them to make sure they are up to Caribou standards."

"Uh okay. But I haven't made a drink since my first couple of days." I'm not lying either. I have only been the greeter. She doesn't care. Well, here we go.

"A latte." *Uh, is this the one with chocolate?* I pour espresso and steam some milk, but I have no idea of shot counts or pumps of flavor. Does just a latte have flavoring? Is there a latte flavoring? Does every latte have vanilla? Kirsten weighs it and tastes it, but it can't be right. She doesn't say anything.

"A medium cappuccino." *Uh, is this the one with chocolate?* I don't know how to froth the cappuccino foam, and I put water in it. It's a watery espresso milk drink. That's kind of how all the drinks I make turn out.

"A white chocolate mocha." *Finally the drink with chocolate!* I use dark chocolate and I don't know the espresso shot count. I also steam the milk instead of combining it with the chocolate in a pitcher. At this point we should stop the whole charade, but Kirsten presses on.

I stumble through. I'm really rattled not knowing the basics of these drinks.

"An almond tea latte." I have no idea how to do it or what pitcher to use. *Do we have almond flavoring?* Is this a trick question? It is not. A tea latte? *What the hell is that?*

"A grilled cheese sandwich." *Sandwiches I'm a god at!* But my confidence is so shaken after the bar debacle that I put the sandwich in wonky. The brown parchment paper folds over and creates a half-cooked sandwich.

Stephen is watching and later asks how much time I was on the bar.

"Roughly a day and a half with Kirsten. Otherwise all greeter."

"It takes a lot of practice to be on bar." I don't know if Kirsten is trying to sabotage me or just doesn't care. She never fails me on the test. She never brings it up to Christian. I decide she doesn't care about my future.

I decide right then and there I have to teach myself to be a barista, no matter how daunting and scary it will be. No one is going to teach me.

The angel and devil on my shoulders have a conversation.

"Who gives a shit about not knowing the bar? It is intense over there! Obviously no one cares if we don't know it."

"We need to learn the bar, no matter how hard it is, because in the future we will be expected to know it. And to be good at it."

"No wants to train us on it! So we can slide by and not worry about the extra aggravation."

"If we learn the bar we will not have anything to be afraid of at Caribou. We are in training. It's our time to learn and if we don't utilize this time it will come back to haunt us."

I know I have to learn the bar. It's just not going to be fun. And a few customers are probably going to get pretty pissed. In the movie of my life it would make sense to cue the montage to 80's music of me learning the bar. The problem was no one wanted to teach me the bar or give me any time on the bar. The montage would basically be me whining to let me work the bar. Then quickly switching back when things got too busy for me. I know, pathetic.

CHAPTER 10
BARISTA MOVIE MONTAGE

Dear Starbucks customer who comes to a Caribou and orders Starbucks drinks,

I do not know what a frappuccino is. If you say tall, grande, venti or whatever shit you are saying, I will simply say ,"So you want a large?" It's is not my job to figure what you get at Starbucks and what it will be here. Why are you ordering a Starbucks drink here? Would you order a Big Mac at Burger King? Would you try to buy a Civic at a Ford dealership? Then when you get the fucking large drink you stare quizzically and ask is this a small? No, it's a fucking large. And if you want a small why didn't you fucking say small? Why did you say tall if you knew we served smalls and then said yes when I said large? Why are we playing this game?

To become even a low-level functioning barista I am going to have to really work hard at something that scares me. It's not something you just pick up by being at the coffee shop. You really have to pay attention.

First I have to literally figure out what these drinks consist of, so I write down every drink combination. Being at the register I kind of know what is in the drinks, but not near the level I need to know. I don't need to write down thousands of drink combinations. I've learned that these drinks are not really all that different. A little milk, a little espresso, sometimes chocolate, and a few different toppings make up three-fourths of the drinks. But within that structure it can be complicated until you know the drink combinations. For some people that takes a day or even a few hours. The numbers and whatnot click in their heads. Others, like me, need hours and hours of practice to remember the combinations.

Every down moment, from driving to sitting on the toilet to watching TV, I think about different drink recipes. I have Gisele quiz me on every drink and I envision how I would make it. I ask friends and family what their favorite drink is and envision if I could make it. "If you have to think about making a drink you are going to forget something else," Kirsten told me.

The Lake store has a Super Automatic espresso machine and until I used a traditional espresso machine I didn't realize how fucking fast and easy it makes espresso. The only challenge is to keep a mental track of how many shots have been pulled because the machine will start filling up a bucket with used espresso grounds. It takes about 25 seconds to change the bucket. And if the bucket is full the machine will not pull shots. We have three espresso machines and on top of each are two compartments, one for regular espresso beans and another for decaf espresso beans. The machine is easy to clean and pretty easy to put back together. The only thing that can go wrong is you run out of espresso beans or the bucket fills up. I did both at the same time in a rush.

"You don't see that very often," Stephen commented.

Each espresso shot is exactly the same volume and timed at the start of each new shift by the barista. There is one notch to switch if the shots are coming out too fast or too slow, but usually they are perfect. It makes life easy having the shots be consistent. I can put the small espresso pitchers under the nozzle, press the button, and walk away and do other stuff like steaming milk. There isn't much to tinker with on the Super Automatic and that's the point. Drink orders come so fast that the barista doesn't have time to be fiddling with the espresso machine.

I receive my horoscope text while I am nervously doing the bar. Capricorn: Whatever task is put before you, give it your full focus; a moment of distraction could cost you in more ways than one. *It's in these moments that I think, maybe there is a God watching me.*

Later in my career, I would work on a traditional espresso machine, which is great if you want inconsistent espresso, full of espresso bean dust, made slower! But coffee snobs love to complain about how the Super Automatic is destroying the world! It is fast, consistent, and easy to use. With all the ways to screw shit up, having the Super Automatics takes one mistake out of the equation, which is great for idiot baristas like me!

Learning drinks also starts with "milk standards," which Caribou believes distinguishes it from Starbucks. Milk should not be steamed to past 160 degrees for adults and 110 degrees for kids. The Super Automatic machines automatically take them to 160 degrees, but the traditional machines require a temperature gauge to be dropped in which is fucking annoying.

Milk at Caribou can only be re-steamed once and it must be below 100 degrees before you can re-steam it. I have no idea where these numbers came from, but I've played around with milk quite a bit and after two steams the bubbles get weird looking. I wouldn't serve a cappuccino or latte customer milk that's been steamed more than twice, but mochas don't taste any different. The foam does look different. Steaming milk takes time, especially frothing, which is that fun coffeehouse sound you hear. It probably makes you happy, but to me it means time. Time I need. We froth the milk, which means putting the steam wand just under the surface, up to 100 degrees and then we steam the milk to 160 on its own. The easiest way to get in the weeds (besides assholes) is lots of hot drinks because then it's milk, shots, milk, shots, over and over again. So to combat this on busy days, I steam a huge pitcher of milk for emergencies, like a 10 drink family order or a bitchy customer complaining I put in two shots of decaf and one shot of regular espresso, not the other way around. I steamed milk 10 times once, just to see what it looked like. It was a little ragged, but nothing awful. You add a little vanilla, chocolate, and some espresso to any warm milk and it's still good.

Whenever someone says any three—digit numbers in the coffee world that means a small gets three, medium four, and a large five. Hot drinks have 3-4-5 of flavor shots and take 2-3-4 in chocolate chips, which go into a plastic pitcher with the milk. And finally hot drinks get 2-2-3 for espresso shots. So yes, when you pay for a medium you are getting the same amount of espresso as a small. Unless, and this is where it can get confusing, if that hot drink ends in a "o," the shots are 2-3-4. I remember Kirsten explaining this too me like how to screw in a light bulb. It was so simple in her eyes. I had to sit down I was so woozy after hearing the shot counts for the first time.

Cold drinks are much easier to make because there is not frothing or steaming. It's super easy! I envied our southern states coffee shops for not having to make as many lattes and mochas. Now, iced drinks come in bigger cups than hot drinks, so the combinations are different. We also have a junior cup for the kiddies, so the flavor shots are 3-4-5-6, chocolate syrup, no chocolate chips or whipped cream, and cold drinks, mind you, are 2-3-4-5, and espresso shots are 1-2-3-4, even though most parents do not get their kid an espresso drink. And again if the iced drink ends in "o", like a macchiato or americano, the espresso shots are 2-3-4-5. It's not so hard to remember when five people aren't staring at you wanting their drink and watching you make it. And commenting you are not the usual barista.

Eventually I got all the drink shot counts memorized. I would still write with paint marker on the scoops of chocolate or espresso and if you frequent coffee shops you might see this. Little cheat sheets. Kirsten didn't like the cheat sheets because she thought people came to depend on them. *As long as the drink comes out right and fast who gives a shit?*

Second step was figuring out all these famous Caribou concoctions. A Mint Condition has mint syrup, espresso, chocolate chips (either milk, dark or white,) steamed milk like a mocha, and whipped cream and crushed Andes. Crushed Andes? I had never heard of this drink or these candies, but it is ridiculously popular. If you say, "I'll have a mint condition," there can be a bunch of options. A Mint Condition is technically made with white chocolate, but some people want dark or milk chocolate. What kind of chocolate, do you want regular or light whip, do you want skim or 2 percent milk? Each drink is a little different, but the same, and a lot of customers have little changes. About 90 percent of people know what they want, or don't want any changes to the recipe. And about 10 percent of people don't know what they want or just know they want it different. Which slows me down at the bar. Often I'm standing there with a cup in my hand as the customer hems and haws about what chocolate they want while the line backs up.

Turtle Mochas have Snickers bits on top with a caramel drizzle. A Caramel High Rise has just whip and caramel drizzle, and the Campfire Mocha has chocolate chips and marshmallow bits on top. It's confusing until you make 1,000 of them and then you realize the menu isn't so big. Caribou drinks can be made into a hot drink, cold drink and coolers, and each is basically the same. And pretty soon, you've got it down. Americano is water and espresso, espresso is simply that, and of course there are lattes. Lattes are our most popular drink and my least favorite to make because you have to steam and froth so much milk. They take time. I begin to hate latte drinkers just for that reason. And if they order a decaf latte? *Fuck you! I want to scream.*

There are four phases to becoming a great barista. Some people never get past phase one, and some people are so scared they never try phase one.

Phase one is knowing the drink ingredients and the menu, like shot counts, flavor pumps, milk and frothing standards, chocolate chip and whipped cream add-ons, and the ability to remember all of this with someone watching. This phase can take anywhere from one hour to months and months.

Phase two is making the drink correctly for actual customers consistently. This is harder than you might think. The pressure is on when you are making a drink that a customer is waiting for. I know it seems simple, but it's real. I would work the bar in the afternoon and it was steady, but not crazy. I could easily make one drink at a time. I was focused on those drinks and made them perfectly. I easily knocked out a mocha and then a latte, and then a cooler. My mind would tell me what to do. There are four phases to a great barista and I was at two. I was really doing it!

Phase three is not only making perfect drinks, but doing everything else that comes with the barista spot. Filling the espresso machine with more beans, keeping the ice filled, keeping my dishes low, keeping the cups filled, keeping my milks filled, because if I need one of things in a rush and I don't have it I am fucked. People don't like to wait for their caffeine. My barista motto is I am always waiting for the next rush. Even if it's a small rush. I learned this lesson on a lazy afternoon with Stephen. Stephen encouraged me to be on the bar to learn it better because I told him I wanted to work the morning rush but wasn't ready.

I worked a good steady lunch rush, nothing crazy and everything died down. Instead of cleaning and filling, we chit chatted about the "Game of Thrones." Then I had to go to the bathroom, and when I got back the drink board was fucking filled! A family had walked in and behind them another family. Fuck, fuck, fuck. I was rattled and mad at myself for wasting time. Naturally the espresso machine bucket started chirping that it was full and needed to be emptied. Then I ran out of beans on the other one. Then my chocolate chips were a little low. I yelled at myself on the inside, and of course I wasn't paying attention to the drinks.

"Those coolers are decaf for the kids, right?"

"Uh…" And the customer knows instantly they are not decaf. *FUCK.* It was a rough rush, but worth it because I learned something. I would always be ready. I never wanted to feel out of control and in the weeds again. Never. To learn to be a great barista there has to be some causalities. And by casualties I mean drinks that are prepared wrong. You can't learn if you don't make drinks in a rush for live customers.

Cut to my '80s, movie montage of all my mistakes while learning to be a barista. I made a Mint Condition without the vanilla chocolate. *Idiot!* She came back and I made her a large one on the house! My goal now is that if I must screw up, to never screw up *that* drink again. I made a mocha no whipped cream with the whipped cream. I even told her I put on extra whipped cream. I made a latte and forgot the espresso. *I thought it felt like I poured a lot milk in there!* I forgot to put the espresso bean on top of the mocha, I put whipped cream on a coffee cooler, I didn't get a sandwich out of the oven in time, I put milk in the oatmeal instead of water and….it looked gross.

I would force my way onto the bar in slow times, even though Stephen, Beck and Kirsten hated being the greeter.

"I have to learn," I plead. They sigh and let me do it.

"This is something I want to do. It's not easy or fun." I wanted to tell them it sucked and I hated it. Because I did. I tried to remember something in my life I concentrated so hard on before being on bar. I couldn't think of anything. Every second I was thinking about what I was doing and what had to be done next. It was exhausting. As I was trying to think of a time in my life when I had to concentrate like this, I notice a customer staring at me from the end of the bar.

"Can I help you?" There wasn't any drink waiting at the bar and I didn't have anything on my screen.

"I'm just waiting for my latte." I made him a latte and then checked the drink screen history. I was ready to yell at Medora for putting a drink in wrong, but nope, there it was! I had tapped it off without making it! *Serenity now!*

I would work the bar until it would get a little too busy for me and then I would yell "tag out" or "switch." Sometimes I would get caught in the weeds because I didn't know how to make something like a past seasonal drink, or there were too many drinks in a row and I just couldn't keep up. Or I diligently made the one drink, but had not started any preparation for the next drinks. I started to recognize customers and their drinks, which was great because I could have the drinks halfway done before they ordered.

I started trying to batch drinks, which means to make two or three drinks at a time. Customers would make life easy for me by ordering quickly and not changing their drink. If two friends both ordered lattes, I could quickly batch the milk and life would be good. Nothing would throw off my pace more than when two lattes were ordered, I started batching, and the friend then asked for skim or whole milk. *I hate you!*

Like with anything, I got better over time, but I never truly enjoyed it. I now knew things I couldn't even comprehend a few weeks ago. I used to spend precious moments measuring out milk for two mediums, now I knew exactly how much to pour through repetition. I now knew when milk was done steaming by the sound it makes, not by sight, and I would pull it out just as the automatic steamer/temp gauge turned off. It's a small satisfying moment to know when milk is 160 degrees before a machine does. I knew the blender takes nine seconds to go through the number two cycle, so I would have nine seconds to wash two dishes.

The barista is an endless, endless set of tasks. The same tasks literally over and over and over again. I would make drinks in a fevered panic constantly moving and filling and rushing because I never wanted to get in the weeds again. I hated latte orders because it was endless steaming and frothing of milk.

Because when the weeds came for me they came bad. I screwed up a cappuccino and made it with too much milk.

"I want it very dry." I had no idea what this meant, so I guessed.

"This isn't dry like Kirsten makes it."

"I can remake it for you."

Fuck. As I'm re-making her drink, while she peers intently over the counter staring, new drink orders keep coming. *You staring at me really help me make drinks lady!*

"This still has too much milk! This isn't like Kirsten makes." Jesus Christ lady! I make it fucking again. *Why don't we call Kirsten in every time you need a cappuccino I want to scream!* I learn then you can't make some cappuccino drinkers happy.

"Cappuccinos are hard to make right with soy," Stephen tells me later. "They don't foam up so well."

"Information that would have been useful earlier!" I mock yell at him. In busy times I start keeping a pitcher of milk with perfect foam on hand, just for those cappuccino drinkers who love foam.

I screw up plenty of drinks on my own though and I get into the weeds. I make a chai latte with espresso. Twice.

"This doesn't taste right." The woman is sweet and nice about it the fucking second time I make it.

"I'm sorry, I'll make that again. Nash, make a chai latte for me." I watch him add chai and milk, but no espresso. Ah-ha! I remember that woman every time I make a chai latte now. If they order a dirty chai then it has espresso in it.

To this day, I remember how to make some particular drinks correctly by remembering the customer's face when I screwed it up the first time I made it. Sometimes I realize just as I'm handing a drink to a customer, I made it wrong. I watch their expressions and either they immediately turn around or they do nothing. I get good at some point and I am finally ready to work a for real morning rush.

In my head, I tell myself I will be the morning barista even though no one talks about it. I think about it constantly, like climbing some huge mountain. I arrive at the store and sit in my car. I pump myself up! I walk in with Beck and I start doing the barista morning tasks. I dive right in and Beck doesn't say anything either. We get all the way to 6 a.m., store opening time.

"Are you ready for this?" she asks. And that's when I chicken out.

"No, I'll be greeter." I try to think of things I have been scared of in my life. There's not a lot, and not even all that much I've been really that nervous about either. Maybe presenting at a meeting or public speaking, but I haven't been nervous about that for many years.

I chicken out more than I like to admit. I can be the barista in the afternoon and at night, and I'm fine. It's something about the morning rush that terrifies me. So many people, so many orders, so many sandwiches, so much milk frothing. I make myself nervous just thinking about the mornings. And then one day I look at the schedule and see Beck's name crossed off. Only my name and Nash's name are on for an upcoming morning.

"Beck and I can't work till 10 that day. You and Nash should be all right," Kirsten says. *Is she fucking high?!* And for the next week it is all I can think about. Because Nash cannot do the bar in the morning because Kirsten has had him at greeter while she does the bar. And I technically can.

I'm fucking nervous as shit and I think about quitting. I fucking hate the bar. I sit in my car staring at Caribou. It looks so nice and pleasant from the outside. Fuck, I don't want to work the morning rush. I'll get in the weeds. I sit in my car and I think I'm going to throw up. The second busiest Caribou in the city on a Saturday is depending on me to be the barista? *Are you shitting me?!*

And then Nash offered to do the bar. I debated in my head. I could avoid this whole thing. I was done chickening out. So even if the day goes bad, at least I know that I didn't chicken out.

And I made it.

At the end of our shift Nash tells me he thinks I am better than him at the bar now, and I feel good, even though I don't enjoy the bar.

"You go so fast, even on easy drinks."

What Nash doesn't realize is that my speed is out of sheer panic for not wanting to fall behind. Constant panic makes me a good barista. It's draining and I wish I could work the bar with the causal confidence of Kirsten or Beck, who seem to enjoy the whole thing.

Sitting in my car at the end of the day, I feel a moment of euphoria. I did it. I had faced my fear. The whole shop didn't come to a grinding halt. I didn't erupt in tears and I didn't quit. I have areas I can improve on--it was certainly not the best I could do. Like I cursed myself when I didn't fill the ice during a lull and then had an order for four coolers and ran out of ice. I had to take precious moments with customers waiting in line to fill the ice! *Fucking fuck! I screamed in my head.*

I didn't monitor the espresso beans and ran out during a semi-rush. Fuck. How could I let the espresso beans get so low on two machines? *That could have been a disaster!* I vowed never to forget. *I think you've vowed that before I tell myself. Shut up!* During any dull time I listed off things to do in my head: check ice, check espresso, clean steam wands, check teas, check milk fridge, walk dining room for plates, start hot water for dishes, knock out a few dishes each lull, and on the list goes.

And that's what a barista does. A neverending, repeating set of jobs. And I hate it. And I start to sweat thinking about the next time I have to do the bar.

A phase three Barista also has to do the morning shit jobs. An already busy morning is accompanied by a bunch of shitty to-do tasks, so teas and bakery are fresh.

The thing about a coffee shop is it creates coffee drinkers. (And oddly enough, I can't write now unless I'm slamming coffee with steamed milk.) I didn't drink coffee before I worked at Caribou, but now I do because I need the caffeine to get through the early morning rushes.

We arrive at 5:30 a.m. and have the store opened at 6 a.m. Now we don't just open and it's chill out the rest of the morning. There are people waiting at the door when I open it every damn day. And they want their fucking caffeine now and they want it cheerfully. Just because it's early doesn't mean we cannot be chitchatty and happy.

I make six tea extracts for the day for the iced teas. It's basically measuring out tea extracts and soaking for 20 minutes. If you ever find yourself making these I recommend labeling the bottles. I mixed them up and couldn't remember which was which and had to start all over. I also got the water wrong and made the most watered down tea extract ever. "Did you make these teas?" Kirsten asks a loaded question. *God I am a fucking idiot.*

We make yogurts for the day in the morning. You might ask, why not do this at night since mornings are already stressful? If you make it at night you lose a day of freshness and would have to throw it away earlier. It's annoying to have to do all this stuff in the morning but it make sense. It just makes the morning an anxious, nerve wrecking living hell. The barista monitors the cooler mix, which isn't hard to make, but if you make too little and you run out everyone hates you. And if you make too much and you have to throw it away, Kirsten yells at you. It's fun!

In the morning, I drain the five-gallon bucket cold press through a filter into pitchers which is annoying to do with customers coming and coming. I try to stock the sandwiches from the freezer, but they all still look alike to me. I forget to pull some or I pull way too much of one. Then we have to throw them out and Kirsten sighs and tears come to her eyes.

"I'll get it from now on," I tell her. The morning list just keeps getting longer and longer. If you make a nice list at home and don't get something done, who cares? But if you forget to make cooler mix, or pull fresh sandwiches, people get fucking pissed, including everyone you are working with.

"Uh we sold out of the Day Breakers," I hear Carlee tell a customer and it's like disappointing my parents.

"You ran out of Day Breakers sandwiches at 9:30 a.m.?" the customer asks. 'I'm human,' I want to yell! 'I made a mistake!'

I don't even think of having the morning sleepies while being on the bar and having a list of shit to do that affects the rest of the day. Because the drinks keep coming and if you aren't thinking about the next-next-next drink while making this drink, you will quickly be in the weeds. And people hate waiting for a drink any time of the day, but combine that with being in a hurry to get to work and I feel hate bullets from the customers. Caribou's goal is to have your drink in your hand when you walk in the door in four minutes.

Carlee is a University of Minnesota student who has red hair and wears big black glasses. She is arty and hip, but instead of being aloof she is super nice. She has worked at Caribou for almost a year and has never learned the bar because of the very reason I wasn't learning the bar. No one wanted to teach her. So I make it my project to get Carlee and another employee, Medora, a little bar time. They panic at first. With my mock bravado I tell them it's easy when you get the pace down. Which is a lie.

You can be a great phase three barista, but not be a great phase four barista. A phase four barista, is a barista who can successfully work the rush ridiculously fast, with few mistakes and by getting the customers their drinks within two minutes of when they order them. To become a phase four barista, you need two things--ears. I am not only making the drink for the person standing at the end of the bar, but I'm starting the drink for the person in line. I've started the milk or drawing the espresso, so when you arrive at the bar it's ready. It's kind of a Zen/in-the-zone thing. Plus I'm eyeballing the door for regulars whose drinks I can knock out quickly before they order.

A bad Caribou manager once told me to improve his customer service scores, he wanted the barista to chitchat with customers. NO! The barista should be listening, concentrating on drinks, announcing drinks, and saying thank you in a morning rush. The listening zone is key.

So now you understand why when a customer changes his order it slows everything down. We've already started making it! *Order right the first time!*

At my sixth week of training I was feeling pretty good about myself. I thought I was a decent barista, heading towards a phase four barista. I hated it, mind you, but I could do it. I was terrified every minute of falling behind, but on the outside looking in people thought I was doing well.

"Why am I off the schedule on Wednesday and Thursday?" I ask Kirsten.

"Christian wants you to observe the drive-thru."

"Oh my god I am so scared of the drive-thru!" Beck chimes in. "I could never work at a drive-thru." I'm a little surprised to hear Beck say that because even with her faults she is a hard worker and competent barista. And if Beck is scared of it I should be passing out in horror.

"Why are you scared of it?"

"I've heard stories that it's just so intense. Danni Kaye had to go there and she said she started hyperventilating." I look to Kirsten. She nods. Danni Kaye had been promoted from Kirsten's store to an assistant manager. I had not heard a bad word about her.

"You'll do fine." The one thing I was banking on was that Kirsten had said "observe." I'm sure they wouldn't put me anywhere that would compromise the business.

I arrive at the drive-thru Caribou at 5:25 a.m. The store manager, Billy, hasn't arrived yet and the four other employees mingle in front of the store. I introduce myself and we wait. I was getting antsy. The store opens at 6 a.m. and one of the employees is pointing out cars in the parking lot. Customers waiting like sharks swirling in shallow water.

A blue Fiat flies into the lot and Billy jumps out and runs up to the door. Everyone bustles in and gets the store going. I stand back and observe how they fill the bakery case. In general, I lay low and kept my eyes down, kind of like in high school when you didn't know the answer, but didn't want to look like you didn't know the answer because if you looked like you didn't know the answer the teacher would call on you.

Billy walks right up to me and throws me a headset. "You're drive thru-greeter. Don't start crying if it gets bad."

CHAPTER 11
HAVE YOUR FUCKING MONEY READY

Dear customer going through the drive-thru,
HAVE YOUR FUCKING MONEY READY! HAVE YOUR FUCKING
MONEY READY! HAVE YOUR FUCKING MONEY READY! HAVE YOUR
FUCKING MONEY READY! HAVE YOUR FUCKING MONEY READY!
HAVE YOUR FUCKING MONEY READY!

"Okay. How does this thing work?" As I heft the headset in my hand.

"You've never worked a headset?" Billy screams. I become scared shitless.

"I've never worked service industry before Caribou."

Billy shows me the on/off switch, and how it beeps when a customer is at the window, where I am supposed to put in the order. It's like I'm on TV! There are two registers side by side. I take the order and then sent it to the other register, where another guy takes the money and serves the drinks to customers out the window. Two people did the bar, and then there was another entire register set for the dining room customers. Five of us have headsets and I was the only one who talked to customers, so everyone could hear what was going on.

I begin taking orders. I hate the way my voice sounds. Nervous. I know my voice sounds a little different than it normally does. I know people are listening. I don't know if I can do this.

My whole life up to this point I had been on the other side of this scenario and now I was working the drive-thru. You may think I'm being crazy here but working the Caribou drive-thru gave me the confidence to do literally anything. Once I faced the drive-thru nothing else scared me.

The morning drive-thru peaked at 9 a.m. and I was busy the next three hours. I hadn't realized how much I knew. Customers would ask what was on the menu and I had to know. When they asked me to explain what was in a drink, I knew. I had to upsell over the headset. I had to do all of this for a neverending line of cars with five people listening to me. Sometimes I couldn't hear or understand the customer and everyone would yell, "Turkey Bacon Mini!"

A few minutes before 9 a.m. the morning got busier and busier, and faster and faster. Billy asked if I wanted to call it a day. "Better people than you can run a store but not hack it here. There is no shame in bowing out right now." I thought about it. How easy it would be to go sit down and have a nice long drink of water.

"I'm good. I can keep going." Billy nodded his head.

"Then you need to do more." He said firmly. At the beginning of the morning I would take the customer's order perched over the register tapping as they talked. Now I was expected to do more. I wanted everyone to work harder around me, so I could just do what I knew how to do. I took an order for a large coffee.

"Ben, that coffee is you!" Billy yelled as he ran by. "You got to get the coffees! And sandwiches! And that bakery," Billy yelled as he ran back the other way.

I'm new, I wanted to say. But he yelled at everyone, so I felt like part of the team.

At the end of the day, I was pouring coffee, getting sandwiches, and running for bakery, while still taking orders. And not just taking orders, but upselling and getting names too. I used to think that it was impossible until I watched a girl named Melissa wander all over the back room, cleaning and filling while memorizing orders. She would return to the register and enter in all the orders before the first customer arrived at the window.

"How many drinks can you memorize?'

"You only have to remember five because by then the car will be ready to pay. And you need to make sure the baristas are listening too."

Yes, just remember five drinks I laugh. Is this girl a fucking genius? I have never memorized five drinks. Just being able to make drinks and remember them for two customers impressed me.

A customer orders a large decaf coffee and I grab the large cup and the sleeve. The pitcher of decaf has only half a cup. I pick up the other two pitchers, but they are empty too. The dining room greeter is responsible for the decaf and she forgot. The whole team is watching me. I can feel them watching me, wondering if I am going to stop the entire drive-thru by brewing some more decaf. I walk over to the regular coffee and fill it up.

"Atta boy. You should think about transferring here," tall Sam tells me. I was one of them! Tall Sam has coffee shop street cred because he was the "left side barista"- the hardest position of the drive-thru. He starts and labels all the drinks for all orders. So if he fucks up on one, it is in the weeds for everyone. It is the most intense position for all baristas.

Competitive people are going to muscle through and fight to do a job. You need that in this job. I wasn't going to be the one to drag the drive-thru down. There were moments when I thought about it, but I didn't quit. And when you get through it once, you can do it again. It's great and awful all at once!

"You're not going home crying so you did okay," Billy says as he slaps me on the back.

"People really go home crying?" I ask this even though I know people do. I myself have thought about it.

"Yeah. Good people too. If you can't take the pressure, this isn't the spot for you." Billy and tall Sam tell me horror stories of the pressure getting to people. Crying is the number one reaction, but people also just walk out, or shake uncontrollably. Billy once had the drive-thru come to a standstill because the barista couldn't handle it and made every drink wrong. "Has Christian told you to feed the monster?"

"Yeah all the time."

"This job is high stress, high burnout. I like all these people but they all could be gone in two weeks. Tall Sam's replacement has to be ready to go before tall Sam quits. Keep hiring."

I am amazed at how much pride all Caribou employees take in the execution of the job. They want to be good and fast, and they are friendly. And it's such a shitty environment. A customer asks Billy name off every breakfast sandwich, holding up the line. Billy bangs his head against the freezer. Another customer says she now wants her drink iced when she gets to the window, which now means her mocha gets re-made and slows down everything. These people are so competitive and they truly want to do a good job. It amazes me. The customers are rude and impatient, but the Caribou employees make their days better.

It was funny to watch the team call out regulars by their cars. "Two large darks is here!" "Here comes Treasure! Get a fucking treat ready!" Billy yells out. The drive-thru has a monitor showing the order area and another view of the cars coming to the window. Treasure is the dog of a high maintenance regular who freaks out if the dog isn't offered a treat.

Billy runs his store much looser than Kirsten, but he is hired up. The team talked a lot to each other, and made jokes, but kept working and kept working hard. It was a shit environment, but Billy made it better. By the luck of the draw I got Kirsten as my training manager instead of Billy.

Not that a coffee shop without a drive-thru is easy, it's just different—maybe even harder in some ways. At a regular two-person coffee shop you have to multi-task all day. The drive-thru has eight people doing the same things over and over. Neither is easier, but they are different. I returned to Kirsten's Caribou a different barista and greeter. I was confident.

Kind of.

CHAPTER 12
NOT TOM CRUISE

Dear crabby old guy,
Yes, our coffee is $1.81 for a small cup. Yes, I know you think that is expensive. Guess what, crabby old guy? You don't need to mention that to me every time you get a coffee and guess what else? No one is holding a gun to your head to fucking come in here! You fucking think it's too expensive, then don't fucking buy it! I can name 50 other places that have cheaper, shittier coffee. Do you think this is chitchat with me? Do you think we are having fun with this banter?

After working at the drive-thru I would ask customers who had not yet reached the register what they were getting while I was pouring coffee for the customer before them. I would make their drink without the drink screen, something I used to stare at for too many precious moments. Re-checking the screen for reasons, like was it skim or 2%, milk chocolate or white chocolate? I would upsell from the bar and then ask the person behind them what they wanted. Still upselling. Boom! I used to be amazed at waiters who remembered everything without a pen and pad. Now I was kind of one of them. I would listen to the order and repeat it once, then repeat it once again if I needed it. I was still scared shitless every moment trying to stay ahead of the next rush, which sometimes cannot be taught. People who do not care about getting their customers' caffeine quickly do not usually last on the bar. They get in the weeds or customers bitch and complain. Customers don't want to wait. Fearing the rush is a good thing.
    Sometimes I'm asked: can anyone be a barista? Yes and no. I can teach anyone who can read to make a mocha. I cannot teach everyone to make 20 mochas, 10 lattes, and five coolers in a span of 30 minutes. Some people just can't handle the immense pressure of morning rushes. It is fucking hard and if you fail people get fucking upset. If you are a perfect barista no one says anything. If you make one mistake someone will let you know. So on your best days you meet everyone's minimum expectations.

Some people fail at being a barista because they simply were not trained in the beginning of their career. Meaning if you are hired and stuck at the greeter position and never work on bar. You become scared of the bar, you feel the rush and you fear it. In the book, How Starbucks Saved My Life, Michael Gate Gill is not on the bar for over six months. If no one, including yourself, makes you work the bar, you will never learn it. Gill thought they were doing him a favor having him clean bathrooms and do shit work at the beginning of his Starbucks career. They weren't. Because one day there will be a call in, and you will be put on bar and literally start to cry.

The barista does 9,000 small tasks every morning that need to be done over and over again with perfect precision and timing. It is not for everyone, and that's okay. The Caribou training program calls for three buddy shifts, one at bar, one at greeter, and one as Super Glue. I changed my training program for new people and made anyone new be on the bar for their entire three training shifts.

In Kirsten's world you had to earn the bar and in my world you have to earn the greeter spot. I can teach someone how to do 9,000 mini tasks, but I can't teach personality as the greeter. Because personality equals upselling and upselling equals profits and more payroll (and higher OSAT scores, which we will get to later).

An un-informed Caribou manager once told me that he wants his baristas dancing around and having fun like Tom Cruise in "Cocktail". If you walk into a coffee shop and the barista is not busting ass getting you your caffeine as quick as he or she can then what is the fucking point? The greeter should be Tom Cruise, not the barista!

A phase four barista, the pinnacle of baristas, might be the most celebrated position in the coffee shop, but after being the barista I realized it was the least important spot as far as making money and being profitable. If your goal is to be fast, make money and make people happy the best person should be on greeter and not be the barista, since the barista is a tasker.

The greeter spot is the most important to the store because they are doing all the customer service. Kirsten spends her whole day on the bar. She should be in the front selling and creating relationships. She doesn't touch the customer until they are leaving the store. The money has already been made. The real reason long-term Caribou employees hide at the barista spot may just be because of the customers. Customers are a lot of work. And by a lot of work I mean unfucking believably annoying and rude. And dumb.

Now that I have learned the bar and the greeter spot, I am now able to take in the scenery, and learn what it means to work in a coffee shop. When I finally figured out how to survive a day working at a coffee shop without crying, I was able to look around and take a deep breath. I realized what I hated the most wasn't the pace, but the people right in front of me--the customers.

There are your average everyday idiots of course. But the worst customers are the regulars who have their own routine, and part of their routine is giving us a hard time.

"Does this have the extra shot?" She sips it while staring at me.

"Absolutely." It did, too. This was not an overconfident sell when I knew the drink was wrong. I heard her order from her lips.

"And it's extra hot?" She sips again frowning.

"Absolutely. I can make it again if you'd like." I'm making other drinks, listening to orders, while she plays her game.

"No it's fine."

I know it's a game because we act out this routine every fucking time! Why does she not remember these moments with me, but I remember her?

I found myself wanting to write customers little letters about how they are such dumb fucking idiots. I wanted them to know how their ordering process, their remarks, their rants, their snipes, and their meanness was not just affecting me, but everyone around them. I thought if they could just read these little letters maybe they would change their ways. When a bad one leaves I start composing the letter in my head. And one day I started writing them down.

Dear customer who complains he drink the ordered was not how it was made at Starbucks,
There are literally four fucking Starbucks within three miles of here. What do you want from me? Why did you come here and not go there if that's what you wanted? Just so you could complain? Then you are a sick fuck!

Dear customer that fucking literally takes five minutes to pick what they want,
You think you think you are being cute. YOU'RE FUCKING NOT! Pick fucking something or go to the end of the fucking line. You standing here is making everyone get their drink way fucking slower!

Dear customer who says to me, as I hand you the drink that you watched me make, that you don't want whipped cream,
Do you take some pleasure in making me run around with my head cut off? Are you some sick sadist or weirdo who gets off making people do shitty tasks over and over again? All you had to say was "no whip." Why didn't you? Why did you watch me take the whipped cream canister out of the fridge, shake it real hard, tip it towards your mocha, squirt the whip, put on a

lid, and then a espresso bean, and then hand it to you and say 'here is your milk chocolate mocha'. Why then do you say, "Oh, I didn't want whip?" Are you dumb? I want take the whipped cream off with my bare hand and give your mocha back. But I can't.

Dear customer who wants a glass of water,
And not the water we have out for everyone. Not the water you can pour and serve yourself. Not that water because you need different water. What if everyone asked for fucking water? Maybe everyone does and that's why we fucking put it out so every fucking one can get their own! Which everyone does except for fucking you! Fucking-a, dude.

Dear flamboyantly gay customer,
I get it. You're gay and out there and loving it. Maybe your sexuality defines you because for so long you couldn't exhibit it. I serve probably hundreds of gay customers a week and I'm from the generation that views all as equals. But your constant sexual innuendos, said loudly, about ordering something hot and black and creamy with a cherry on top are slowing down my line!

Dear customer who turns their hand sideways when I'm trying to give them change,
Hold your hand flat! I give change to some 300 people every day. I know more about change than the FBI. I study change. I live change. I think about fucking change. You holding your hand like an idiot and dropping change all over the place is your fault, not mine. So please don't sigh. Place your hand out flat.

Dear customer who I tell to turn your hand or you will drop your change,
I know what I'm talking about. I do this all day, almost everyday. So don't give me that look. Turn your fucking hand so it is almost flat, but cup it a little so gravity keeps the change in your hand. Since you won't move your hand, you drop the change, you give me a dirty look because you think I'm at fault when I fucking told you to move your fucking hand! And now the line is slowing fucking down because of you! Move your fucking hand when I tell you!

Dear customer who spends literally 20 minutes between walking in the door and ordering,
Something is wrong with you. Hurry the fuck up!

Dear asshole that pays with a $100 bill,
    I got $400 dollars in the safe, buddy, and $125 in the register. Who the fuck are you trying to impress? If you bought $60 worth of stuff it would be one thing, but $2.46 and you pay with a fucking hundred? More than anything you are annoying. I ask if you have another form of payment and you say no. You don't fucking have a fucking credit card? Now I have to change your shitty $100 bill and then eventually run in back to grab more 10's and 5's, which will make everyone wait. Because you don't fucking carry a credit card or a $20. I hope you know you are so annoying. But I doubt it.

Dear customer who complains about the sustainability discount changing from 10% off to 10 cents off,
    Oh it's your lucky fucking day because I'm the guy who made that fucking decision! You fucking found me working the fucking register on a busy Saturday in Minneapolis! So let me have it in front of this busy store and I will change it right back! Oh you are not tipping, then? Oh that will really fucking show corporate! Not giving me a lousy quarter will just teach corporate such a lesson about profitability and fucking with their customer base! You are a fucking hero for not tipping me! You truly are! Have you ever heard of a fax, letter, phone or Internet? Because that would be a much better way to complain than to me on a fucking busy day!

Dear yuppie driving the yellow Lamborghini who parks across three spots in the front,
    You must have the smallest penis in the world.

CHAPTER 13
THE RULES OF SERVING A VERY SPECIAL CUP OF COFFEE

Dear all awful customers,
Failing to prepare is preparing to fail. Have a very special cup of coffee.

"You ever hear about anyone fucking with drinks?" I ask Nash, as we are lamenting that rude people seem to enjoy not only fucking with us, but also slowing down the whole drink ordering process. Why do people want to get their caffeine slower and slow down everyone's drink behind them? And why are they so rude?

"Nah. It's not like we are cooking steaks in back and it can accidentally drop it on the floor." At the end of the day Nash is too nice to fuck with people's drinks or food. I bring up the subject to Stephen and Rachel, but everyone respects not only the company's reputation, but the job itself. We complain about customers' behaviors, but take it. The Caribou employees respect the job and don't see an alternative to putting up with the customers' shit. Some customers are just over-the-top awful. How can they treat people this way? How? I start being pushed little by little, and start scheming and planning. Then I daydream about doing stuff to consistently rude customers' drinks and then I think, why not? I prayed a retirement home worker would spit in one rude customer's food every night. Actually, I'd hope someone was doing something awful to all of the horrible customers I had. I found myself wishing justice on these people who made my life a living hell.

Larry Wenylls is the guy who pushed me over the edge. This is his real name because I want Larry to know there are repercussions. I want Larry to know he got his comeuppance.

Larry is tall, white, balding and looks a lot like Robert Dobak in "Step Brothers." Larry selected three separate pounds of coffee and wanted them ground for a paper filter on a fucking busy Saturday morning. Three pounds to ground is a lot. It's takes about 45 seconds per bag. I sigh because grounding this much coffee could get us in the weeds.

"Okay. I will get those ground up for you in a minute." Larry sat down, not ordering anything else, and I quickly rang up the next four people. After the fourth person there was no one and I could ground Larry's coffee, so I was thinking I was lucky. I thought that would be obvious to Larry or anyone in his position. As I began to quickly take the fourth person's order, Larry screamed.

"Are you gonna ground that or what?!" His voice boomed. The coffee shop with roughly 50 people in it was suddenly silent. "God damn it!"

"I will in a moment, sir," I said calmly. I couldn't believe he yelled. Worse, Larry then slammed his hand down and kicked the table. Kirsten looked at me and whispered, "I'll help you in a second." She gave me the *this guy is such an asshole* look. He was beyond an asshole.

"You better help him," the fourth customer whispered to me. I ground Larry's coffee and that's when I decided to implement what I call giving a deserving, over-the-top-rude asshole or bitch a "very special cup of coffee." Larry pushed me over the edge from a daydream to reality. I burned Larry's face into my mind, and like Arrie Stark, I repeated his name nightly. And others I began to add to my list. Larry Wynell, Easy, Mona, cappuccino woman, tennis hat lady, ice tea rich lady…

Ryan Reynolds said it best in the movie, "Waiting": You don't fuck with people who handle your food. But I was on stage in the coffee shop, not able to take Larry's cup in the stockroom or bend down behind the bar. Plus, I'd lose my job and wouldn't be able to support my family. Everyone was watching, and the ruder these customers were, the more they focused on watching us make their drinks. I think they fantasized about catching us spitting in the coffee. To prove their rudeness was necessary. "You have to keep these coffee shop people in line," they'd cackle to each other. Only two percent, mind you, of customers are awful. But that two percent has to be punished justly. This had to be very carefully planned out and prepared. First, I decided there needed to be some rules. I was not out to destroy everyone's coffee. That is not how a coffee justice sniper operates. (That really doesn't have that great of a ring to it.)

When I worked at JC Penney there was an urban legend about an asshole customer who came to the store most days and was a colossal dick to everyone. Before the customer left he would always spray himself down with a particular cologne sample, which was set out on the counter. For revenge, one employee took the cologne and peed in it. The entire store watched as the dickhead sprayed pee on himself. The rumor was he knew instantly the container was full of pee and ran out of the store while everyone looked on. The guy who peed in the cologne was fired, but was a hero. This urban legend inspired me.

The Rules of a Very Special Cup of Coffee

1. It can only be for a dick customer. Not someone you personally don't like , like an ex-boyfriend or girlfriend.

2. It cannot be for bad tipping. Has to be for an awful dickhead or ridiculous bitch.

3. You cannot give a very special cup of coffee to a pregnant woman no matter how big of a bitch she is. I have been around pregnant women and know they just get crazy.

4. You cannot destroy an entire batch of something to get back at a dick customer. So you can't line the cold press bucket with your used toilet paper to make one bad customer eat your shit. It has to be drink specific. This rule cannot be broken under any circumstances.

5. You cannot give a special cup of coffee to someone who orders a drink you don't like or respect. For example, I cannot give a special cup to decaf drinkers because I do not respect them. Nor a whole milk latte because it takes forever to make.

6. You cannot give a special cup of coffee to someone who wants coffee at an inopportune time. Like if they are knocking on the door to get in at 5:30 a.m. or if they show up at 9:59 p.m.

7. You cannot give a special cup of coffee to anyone who will not participate in any of our promotions or donation drives or is unwilling to be upsold.

8. It cannot be given to a regular who you do not like and you know personally. They have to be above and beyond mean. You ex-girlfriend's new boyfriend for example.

9.   You cannot give a very special cup because of politics, unless they are a preachy dickhead–and the same goes for religion.

10.   You cannot give a very special cup of coffee to someone who orders a large order and is dumb about the process.

11.   You cannot give a very special cup of coffee to someone based on appearance or any protected status. We do not give special cups of coffee to anyone based on sexual preference, color, nationality, religion, gender or age.

12.   You cannot give a special cup of coffee to someone you simply do not like for no explainable reason. They have to do something horrible to deserve a special cup of coffee.

13.   A special cup cannot be given to someone just because they are dumb or stupid. They have to be mean to get a very special cup of coffee.

14.   It cannot be over a mistake I made. Unless they are ridiculously over-the-top rude.

       For example: They want a Caramel High Rise and I accidentally make a Mint Condition. And they say, "I'm in a hurry of big meeting!" That's okay. I understand being upset over that.

15.   A special cup should only be served once per awful incident. A rude customer cannot be given a special cup of coffee every day, unless they are over-the-top-awful and mean every day.

16.   You cannot give a special cup to another employee. If they found out, you'd be cooked.

17.   You cannot talk about fight club–errrrr…, you cannot tell anyone about serving a very special cup of coffee. Anyone. Even your family. You do not talk about a very special cup of coffee, even though it would feel so good to do so!

18.   You cannot give a special cup to a famous person, just because they are famous. Amelia Santaniello is a local celebrity newscaster and is consistently a bitch to us. Not a super bitch, but still a bitch and rude. Even though she should be nice to us

so we watch her show. You cannot give a special cup just to be and cool say to your friends, "Hey! I gave Amelia Santaniello a special cup!" She has not received a special cup for being rude. Yet.

19.   You cannot give a special cup to someone for a being dickhead outside of the coffee shop, like a politician who lied, an athlete who lost the game, or a public figure who just plain pissed you off.

Narrator: He was guerilla terrorist in the food service industry.
Tyler Durden [urinating]: Do not watch. I cannot go when you watch.
Narrator: Apart from seasoning the lobster bisque, he farted on the meringue, sneezed on braised endive, and as for the cream of mushroom soup, well...
Tyler Durden [laughs]: Go ahead. Tell them.
Narrator: You get the idea.

For all of for you "the sky is falling!" types, be comforted by this–good people cannot receive a special cup. The special cup is a sniper, only punishing those who deserve to be punished. The rules have to be followed because it would be easy to ruin a batch of coffee and give it to everyone. That's not fair or just. And I didn't want the Larry Wenyells of the world getting off easy in the world thinking well everyone drank it, not just me. Only you did, Larry!

Now that I had the rules and gumption, I needed to figure out what exactly I was going to do to these drinks. I knew I wanted to do something bad to them, but it to be extremely calculated and quick, and none of my coworkers could suspect. The customers also couldn't suspect a fucking thing, so I couldn't take their drinks to the back room.

And so I found myself peeing in a large hot Caribou cup in my bathroom at home. I was worried Gisele would burst in and think I was crazy. I will admit that I probably am. I peed in the cup and swirled it around, coating the cup, and poured it out. I wondered if the customer would instantly be able to tell? I wasn't going to test it.

After drying the cup, I now had the conundrum of getting the cup to the exact customer. Timing would be everything, as I had to be on the bar, and they had to order a large hot drink, and I had to have it near so it would look like a regular part of my routine. The moon and stars would have to align for me to serve a very special cup of coffee.

My next few shifts I put the cup underneath the bar, behind some stuff but still reachable when I needed it. I practiced how I would grab it if anyone deserved it. Having the cup there comforted me for awhile and I began to think I would never use it. I had planned in my head if a customer deserved a special cup I would make the drink in a large even if they asked for a different size an act and then act like I was an idiot. As I was on the bar in a rush I would daydream about giving a special cup to someone from my past. And there he was…Larry. I grabbed the cup and made sure Carlee didn't notice. No one did. I grabbed two others and placed them near, but I knew which one was special.

Larry was with his wife and she ordered a latte. He hemmed and hawed and I finished the drinks before him, but my ears were on him.

"Oh hell, I'll get one of those fancy lattes too. Give me a medium one." *Milk and espresso is so fancy!* Before Carlee could say anything I yelled, "Large for 30 cents more? Good deal!"

"Sure," he said smugly. It was on.

My hands were shaking. I was so fucking nervous and excited. Play this cool I said to myself. Abort! Fuck it! I'm doing it!

I put the latte on the serving counter and I watched Larry pick it up. I wanted to say something cool, like here is your very special cup of coffee, but this isn't the movies.

"Have a good day," I blurted out too loud, with a frog in my throat, blushing and sweating from excitement and nervousness. I wish I had video of me then because at the moment the latte touched Larry's lips I regretted everything! What if he instantly whipped around and started yelling? What if he had a gun? What if he calmly said he was going to have this tested for pee and if it tested positive he would destroy Caribou and me? What if I went to jail? What if I'm fired and I can't support my family? These thoughts go through my head whenever I serve a very special cup of coffee. They vanish instantly as I go into a euphoric state, and justice is served. Giving someone a special cup of coffee who has treated me and every service person like shit…is one of the greatest feelings in the world.

A woman comes in a couple of times a week and orders a large ice tea. She drinks the entire tea in front of me. Every time she comes in, she says I didn't put enough flavoring in it. "You never make it right, so put in some more and fill it up." The first time fine, the second time okay, the third time…special cup.

My job in the coffee industry takes an interesting turn when I start dispensing justice. And I love it.

I mix things up with the cups and have some movie-worthy scenes in my life. I make myself throw up into a cup, I take a shit into a cup, and both acts are a lot harder to do in a cup than you'd think. I stuck my finger down my throat for 30 minutes and drank a whole jug of orange juice before anything came out. And shitting in a large Caribou cold cup is not easy. I'm not going to go into that, but lets just say it's messier and takes longer than you would think! I decide not to masturbate into a cup. That just seems to cross the line to maybe a little psychotic. I realize that line has probably been crossed by the other things I've done. And of course I do the classic spit in cups, but that just seems so boring these days. I started experimenting with throwing up different food items and drinking weird vegetable juice too because it stunk. Then I thought, Jesus, I'm already peeing and puking and pooping into these cups, I think that's bad enough.

It's an art deciding quickly if someone deserves a special cup and then quickly grabbing the cup and implementing the whole thing. First off, I'm at the greeter a lot and sometimes I have to yell, "let's switch!" Or I tell the barista to go get ice or more bakery items, or I say "Sorry I made a mistake! Is a large okay for no extra charge or would you like me to make another one?" The real dickheads complain about the extra espresso or milk, but always take it.

The real art is serving it to them without staring at the drink while they take the first sip. The art is not saying, fuck you, you fucking fuck for being such a fuck! How does my fucking piss taste, you asshole? How does it feel to drink pee for being such a dickhead? Why the fuck do you treat people like you do? What the fuck is wrong with you?

The real art is not letting those emotions show on my face.

Then I have to deal with whoever is on greeter or bar because they were just treated like a piece of shit, and probably wondering why I gave the asshole or the bitch a free large drink? I want to tell them, but I can't. No matter how much I like or trust them.

Would I give special cups to regulars? If they deserved it. But only once per incident I decided, which became a rule. I would pretend I was in a very special cup courtroom with different baristas debating whether or not a particular dickhead or bitch would get a cup. "They were rude, but was it over-the-top-rude, your honor?" The other lawyer would chime, "This is the fourth occasion of complaining in a loud tone that there was not enough cinnamon in her latte and is anyone here smart enough to know what a 1/3 of a cinnamon packet means...your honor." Special cup, the courtroom cheers!

And then "Easy" walked in. A regular. It was on.

Easy was a large, incredibly large actually, black man about 50 years old. Picture Biggie Smalls at 50 years old and that was Easy. I knew Easy always got a large coffee with steamed skim. I grabbed the cup and flew over to the coffee before Beth could pour it into a clean cup.

I met Easy one of my first days, as he was a regular who set up shop at one of the tables. Kirsten didn't know what he did but said he was really successful. I listened to Easy do business and he seemed to be in the insurance business. His guys came into our Caribou, dressed like cheap insurance guys, and it seemed to be their office.

Each time Easy came into the store Kirsten and Beck yelled "Easy!" like he was Norm from Cheers. I didn't think much either way of Easy until I was at the greeter and a survey popped out.

The surveys are how we get our OSAT scores, which I'll explain in more detail later. The basics are you take a survey online about how we did and if you bring that back in you get a dollar off. This whole six-second speech seemed to rile Easy up.

"Why don't I get a dollar off now? I'm here every day? Ain't that a comment on the service? I'm here every damn day."

I try to keep a jovial tone because I know he is a regular. And because I have to. It's my job to be jovial with all people. "I think the home office would like to know right from you. And it's your chance to tell them what you like or don't like." This apparently gave Easy permission to complain about things he didn't like about Caribou. But, unfortunately to me, not the survey.

"At Starbucks I put my phone up to the register and it pays. You do that?"

"Ah no."

"Well why not? That's what I don't like about Caribou."

"I don't think we are quite there technology wise." I try to turn around, but Easy keeps going.

"And I get a free coffee after buying 20. Why don't I get that here?" Beck gives Easy his coffee, but he keeps talking to me from his seat across the room.

"Gotta take a survey. I'm here every damn day." What a dick. Easy is loud and thorough with his embarrassing of the coffee shop guy who has no control over what he is complaining about. I knew Easy had a large coffee every day. It was on. Not only did Easy continue to embarrass me that day, but the next few times I served him he kept right on as if he never left the shop and was still complaining.

When I served Easy his special cup of coffee (pee) it was kind of anti-climatic. He drank it, I smiled, and I smiled more when I saw him an hour later draining the last drops and smacking his lips. Justice. But I still wanted the people to know that they are punished when they do not treat people humanely and decently. I couldn't think of a way to let a bad customer know what had been done without compromising my job. It bothered me. I had been working at Caribou Coffee for a little over six weeks and it felt like 10 years.

CHAPTER 14
REGULARS

Dear "regular" customer,
*   You need to get help. It is not normal to pretend we are your close friends.*
Some employees might think it is cool, but I do not. Go away.

The term "a regular" can describe a few different types of customers. One type of regular comes to the store every day, likes the service and the people, orders their drink, and leaves with a smile. Another type of a regular comes to the store every day, expects their overly complicated drink to be remembered and made perfectly, but still is rude. Every day. And yet another type of regular comes to the coffee shop….and stays all day.

Everything good about regulars can also be bad about regulars. Regulars are good for business because they are at the shop every day. However, some regulars begin to affect our profits and time because they are taking more than they are spending. They want extra refills or anything you can think of for free because they are a regular. Regulars can become bullies and take advantage of our kind ways. Worse, some regulars use the OSAT survey to hold us hostage and meet their demands.

"When I get one of those little surveys, I'll be sure to let corporate know."

Regulars have a usual drink, which speeds up the line because the barista can make it before they even order. The bad part is that regulars' drinks become overly complicated and more time consuming to make. Plus, a regular wants you to remember their drink and are let down if you don't remember every specific little aspect of the drink.

These people wanted to tell me about their lives. Some wanted to be my friend, some bragged about what they did or told me about themselves. Some would start talking to me and my coworkers like we were all old friends as soon as they walked in the door. Some would invite us to do things outside of work. Worse, they would be upset when we didn't show up. Even worse, they would then awkwardly complain while in line that we didn't show up.

Kirsten was interested in some of the customer's lives. She was like a sounding board to some, a psychologist to others, and a mentoring coach to others. The customers saw her every day and she listened. Sometimes while she was on bar, the line would back up because a customer was describing an event in their relationship or at work, and there was Kirsten, brow furrowed, listening intently. She created extraordinary experiences for them just by listening. And that was what Caribou was about. And there were some—Kirsten, Stephen, Beck even—that were so good at it was scary. When you have that personality and engagement it makes people feel like the workers at Caribou are their friends.

Once a college-aged regular named Danny came into the shop and didn't even order anything. He wanted Kirsten's and my opinions on how to best proceed with a girl he just met. He didn't ask his friend, his sister, Facebook, Twitter, not ever his mom. He asked his local Caribou workers.

I have looked deep into the heart of Christian, Kirsten, Stephen and lot of other Caribou folk and they are not faking. They are legitimately nice people that care deeply for others. They are not faking being nice and interested to just sell coffee. If anything their genuine love of customers can get in the way of speed and sales. They look past the rude customers and crazy needs. They look to the good of the coffee shop. It amazes me.

The regulars of all shapes and sizes fascinate me, disgust me and, annoy me, but for the most part they are nice. Some regular customers are awful, and the problem with awful regulars is they keep coming back.

I saw regulars for anywhere from one minute to 10 hours a day, and I couldn't help but wonder who they were outside of the shop. Liz would later accuse me of prejudging them, but I was always interested in if who they wanted to come off as being was the same as who they actually were.

Regulars can be described by coffee shop workers in one of three ways. The regular's drink order is the most common. "Medium skim white chocolate mocha no whip was in today and actually got a blueberry muffin."

Physical appearance or if a customer always wears a particular article of clothing is another way. "Beer gut was here with a new lady." "Tied died t-shirt lady complained we are out of ho-ho mocha again." These names are as common to me as Judy or Doug.

And if we call a customer by their first name it is either very, very good or very, very bad. One customer, Paul, started out as two large blacks, then as we got know him he became Renaissance Festival Paul because that's where he worked, and finally he was just Paul. He was a nice guy, maybe talked to us a little too much, but he was one of the good ones.

"Anne was here today," Jenn tells me.

"How'd it go?"

"Too much froth." Ahhhhhhh! We both laugh. You can't make some regulars happy. And that's why they keep coming back too.

I met tall, bald John my first day and I was at first very intimidated by him for a few reasons. Kirsten said he was super rich, super successful, and it was one of my first few days so I felt like I was going too slow. It didn't help that I got coffee grounds in his coffee, either. You get a look into the inner world of strangers when you are at your worst. How do they react to you being horrible at a job they deem easy? Sighs, harrumphs, staring at the ceiling in a *why God is this happening to me* look? It's actually not happening to you, John, it's happening to me.

I asked bald John if he wanted a muffin and he abruptly growled, "No, just coffee." I never asked him an upselling question for a while after that. I asked Kirsten what he did because she talked to him a lot. She didn't know, but thought he was rich. Kirsten thought everyone was rich. (In her defense, we worked in a ridiculously rich area.)

Then one day, I saw John riding a girl's 10-speed bike in weird clothes. I cut across three lanes of traffic and followed him. He rode his bike to a house that was being painted. He was a painter? I watched him painting. Was he being rude to me because he hated his life and he could take it out on me? But we are just two regular guys! He can't stand the occasional offering of baked goods without getting rude? The delicate genius can't be bothered?

After the painting incident I wasn't imitated.

"Would you like a delicious chicken apple sausage Day Breaker with your coffee?"

"No, just coffee."

"Would you like any beans this weekend? Great if you are going to a party or something."

"No just co-."

"Beans are great for a house warming gift or for entertaining."

"Just coffee."

"How about a chocolate chip cookie? They're my favorite. Any time is a good time for a cookie," I say with a cheesy smile.

"Coffee." His voice gets quieter. He doesn't know what's going on.

"Now have you checked out our new fall merchandise? Tumblers and fun mugs?"

"Ah…"

The coffee shop gets eerily quiet. Kirsten stares at me, not knowing what to do. I carry on like he's any old customer. We stare each other down in some perverse battle. Some regulars believe they are beyond being upsold or even talked to about anything other than what they get every day. My new favorite ploy is to slowly, painstakingly, upsell them on any and everything. It can be pretty uncomfortable and it is my favorite part of the day.

Mona is a typical old lady who lives in a changing city. She has the same routine every day. She wears a fanny pack and carries an umbrella and a cheap blue coat every day. She doesn't come from money, but seems to have family who are all far away now. She comes to Caribou every day to writes letters. When I first met her she didn't even order a drink.

"We don't sell stamps," I tell her after she waits in line for stamps.

"Oh, sometimes Beck or Kirsten will give me one."

"They aren't here," I say cheerily. She waited in line to ask of I have a fucking stamp?! I have no idea where we keep stamps and I can't leave to go find one. And even if I did know where they are kept I still wouldn't go get one.

Mona likes a medium skim latte with lots and lots of extra froth. Creamy froth too. After Mona's drink is prepared she will taste the froth and then judge the drink. If it's to her liking she smacks her lips and says, "Oh that's good." If it's not to her liking she harrumphs and walks away. She basically judges your skills in front of your face. It hurts your feelings if it's not to her liking. The mark of a really shitty regular customer is that their drink has some debatable, judgeable component to it, like extra creamy froth but not overly creamy or extra hot but not too hot.

After judging our barista skills and making us feel like shit, Mona retires to the dining room. She returns later and would now like to add a decaf coffee to her latte. This leads to my first real confrontation with a regular. Because they come every day they think they should be treated different and get some extra benefits.

"So now you want a cup of decaf?" I ask Mona as she is handing me her latte cup.

"No I just get a refill of decaf."

"You haven't had a original cup yet though." I frown to her. Caribou allows one free refill of coffee if you stay in the store.

"I always get just a bit of decaf," she says sternly.

"For free?"

"Yes, just a bit." Her tumbler is about three-fourths empty.

"Yes, but of decaf. If you buy a cup of coffee you get one free refill. But you had a latte." Beck hustles over and fills up her decaf.

Every time Mona comes in we lose money. She seems to think she is doing us a favor though. Mona also doesn't tip, but says each time, "I just tip my favorites and gave Beck $10 not too long ago." *Thanks for pointing out I am not one of your favorite.*

"Did Mona really give you a ten dollar tip?" I ask Beck.

"She did. A long, long time ago. I don't think she has tipped anyone since or before."

"I don't get tips so you're really hurting Beck and Carlee anyways," I tell Mona. She doesn't care because it's not really about who gets the tip. This is the game I play with Mona.

That's the conundrum with some regulars. They are annoying, but spend money consistently, and sometimes are so aggressive in what they want because they know we are supposed to be nice. We are nice. Too nice sometimes. People can mistake friendliness for weakness and take advantage. They are called regulars.

Now you might be sitting in your chair thinking, 'I work in a cubicle and never see anyone until I go to the coffee shop and then I chat with the barista and greeter, so am I weird?' NO! I understand and appreciate wanting human interaction. And I am a great guy to chitchat with at the right times. The 8 a.m. rush is not the right time, nor is it cool to hang out at said coffee shop every other minute you are not at work. That's weird.

Kenneth is a 50ish-year-old man who sets up camp each day and conducts some sort of business on his laptop. Kenneth is also "allergic to caffeine" and it keeps him up for days if he drinks it. According to him. One day he tries our new white tea sparkling juice and complains it kept him up all night because there is caffeine! Kirsten fusses over him, but there shouldn't be any caffeine in the tea. The real question is why does he hang out in a coffee shop? *Beats fucking me!* The best part is he doesn't ever fucking get anything and most days will leave his stuff and go get a Jamba Juice. I ask Kirsten why we let him sit here if he doesn't ever buy anything. "He's a regular, Ben!"

"But he doesn't buy anything. He's a regular, but not a regular customer!"

"Sometimes he buys a cookie," she shrugs.

Regulars are also more likely to complain when anything isn't up to their high standards. If you hang out in a coffee shop all day you have no life. Or you had a life and that life is over, so you have to come up with shit to get riled up about. Like a coffee shop being out of something on our mix-ins table. Even though you don't use said product.

"Looks like the raw sugar is out," Richard tells me as I'm working a rush.

"I've got like three right here. How many do you need?"

"None," he replies. Jesus, don't get mad at me if we don't have something you want, but I have it right in front of me. After the rush I check the mix-ins bar and there is plenty of raw sugar. It was under another packet of regular sugar that had fallen over. What a dick.

On my first day as I was meeting Christian, a white bearded gentleman in his mid 60's approached us.

"Now is this guy in charge of you?" he asks Christian.

"He will be someday," Christian replies. I hadn't seen Christian annoyed until Richard.

"Ben, this is Richard."

"Ben, I've got a great idea. The first customer each day gets a t-shirt that says, 'I was the first customer today.' I think it would really sell. And people would know I was the first customer."

"I'll send that up to the top." Christian just shakes his head as Richard walks away. Regulars can own us. Every instinct for Christian and me is to tell the guy to get away from us as we are obviously working. But regulars are fixtures and can control the OSAT game too. And it's a customer service industry. It's the game.

Richard, like Mona, has a complicated drink that he likes just perfect and will tell you if it was made correctly or not. Really great guy! Richard gets a medium skim latte with two shots of raspberry flavoring and two shots of sugarfree raspberry flavoring. Richard also likes it made hot, but then poured over ice into his own cold cup. So he will order an iced raspberry latte, but that's a lot different than it is made. If I'm on greeter I have to tell the barista it's Richard's drink or tell them how to make it. If I'm on bar I have to notice it's Richard because on the drink board it won't be the way he wants it. All in all, he's a pain in the ass.

"Why do we do that for him?" I ask Kirsten.

"He's a regular."

"But he's a dick and a weirdo. Why are we kowtowing to a bad regular?" She shrugs. Richard is a fixture. Like Mona, Richard does not tip unless Medora or Beck is working. He tells Medora she should date a guy from his building and he shows her a Facebook picture of the guy. Medora is a young and pretty, but from a small town in Wisconsin and a little naïve. She has intense eyes and is hated by Beck for some unknown reason. Of course when given the opportunity to be barista Medora excels with great determination and to Beck's chagrin.

"It's probably Richard doing some weird catfish shit." I agree and I decide if Medora ever goes missing I will promptly point the police Richard's way.

Richard holds court each day at the same table with a nerdy crew of other losers, who read their iPads, newspapers, and $200 Toshiba laptops and laugh at Richard's wild thoughts and funny comments. I eavesdrop on their gathering and it is as depressing as it sounds with lots of re-used jokes and standard one-liners. The group stands out to me because of their odd assortment of flip down sunglasses, flip flops with socks, fanny packs, outdated baseball hats, and bandages on odd places on their legs.

But these regulars at Caribou don't shun or look down upon us simple service industry workers. No, worse than that, these regulars want to be our friends. We are the cool kids. Not them. And they want into the club. I nod at the regulars, but I never say much or open up. Richard hobnobs with the social elite, a bunch of weird old people, and Beck and Kirsten think it's so great.

One day Richard doesn't show up. And then doesn't show up for a few days in a row. And Kirsten and Beck are concerned.

Good for him, he got a life, I think. Kirsten talks to the other regulars he sits with and they haven't heard a thing from him either.

Kirsten wonders how to get his phone number to call and see if is he is all right.

"No one has an email, Twitter, phone number, or Facebook for him?" I ask her.

"Nope. They don't know how to get a hold of him."

"He spends all day with them. And us." I feel sad for Richard. Wondering if he is alone dead in his apartment with no one to check on him. 'Is he dead?' we all wonder, but won't say it. Did he get arrested? Did someone offend him? It's the best few days of my life!

Richard shows up a few days later. He had minor surgery. Beck and Kirsten make a fuss over him. His cronies at the table let him hold court and share his story. I watch Richard and I don't know quite what to think. I feel bad that his relationships at Caribou are not deep. No one could get a hold of him and he didn't let anyone know he had surgery beforehand for God's sake.

But at least he has Caribou. These are not real relationships but it's something for Richard. Richard's lot in life does not include a normal social functioning personality. He seems to have found a place, though. He should drop down on his knees and thank God for Caribou coffee and Kirsten and Beck and Stephen and Medora.

I have a similar moment with a lot of regulars. On Mother's Day the store was packed and I was busy as shit. And then I noticed Mona sitting at table all alone, writing a letter. The store bustled with activity on a family day, but Mona did what she does every day. Sit in a comforting coffee shop and do nothing. Alone. And it dawned on me the regulars are here because they are alone. Normal people don't spend nine hours in a coffee shop. They have friends and family to go home to and a whole other life outside of the shop. I felt bad for Mona for sitting all alone. Until she came over and butted in line to a get a re-fill of decaf for her fucking latte!

CHAPTER 15
BE THE BALL

Dear customer who says working at a coffee shop looks so relaxing,
 First off, that you think what I'm doing right now looks relaxing leads me to believe I am making this look really easy, or maybe you are blind. So you've always wanted to work in a coffee shop, huh? You wouldn't last ten seconds. I'm not being a dick. You just wouldn't. Either way, you standing here telling me how relaxing this is is actually creating stress because you are holding up the fucking line!

Christian meets with new hires every week through their training period. He has never missed one with me and I know it's something small, but I am impressed. These meetings stay away from the hell of the floor and the bar, and focus on family, outside Caribou interests, and coffee flavors. Even as we talk my eyes drift to the front door, anticipating the next rush. I start to learn why Caribou is different from Starbucks.
 Caribou buys only coffee that was grown over 3,000 feet. My question for Christian is when does that supply run out? I was under the impression that the reason why we weren't growing faster was because there was only so much good coffee.
 "There is an unlimited supply. I don't know how to answer that really, but it's a great question."
 "So why are we only opening 25 stores and not a lot more? We have a better product and a better environment than Starbucks and McDonalds." Christian smiles sheepishly. "Well, we tried that a few years ago. We were going to open 75 stores three years in a row. The first 25 failed."

"How did they fail?"

"We know our area. Right now I know a store on highway 100 and 394 with a drive-thru would attract new business and not take much from the surrounding stores."

"Right."

"But we didn't know the areas in Atlanta, DC, or Chicago. We picked the wrong locations."

This is interesting to me because I thought Caribou could only grow so fast because there was only so much great coffee. Nope. They didn't hire market analysts and people in the know from the areas before picking locations. Starbucks makes it look easy.

"We actually quietly closed down a store in Chicago." It makes me feel kind of sad for Caribou because they are nice people. Christian is a good guy and loves his family and seems genuine. Everyone at Caribou seems genuine. They just are not great business people. They have a better product and a great environment, but they don't know what to do with it. They are the second biggest coffee house in the country and seemed destined to stay that way.

"Leslie, our VP of operations, always says we are at our gawky teenager phase right now. Making mistakes and doing dumb things. But it will help us in the future."

"I'm confused why we would build a Caribou without drive-thru? The inside would still be the same and attract dining room guests, while the drive-thru would attract those who just want it quicker."

"Yeah, that's a good question." Christian answers every question thoughtfully and deliberately. I notice he has two new piercings on each ear. His hair is graying and he leaves a little spot of beard below his bottom lip. He fits in at Caribou.

Christian tells me about a trip to Costa Rica with Caribou to see the entire production process. Caribou's main coffee bean finder is a guy named Chad, who Christian tells me is traveling constantly.

"Does he have a family?" I hate leaving my family for the day and this guy travels for months on end to find coffee beans.

"He has a husband, who also travels a lot."

Christian says it was a life-changing experience watching migrant workers swarm out of the mountains with huge bags of beans, weigh them, get paid in cash, and then head back out in the sweltering heat to fill the bags up again.

"Chad works with all the farmers to become Rainforest Alliance certified, so this farm had housing and a clinic for the workers on site."

"Is there pushback to become Rainforest Alliance Certified?"

"What do you mean?"

"Is the farmer in Costa Rica doing all this stuff to keep our business or because it is good for his people and home?"

"We'd like to think both." Christian tells me that the La Minita Peaberry Farm coffee, only sold at Caribou, was not originally Rain Forest Alliance certified. It was almost to the point where Caribou could not carry one of its signature coffees because the farmer wasn't certified. At the last moment the farm was approved. "We were sweating for awhile. You'll see some people come just to buy La Minita. That's their only visit to Caribou all year long."

Christian shows me pictures on his phone from his trip, including one of different bags of coffee beans. "Here are our beans." The bag is full of lush, brown beans. "Here are Starbucks' beans." They are noticeably lighter. "And here are McDonalds' beans." It looked like sand. "Starbucks and McDonalds will buy any beans just because they have so many outlets. We are smaller, so we can better monitor the quality."

Casually talking with Christian about big business ideas and coffee culture takes me out of the service industry world and into the cushy corporate world. It's a few moments away from the hell of working in a coffee shop. The next rush is coming as I stare at the front door. Christian asks me how things are going and in that one second my coffee life hell flashes before me.

My God, this job is awful. I hate it and I'm not good at it. There are moments when I'm on the bar and I literally blank on how to make drinks. Even the easy ones like mochas and lattes. *Now how many shots of espresso go in the iced latte? I've got no fucking clue!* I scream at myself in my head. There is something in Kirsten's personality that makes her like this work. She is energized by it and thrives in the busy craziness of it all.

I watch Kirsten constantly moving, constantly filling, constantly cleaning, seamlessly making drinks, doing dishes, doing extra work so the next shift is set up for success. Kirsten never walks out of the backroom without something to bring to the floor, "an old waitress trick", she told me. Sometimes I just can't literally think of anything else that needs to be brought to the floor from the sales area, so I grab a handful of straws. It's really pathetic, I know. All of you waitresses are yelling, 'what a dumbass' at the page right now.

Stephen tells me he is quitting in less than two weeks and moving back to Mississippi. He said things just aren't working out here with school and life. Another employee, Gabe, tells Kirsten he got a full-time job bartending, but he promises to work out his shifts. She worries he won't show up.

Kirsten has five interviews set up, but barely has enough people to run the store. We make the schedule and we are 60 hours short.

"We could use those people on Saturday and Sunday," I say. She knows.

"We could have four people those days Ben!" Is she arguing for my point or against my point?

Kirsten tells me one day I must punch out for breaks and work only 47 hours a week! Poor Kirsten. She is telling me I need to punch out for 30 minutes, "by law" she quotes. I laugh. With only two people on all day it would literally be impossible, unless she wants to lock the front door. Tomorrow I'm on the floor from 9 a.m. to 6 p.m., no breaks scheduled, and I'm already at 46 hours for the week.

Kirsten texts Rachel to see if she can work the weekend. Kirsten complains that no one can work Saturdays and that's why it's so hard to schedule properly. I should note again Kirsten's hours are under her planned scheduled hours. Kirsten's store cannot use over 30% of its payroll to sales. What is Kirsten at this week? Fucking 16%! Lets just say she has hours to give to people.

It turns out Rachel is working at another store to pick up hours. Fucking Kirsten! It gets so busy that customers ask if someone didn't show up.

I pray for rain every day and tell Gisele to do the same.

"I don't want it to rain," she says. "Matt and I will be stuck inside all day."

"You do it!" I scream. "Pray for rain so that goddamn store isn't so busy."

When I see red skies in the morning I sing out in glee! "red skies in the morning, sailors take warning!" I hope people see the red skies and don't come to the store. What I have actually noticed is that red skies in the morning, sailors take warning, is a shitty indicator of bad weather coming. Many morning skies are red, but the bad weather never comes to save me.

The night before Mother's Day, Caribou sends out e-mails, texts, and Facebook updates that tomorrow will be a 'buy one, get one free day' to celebrate Mother's Day! Oh God, it's going to be brutal. I look over the schedule and realize Nash leaves at noon. Stephen isn't in until 4. Just me and Carlee.

That could be a long four hours for me. I start to sweat a little. I still don't know the drink combinations! Yes you do I tell myself. I should have jumped in the bar more and faced my fears. You did! I tell myself again. But I didn't. And it has caught up to me today. You can do it! Am I crazy? No you're not!

I can't put Carlee on bar? Can I? Being a barista at a coffee shop has really turned me into an asshole. Carlee has never worked the bar more than a lazy afternoon, but now I'm thinking about throwing her onto the bar on Mother's Day just so I don't have to face the rush! Hopefully our customers will go to the Susan G. Komen race near the Mall of America and leave us alone. That is wishful thinking.

My God I'm praying. That is what Caribou has reduced me to. Praying. I think about calling in sick. There is no one to call to replace me. I thing about not showing up. I can't. So I begin to build myself up. I only listen to uplifting energetic music. *You are a god. Be the ball.*

The morning is busy, but we manage with Nash, Carlee and I. At noon Nash has to leave. He shakes my hand and says good luck. "I have to go," he says apologetically.

"Go. I got this."

The line is out the door, but Carlee and I push through. I keep milk frothing and steaming. I spin and drop a pitcher into the sink and keep the water running. As I blend a cooler I finish washing the pitchers. I keep my ears open and listen to every customer's drink, but sometimes it gets too loud. *Stay ahead of the drinks.* I scream out customer names, not wanting my serving station to back up with drinks. Or worse, have a customer grab the wrong drink and fuck up my whole flow.

"No! That's not your latte!" I scream at a customer. "This is your vanilla soy latte!" I hand her the drink with a smile. Us crazy baristas! I get in the weeds for a moment, but two large coffees bail me out. That is Carlee's responsibility. I throw in turkey sausage minis at once and a small timer counts down in my head. I race around making drinks, doing dishes, frothing milk, and pouring espressos while the sandwiches cook. I open the oven one second before it's supposed to be done without even looking. We are going to make it! We are really doing it!

And that's when God punishes me.

"Can you make us three French presses of three different coffees and serve them to us so we can do a blind taste test?" a couple asks Carlee.

"It's Mother's Day," I say. They've got to be fucking kidding me. They've got to be. They are not.

"Can you do that? We will pay right now." Oh, you'll pay first? Oh, okay, then yeah I'll do it. Fuuuuuuuuuuuuck! I will have to run in back and grab three bags of beans, I have to measure out one cup of each bean, grind it, find three French presses, fill them all with hot water, and wait five minutes and then pour. The barista law is you'd rather make one person upset than 20 people. No special cup though, if you were wondering. You can't give a special cup of coffee for huge requests on busy days.

Lauren walks in and I know we made it.

"Wow, 4 p.m. already? That went by quick, huh?" I say to Carlee with my normal false bravado. I look at Carlee and she looks like Shelly Duvall at the end of the "Shining."

"Yes it was fine," she says robotically.

Carlee and I make it through the Mother's Day massacre. I sit in my car after Mother's Day and I'm feeling a little giddy. I want to yell and scream and shout and cry and sing! I can't believe I did it. And as happy as I should feel for doing a great job I can't be happy or satisfied. I sigh. I know the next rush is just a day away. My euphoric state ends and I become nervous and agitated thinking about Monday's rush. Mondays are brutal at the Lake store.

"Westin quit," Kirsten tells me as soon as I walk in the door.

"Have we hired a Westin?" I have no idea who Westin is or why he quit.

"Westin the store manager at Southwest." Oh, that Westin.

Christian had a store manager quit unexpectedly, but Christian practices what he preaches. He feeds the monster. I'm in line to run my own store after roughly 10 weeks. I was scheduled for 12 to 13 weeks of training. As Kirsten tells me the good news, all I think is that I can barely do the core requirements of this job…and now I am in charge of a store? I wanted to get away from this craziness of the Lake store, and now I am longing to stay near the familiarity, the low expectations, the fucked up comfort zone, but a comfort zone nonetheless. Kirsten suggests we tell Christian I'm not ready to be done with my training so I can stay and help. *Uh, yeah. That's an idea. And it wouldn't really be a lie.*

Christian meets with me and asks if I'm ready. "Absolutely." *I don't know where I get this overconfidence,* I think, as I'm talking with him. He obviously doesn't notice.

With no fanfare, no cakes, no cards, no teary hugs, I leave the Lake store to manage my own Caribou Coffee. Then Kirsten calls me and begs me to cover one last closing shift. "Absolutely."

On my last night at the Lake store my wishes are answered and a thunderstorm looms. But like a foolish man making wishes from a genie that backfire, my thunderstorm doesn't save me from customers. It attracts more.

I was training Lauren, a high school student, that Kirsten had hired on the spot. The only thing worse than having to learn to run a coffee shop is training someone to run a coffee shop. I do my goddamn absolute best to not act like Kirsten. Lauren is doing great, but still is learning the register. I have to monitor her body language to detect when she can't find a drink. She forgets to pour a coffee and the customer stands at the end of the bar.

"Uh, can I help you?"

"Large coffee. I haven't gotten it yet." I want to yell at Lauren for screwing up the line because I have to rush over and pour the coffee. I don't. It was a simple mistake. She is doing a hell of a lot better than I was at the same stage.

As I'm training Lauren I notice I'm really sweaty. I check the thermostat and it says 82 degrees. When I try to turn down the temp it prompts for a pass code. I text Kirsten and she says to call our service line. So in the middle of a training someone new, who was doing great considering she should be doing a buddy shift right now, my jeans are getting sweaty, and we have customers coming in and out. The service line people tell me that only the store manager has the pass code. Kirsten is no help. They are no help. Right at this time the thunderstorm strikes. And, everyone in an 8-block radius comes to our coffee shop to stay out of the rain and get something to drink. Fuck.

The air's out, humidity strikes, and the coffee shop fills up. Only every other customer complains about the heat. It starts getting so warm the chocolate chips are melting together. I have to drop a ball of chocolate in the milk and now stir it loose, of course after fucking up the first ones that were like backwashed chocolate milk.

My jeans look like I've wet myself. I open both doors on either side of the store, but that only does so much good. I'm in a run of 10 coolers when I knock the milk chocolate syrup on to the floor. Lauren stares at me, the customers stare at me, and I....start laughing.

I was sure managing my own coffee shop could not be any worse than the Lake store. It just couldn't.

CHAPTER 16
A BUNCH OF FUCKING IDIOTS

*Dear customer who, while I am in the middle of the weeds and, bumbling
employees, spilled coffee, boiling burnt milk and, missed drink orders, says "I
can already tell you will turn this place around.",*

*I want to hug you and cry on your shoulder. I want to have a Robin
Williams/Matt Damon moment where you tell me everything will be all right
and to let it all out. Thank you will have to suffice.*

I walk into my new store on the Monday of Memorial Day weekend, and
customers are everywhere and not moving. *This isn't good.* Noreen, a 23-
year-old woman was on register staring at another 21-year-old with a
cockeyed Twins hat and saggy jeans on the bar. Neil was in epically bad
weeds. Dishes and steamers were stacked at the sink, customers were
sighing heavily, an unhealthy silence over the coffee shop, but Noreen just
stood there and watched him drown.

I had never met these two people. "Hey, I'm the new store manager Ben.
I'm here to help." They didn't have any reason not to trust me. Strangers
don't offer to help a drowning coffee shop. I dove in and we got through the
rush. I noticed a handwritten sign on the register that said, "Please pay with
credit card if possible! Thank you."

"What's with the sign?" I asked Noreen.

"It's a holiday today and the bank is closed," Noreen informs me. "So we
have no change." The idiots didn't get extra change for the long and busy
weekend! I spend my first day walking around the neighborhood buying
change from local stores. The store sits in a ridiculously wealthy area, but
it's a neighborhood Caribou, with limited parking, and is attached to a
Bruegger's Bagels. There are roughly 20 other businesses in the
neighborhood, including a fancy liquor/cheese store, a yoga studio, a Co-op,
a running shoe store, two restaurants, and a slew of yuppie stores I never
enter and can't understand how they stay in business.

Westin was the most recent store manager and he lasted about three months, which was three months longer than most thought he would last. Westin is the guy Nash told me about that everyone yelled at. Westin was overweight, slow, and he didn't feed the monster with the right people. Plus, he had a few things out of his control going against him.

Westin was tasked with taking over after the neighborhood favorite: Tori. Tori was unfailing happy and cheerful, had fun, danced and sang and could make lattes super quick. The neighborhood and the employees loved her. Men and woman loved her. Tori came to the store once and while I was chitchatting with her two different customers hugged her. *Yes, fucking hugged her.* I can't imagine for any reason, ever, hugging any customer. Tori was transferred to a slightly larger store only five blocks away, but the store and the neighborhood didn't like her leaving. They all took it out on poor Westin.

Tori's right-hand man was shift supervisor Brennan who was also promoted after Tori left. (In part because everyone wished Brennan became store manager, not Westin.) So Brennan and Tori were gone and everyone nagged and blamed Westin, who was slow, and didn't dance or didn't sing, and wasn't Tori and Brennan. Tori and Brennan had worked there for three years, which is absolutely unheard of in the service industry. The three years spoiled the neighborhood and it's an area already known for being spoiled.

The Pucketts started Caribou Coffee at the 44th and France location in Edina, Minnesota, attached to a Bruegger's Bagels, almost 20 years ago. The story goes they went to Alaska after business school and got the idea in the wild for a coffee shop that serves great coffee with great personality.

Tori told me she met John Puckett a few times when he came into the store. She said he was a little weird and would say kind of strange things. She wouldn't elaborate, but I did learn the Pucketts also started Punch Pizza. He started two successful franchises, so he can't be that crazy.

My store is not glamorous, nor big, and it struggles financially for a few different reasons. After 1 p.m. there are maybe 30 customers for the rest of the day. The store opens at 6 a.m., and starts getting busy from 8 a.m. to 11. At noon a lunch crowd and yoga class ends, so we have another rush. Then it's dead. On the weekends the morning are just as crazy as the Lake store Caribou, but scheduling is challenging. The store must stay under 30 percent of its sales for payroll. For eight hours a day the store is basically empty, so scheduling three people on the busy times hasn't worked.

The stockroom is downstairs and it doesn't have a desk, so poor Westin has put the computer on bakery shelving. The floor is littered with paper clips and pens that fell through the racks. The office and basement remind me of the basement in the movie the "Silence of the Lambs". Since the stockroom and office are downstairs it's a long walk with angry customers waiting when you get in a rush. You have to be particularly prepared so you do not have to run downstairs all the time.

Above the shop are apartments, and right next to the stockroom is the tenants' laundry room. It's always odd to be running down to the office for change or cups, and seeing this old guy in his sweats and a laundry basket. Sometimes it's spooky.

The coffee shop might not be new and shiny, but it's homey. It needs to be completely torn down and rebuilt, but instead Caribou has adapted by adding things where they don't fit. The store doesn't make enough money for a remodel, but it sits near money. Old and new money collide in the area, as the store sits on a busy corner between the city and the one the most prestigious suburbs. Since Westin had to take the brunt of associates and customers missing Tori and Brennan, and he was not equipped deal with a regular store, he abruptly left to sell vacuums.

A Caribou saying is 'never sweat it, it's just coffee.' But it is so much more than just coffee, and Westin did not get the hang of the bar, the pace, or the constant turnover and hard conversations. I was left with a few pieces, but not much. The first few weeks at the store were a lot of long hours and stress. Westin took over a full team, but no one respected him.

On Westin's last day he stops by the Lake store and gives me the keys. "Boy, this brings back some bad memories."

"How so?" I feign ignorance.

"Brad and Beck and Kirsten…ugh. It was the worst."

"Yeah, they have interesting training methods."

"How has it gone for you?" Westin asks.

"I worry about the bar sometimes."

"Yeah I've never been good at the bar. The pace was a lot different than I expected."

"Yeah no kidding!"

"I thought I would be managing, not doing the bar. I could never hire enough people to not have to work the floor."

"What's the store like?"

"It's quiet, but a lot of good people. Just promoted a few and they are all good." Westin lied really well. Or he didn't know what good meant.

After working with Kirsten, I thought everyone would love me at my new store. We would have fun and do things a little different. We'd focus on selling, upselling, and making the store run better and different than every other Caribou. It would be so easy, I thought. We will crush every goal! And the team, well how could they not like working for me? As you can probably guess it wasn't quite that easy.

My plan was so fucking simple. First off, I wouldn't hire zombies with philosophy degrees who would question everything. I wanted sales personalities! I would put all my best personalities at the greeter position to upsell the fuck out of every Caribou customer. I would sell all larges, I would add flavor shots to every drink, I would add a piece of bakery to every fucking thing. We would do it with a smile and send a bag of beans of home with them as well.

The problem with the service industry is that I just can't fire everyone because I need people to cover hours. I need two people in the store at all times either I or a shift supervisor must be one of them. A shift supervisor has been signed off by Christian to have keys and alarm codes and can handle emergency types of things.

I wanted to be at the greeter spot to see if I could upsell and raise the numbers. Every day we monitored five measurables: Total beans sold, number of larges out of 100 drinks, total ticket to last year, customer count, and sales to last year. What I discovered is not very many people at the store could effectively work the bar in the mornings. Or sell. And if you can't do the bar and you don't know how to sell then I don't really need you.

"We don't need to do much upselling here," Noreen tells me. "We have all regulars and they know what they want."

"Uh-huh. I would probably completely disagree. The one thing I have discovered in my time at Caribou is no one really knows what they want. And even if someone gets a cup of coffee everyday who is to say one day they might not want a blueberry muffin?"

"They know." *Shut up!* I want to yell. I start making a list of how many people I need to hire and who I need to get rid of soon. I have noticed in my career that when a new manager arrives there is natural turnover. Not necessarily because the new manager is good or bad, but because people just leave when new management comes in.

I can tell Noreen is not "in" and not surprisingly, she e-mails me her two weeks notice. She apologizes, but blames the whole process of being promoted to shift supervisor too quickly. *No shit.* I want to tell Noreen how awful she is at this job and I would have fired her anyways, but I can't. How she can just stand there while there are a million things to do is truly amazing. I need her to work out her two-week schedule and to her credit she does that. I hate her, not as a person but as a worker, and she is so awful at her job, but I need her and need to be nice to her. I can't let on that she is so awful because I don't want to have to work or fill all her hours. If she quit I would be there all fucking day. I think about giving her a special cup of coffee, but that is against the rules.

When Noreen is on greeter she flies through the customers, not upselling, not really chitchatting, so the bar is overrun with drinks. A good greeter can make natural conversation and upsell, and that gives the barista few precious seconds to get the drinks going. When you are at your local coffee shop and the line is backing up with drinks, the greeter should be slowing down. They are just as important to getting your caffeine quickly and properly as the barista is. When Noreen is on the bar, she does one drink at a time. Never looking ahead, never thinking about the next-next drink. It's hard to watch a bad barista. Painful!

"Have you ever thought about frothing extra milk for the next latte order?" I ask Noreen. She cannot begin to comprehend how to think about the next drink. On days when I'm not there she is in charge! My God!

Neil is the other shift supervisor and I discover quickly that Neil can't handle the pressure of the bar. Nor can he upsell. He can hardly run the register, actually. He stares at it like this is his second day. I overhear Neil talking with Noreen after she announces she is leaving. They discuss how quickly they were promoted and the pressure of it all. I laugh as I think about liberal America, namely my dad, lambasting corporations for not paying people a livable wage or giving them opportunities for advancement. And here I am again trying to find people who want more responsibility, more money, and the chance to move up in the company. Neil and Noreen are done with high school, aren't going to college, and have nothing going for them. It seems like a better job would be good?

Neil wears a cockeyed baseball hat and jeans and t-shirt, which are ridiculously baggy, every day. He is super quiet and I practically fall off my chair when he tells me he is a rapper. He wants to be a big star and is constantly working on his music.

"So you've done shows and stuff before?"

"Oh, no. I haven't got the nerve up yet. But I've recorded a lot of stuff," he whispers. I'm not surprised by his answer; he seems afraid of the customers. When it's busy he just crumbles under the pressure of a lot of orders in a row. Which we get every morning!

"Have you ever thought about pulling the shots as you are frothing the milk?" I ask Neil after a rough shift. He looks at me like, 'wow, I never thought of that.' It doesn't help, though. The bar is not easy, and Neil is not cut out for it. He doesn't have a car, so has to take the bus to work and can't get there until the afternoon except on weekends. He has been working Saturday and Sunday mornings, which are the two busiest days. Westin promoted him even though he didn't have a car. You may think that's not a big deal, but the shift supervisor brings the day's cash deposit to the bank. Westin didn't think that one through. If a deposit isn't made, it flags on a report and the home office accounting people have a nervous breakdown. A deposit must be done every day and typically by 2 p.m.

Neil also cannot be counted on to fill shifts if someone calls out or gets sick, unless it's at a scheduled bus time. And buses aren't coming to the hoity-toity area very often. So not only no car, but he's not comfortable on the bar or register. All in all, he's no fucking help. Westin just promoted Neil so he himself didn't have to work every hour.

I ask Neil how the weekends go for him because the bar doesn't seem like his strength. He agrees and then tells me he wants to transfer closer to a downtown store. And again I want to say you "fuck and you're fired," but I need Neil. I tell him "Hold on a few weeks and we will figure something out." In his defense, he at least does stay.

Every day I dislike Neil more and more. He can't do the basic job and he is literally a warm body. He somehow does the exact opposite of what I want done. It's really quite amazing. I begin to hate him. I don't ever plan on helping him get a transfer. If he reaches out to another Caribou and facilitates a transfer, good for him, but I'm not doing shit for him. I dream of the day he is off the schedule. When I work with Neil and Noreen, more than anger or hate or annoyance, I feel sorry and apologetic to the customers. Sometimes I want to announce to the busy shop, "Things are going to get better! Trust me. Just give me a little time." If people complain or get annoyed, I don't think about a special cup. They deserve to be pissed.

I start to interview people daily, looking for anyone with service industry experience or coffee shop experience, and personality. I can teach people how to make mochas, but I can't teach personality. It's not a science and sometimes I know within 10 seconds that it isn't the right person. Some are crazy, some are stinky, some are overqualified, some just want a job quickly, and it's my job to find someone who will fit and stay. Some want $20 an hour and we start at $8 and $9, plus tips and free coffee! Some want a guaranteed 40 hours a week, and some want to know if it's a lot of work. *That's a great question to ask an interviewer!*

What I really think about when I'm hiring is Beth. I worked with Beth on a weekend at the Lake store and it was almost the worst day of my life. She didn't chitchat with me, she didn't have fun, she didn't talk, and I had to spend a six-hour shift with her. It was fucking hell. At the end of our shift Beth apologized. "Sometimes working here makes me really crabby."

"Why do you work here?"

"I work in front of a computer all day."

"So you like the people interaction?" She sighed. It seemed to me sitting in front of a computer would be a perfect job for her. Beth never showed up again to work.

At the end of the day, I want to hire people who I wouldn't mind hanging out with for 8 hours. I don't want to hire any Beths, because not talking for six hours to someone who hates the job, hates their life, and doesn't want to be there isn't fun.

The worst part about interviewing so many people is they keep calling back to see if they got the job. Even when I tell them we went with another candidate. One creepy guy started hanging out at the shop and told Jenn he enjoyed the interview so much he became a customer. When he saw me he would tell me to keep him in mind for any new openings. Crazy people!

I hire Jenn who was the barista at D'Amico and Sons, so she has bar experience and I think will be able to handle a rush. Because no one else in the store can.

The problem with the store is that there are very few people who can literally make drinks quickly enough to handle the morning rush. They were spoiled because Tori or Brennan did every morning shift. So they were just greeters, and they weren't taught much there. They all cling to the thought that every customer in the neighborhood knows exactly what they want. I tell them they are wrong.

Colton is a neighborhood guy and probably go hired because Caribou encourages hiring locals. I'm sure when I was his age I was an idiot too, but I can't stand him. Tori kept him because he "made her laugh." I want to strangle him. I'm down in my office and I hear a bang-bang, bang-bang, which is a signal to come up and help in a rush. I run up and Colton says, "You have an americano on the board." One customer is standing staring at us like two idiots.

Is someone there fooling with me who put him up to this? It would be funny. Nope. He called me up to make one drink. Which is just water and espresso.

"Did you call me up here for one drink?"

"Uh, yeah."

"Do you know how to make an americano?"

"Yeah."

"Can you do the bar?"

"Yeah. I help out a lot there."

"Here's your chance. You're on bar." Colton's eyes go wide. He is obviously not ready for the bar, nor has he ever helped out much on it. It takes two small rushes for me to quit humiliating him. He can't multi-task and if you can't do that, the bar is not the spot for you. Not the end of the world. Let's see if he can sell.

"Colton, now the next customer that comes, ask them if they'd like a piece of bakery." A customer walks in and orders a drink.

"Would you like a piece of bakery with that?" he barely whispers.

"Colton, are you nervous to talk to customers? Are you nervous to sell stuff?" He doesn't answer. My rules of upselling are easy and they work. When I started at Caribou I was skeptical whether upselling and "suggesting" truly worked. It does and it is amazing what people will buy if you offer it and tell them you like it. If they order a small it can become a large for only 60 cents more. "Would you like to treat yourself to a large today for 60 cents more?"

If they order a medium, a large is only 30 cents more. FOR ANY DRINK. So it's pretty easy to remember. Always offer a piece of bakery. I always offer something I like. "Would you like a chocolate chip cookie? They are my favorite."

If they order a large or medium drink I would then ask if they want to add an extra shot. There is always, always something to add that makes sense.

Customer: "I'll have a medium latte."

Colton: "That will be $3.85."

Me: "Colton! Upsell!"

Colton: "I think she knew what she wanted."

Me: Rolling eyes.

Each shift Colton works it becomes increasingly clear he has some sort of phobia about upselling–or selling in general. He tells me he is transferring to Tori's store. I know for a fact he hasn't talked to Tori about transferring and Christian wouldn't allow it anyways.

"Things just aren't working out here, you know."

"Colton, I could sense that. Good luck and I'll take you off the schedule." Colton moodily comes into the store twice after that day looking at the schedule.

"Do I have any hours this week?"

"Nope. How is it down at Tori's?"

Anthony is a 35ish white guy who plays in a rock band, has a fauxhawk, has what he calls a "sugar mamma," and is horribly inept at all things coffee shop related. He will not do the bar, because everyone has told him, he tells me, how great he is as greeter. He has a real talent for what I call "down selling." A customer will say, "I'll have a latte." "Oh a small one?" Goddamn it! Worse, in semi-slow times Anthony will sit down in our little dining room and wait for the next person to come in. Even though we have literally 150 million things to do. There is Anthony sitting down and Noreen watching him. I tell Anthony not to sit unless he's doing something. Which really means to knock off the sitting. Anthony hauls over the drink carriers to assemble. Which can be assembled in about a half a second and put away in two seconds. He takes the 45 seconds to haul them over and sit down. What a fucking idiot.

I watch Anthony work and I notice he doesn't empty and rinse the coffee urns.

"Is there any reason why you don't rinse out the coffee urn three times after it's empty?"

"Ben, it's so busy in the morning we don't have time. We might be small, but the rushes are intense." I should note Anthony, Noreen and myself are the only ones in the shop. I lie in bed and worry at night what these people do when I am not there. When I am there they must be on their decent behavior, which is horrible. What are they like when they are screwing around?

"What is your favorite part about working at Caribou?" I ask Anthony.

"It's super chill here and no one really cares what we do. This is a primo spot for you, bro. The head honchos don't care what goes on at this store, so we don't have to do that selling shit."

"I need you to do that selling shit."

"Aw come on, bro! We thought you were going to be cool and chill?"

"Is it that awful to ask them for a large or a muffin?"

"Every new manager starts off with the same things, but we don't change."

"It's only been Tori and Westin."

"Whatever you want bro."

I start counting the days when I don't need Anthony.

One day I stood outside the store. I wasn't on the schedule but I had to pick up my Day-Timer. I dreaded walking in and I braced myself for hell. The store was quiet. At least the line wasn't backed up. Two customers stood at the shelves of packaged coffee. They looked at me awkwardly. Anthony and Noreen were sitting down in the customer area. You can tell if someone knows they are fucking around when you catch them fucking around. If they quickly try to look busy, then they were consciously fucking around. If they don't try to act busy or come up with an excuse than they are a lazy dumbass. Noreen saw me and immediately jumped up. "What's up, Ben!?" Anthony yelled and continued to recline leisurely.

"What can I get for you today?" I ignored Anthony and helped the customers.

"Dude, it's been so slow today. Nothing hopping."

"What about them?" I said quietly.

"There were looking around for awhile." *Drop it*, I say in my head. "Were you guys shopping?"

"Ah no." The customer replied.

"Sorry about that," I say. "These are on me." I really should have given Anthony and Noreen a special cup. I am definitely thinking about it. I imagine a website where I could plead my case and people of the world could help me decide their fate.

I wanted to scream and yell, 'there was a millions things to do! It's a fucking coffee shop for god's sake. More people are coming so get ready for the next rush. Not to fucking mention there were fucking customers in the store!' I didn't yell. I needed them for a while longer. "Bro, I thought they were shopping," Anthony continued on.

On a particularly awful day, Westin had scheduled Anthony and Colton together alone in the morning. He obviously didn't care about the store at the point he created the schedule. I added myself to the schedule and I thought between the three of us it wouldn't be that bad and I could show them how it was done while having some fun and being a little competitive. I would be on bar, Anthony and Colton could switch off between greeter and Super Glue. They both hopped on the registers and funneled through about 30 drink orders in about six minutes. My screen was filled up. I was running out of mocha and latte pitchers, my ingredients needed re-filling– we were in the fucking weeds. The two idiots kept taking orders as quick as they could.

"Hey! I need you two to slow the fuck down! Anthony, get off register and help me out!" I switched tones. "Here's your milk chocolate mocha, sir," I said in my cheeriest voice.

"You have shit all over your hair," the customer replied.

"It'll have to wait today."

The greeter position is supposed to do two things: sell more stuff and suggest a larger size, but more importantly, the greeter spaces out the drink orders for the barista. Anthony and Colton asked what they wanted and nothing else.

It was the first and last time I swore in front of customers. I texted Kirsten about the incident. I worried about a customer complaint and Christian firing me.

"LOL I've been there," she replied.

Vanessa was a 50ish woman who was hired by Westin because "she would probably clean good." That's really the last thing I was worried about. I sit down and have a chat with Vanessa and it doesn't go well.

"This is a really easy job because it's just serving coffee," she starts out when asked why she likes working here.

"Wow. I'd really disagree when people say that. We do a million things often at the same time. Upselling, product knowledge, incredible amounts of multi-tasking, we have to know customers, and stay professional. It's an incredibly tough job."

"But besides that it's just handing them coffee." This conversation is not going how I envisioned.

"If you are just handing someone a cup of coffee this isn't the place for you."

Vanessa explains how she is worried about how Larry will be treated. She tells me Larry has Asperger's and can only work at night when it's slow. Christian had mentioned Larry and said he didn't want to tell me much, so I could make my own opinions. I had worked with a few kids with Asperger's at Wal-Mart, so I had a jist of the condition.

"My understanding of Asperger's is it's not something a social environment like this would be good for."

"Well, it's just handing someone a cup of coffee," she replies. Oh boy.

One busy Sunday afternoon I'm working with Larry at register. I have an order for nine straight coolers, so I am in the zone. I can tell it is taking a little longer than normal at the register, but I wasn't paying attention with all of the different cooler concoctions. All of a sudden Larry looks over and says we need change. I was a little upset because you should always say you need change before you really need change. But this was unlike anything I had ever seen. Larry had literally given out all the change. So the last few customers had gotten dollars worth of nickels and pennies back. The cash drawer had all $20s in it. Every other compartment was bare.

"I didn't have time to tell you I needed change." In that instant, I think about just fucking losing it on Larry. I'm fucking 8 fucking feet away and it's not even fucking that busy! God fucking damn it how the fuck did you give away all the fucking change and how the fuck didn't you say anything to me?!

I laugh a little.

"I'm more impressed than mad really. How did you even do that?" I turn to the customers.

"Folks," I look to the customers in line. "Drinks will be on the house if you bear with me. I need to get some change." He gave away all of the change, I later tell any friend that will listen.

I tell Christian about my day with Larry, and he said he thought something like that might be going on. Brennan and Tori covered for Larry and would either do everything for him or tell him EXACTLY what to do. It's a very Caribou thing to do, but it was really hard on the store.

"Brennan would literally tell Larry everything to do. Otherwise Larry would just stare off into space," Christian tells me. "He said it wasn't that bad though." But it is. Larry fill up the coffee, Larry clean up that spill, Larry now re-fill the ice, Larry wipe down the tables. I would get busy with my own things and forget to monitor Larry and he would stare off into space. Or worse, go sit down while I'm hurrying around cleaning.

"There is a place for Larry in this world, but a coffee shop is not the place. It's not fair to the other employees who have to do more and have higher expectations."

Christian nods. He had these same conversations with Westin.

"I don't want to be the asshole who fired Larry, but he can't be on the schedule for 20 hours a week. It's killing the store. The basic expectation is for everyone to be able to make a latte or, a mocha for customers. Larry can't."

"Can he contribute at all?" Christian asks.

"He is a warm body." I begin to see why Neil and Noreen were going home crying every night having to work with Larry and Colton and Anthony. They are worse than no help, they create more work for anyone in charge.

Arnold was a senior in high school and he could manage at the bar and he could sell. Arnold's problem was that he was weird and annoying. He hadn't left the safety of the neighborhood in almost any capacity, but wanted everyone to think he had bedded a thousand girls and traveled to a thousand lands. Each day he wore a light blue dress shirt, pink shorts, and dress shoes with no socks. That description does no justice to just how odd he looked, like Pee Wee Herman working at a Caribou. His mother dropped him off at work, and he would kiss her on the cheek. Arnold couldn't drive and rode a 10-speed girl's bike. I'm not making fun of Arnold's clothes and transportation because he is poor. He chose to wear and ride what he did. I asked him. "You choose to wear pink shorts and ride a girl's bicycle?"

"Kind of retro, I know. The ladies like it." I heard Jake, another employee, do a spit take in the back laughing. Arnold told me he is going to Thailand for a gap year to kick-box. He did not appear athletic. Or coordinated.

"Did you play sports or anything in high school?"

"No. I'm taking a gap year then attending Iowa University, then doing an internship in DC."

"Iowa, huh?"

"Yeah, I didn't study enough in high school so it will fit my academic needs."

"Then to DC for a internship?"

"Yeah my parents are making me." Arnold frowned as if his parents were hard, driving, and demanding socialites and successes.

"What do your parents do?"

"A kindergarten teacher and a carpenter."

Arnold, of course, had a hard time keeping his lies straight. I would later learn Arnold, or Arn or Arnie, would just be spending a year in Thailand with a exchange program family. No kickboxing.

I didn't schedule myself with him because he became increasingly odder. I knew Arnold thought I was an idiot because of all the lies he told me. Arnold wanted 40 hours a week and I started scheduling him about 4, hoping he would go away. He didn't though. Arnold was crazy and an idiot, but he loved Caribou. He was protective of it in a weird way. He loved it there. It was part of his identity, as he didn't have many friends. It gave him friends and a social place to go. One week I had Arnold on the schedule for 36 hours and it was almost the worst week of my life. Arnold at least could manage the bar, probably about a level two barista. In a mad rush he wouldn't crumble, but would start doing tasks he didn't need to do. He would fill his Splenda packets in a rush. I think it was a mental defense mechanism in response to the rush. Someone should study this stuff. I would switch with him when it got too busy. He was folksy with the customers and he tried to upsell whatever I challenged him to sell.

When Arnold left Caribou he scratched his name under the chocolate chip rack on the bar. He will be apart of Caribou forever. I was happy to see him go.

I think about this cast of characters Tori and Westin had assembled and they are lush, crazy, interesting people. They have personality and are different and you might be reading this and wonder why I want them out. They seem like great fodder for writing and you are right. They just suck so fucking bad at the job. They belong in a trendy coffee shop uptown where people do not care about two things and two things only: speed and caffeine.

Westin's other two hires I love! Jake is smart, cleans, upsells pretty good (after I told him to upsell), and is fun to work with. He doesn't make mistakes twice and he is willing to learn and do whatever I ask of him. Jake's father is a surgeon, but even though his car payment is more than I make in a month he is down-to-earth. I call him to fill in shifts and he says he can't because he is on the yacht. Cool.

Leslie is the exact same way except she is a girl. She is local too and her father is the president of a local company. Both Jake's and Leslie's parents are ridiculously rich, but they are both hard and conscientious workers. They would have been awesome hires if not for one thing...they are college students. You might not think that's not a big thing, but at a Caribou with only 13 associates it's a huge deal. College kids are going to be leaving and that leaves me in the shitter. Three months moves pretty quick. As I tell Jake, right when you become basically an expert at running the store, you will be leaving.

I use Jake and Leslie to cover hours as I get rid of the idiots. And I still continue to hire over the summer because they will be leaving. Most college kids want as many summer hours as they can get and I understand that, but I have to think of the business first.

I try to explain to everyone that every extra upsell and sales means more hours. I need two people at a store at all times. I do 75 percent of my business before noon. But we are still open until 8 p.m. because Caribou wants consistency amongst their shops. The Lake store has evening business because there is a lake next to it. Not my store. Everything in our neighborhood closes at 5 p.m. and the Bruegger's even closes at 3 p.m. on Saturdays! So I'm wasting payroll to stay open. Payroll needs to be under 30 percent of my sales and it's a challenge. Some days we have literally no customer for hours. The location has grown old and in a five-block radius there are two more Caribous and a Starbucks. In a two-mile radius there are tons of coffee shops, gas stations, McDonalds, Starbucks, and other Caribou. The morning business is consistent, but there is no new business to grow in the afternoons. So we have to squeeze every penny out of the morning customers. If we can increase our sales I could add a third person to the busiest days–Friday, Saturday and Sunday–which would make everyone's lives easier.

What makes everything slower at the shop is the 'Coffee Asshole Dickhead Snobs' favorite gripe in the world. The espresso machine. At the Lake store we had the Super Automatic espresso machine, which makes a consistent volume, taste and texture shot with one push of the button. Coffee snobs complain, and I read this complaint all the time, they want the traditional machine. Why? Because they are idiots!

The traditional machine starts with the portcullis, the big metal thing you see baristas banging. The bean grinder is separate, so the portcullis fits underneath the grinder and you give two clicks of ground espresso. Then you brush off the excess, touching it of course, and wedge it into the spout of the espresso machine. Which basically is this huge old concoction to run hot water through the espresso. It is five extra steps to do what the Super Automatic does in one push of a button. The problem is there are now five ways that your espresso shot can come out different. Too much espresso, not enough espresso, and if you fit the portcullis in at different angels the shot comes out too thick or too thin. Now, you've met my cast of Caribou workers–they can barely figure out the fucking register and now we are throwing this at them?

The traditional machines have a steam wand, but it is not automatic either. You have to drop a thermometer in the milk each time you froth or boil. It's messy and splashes and you feel like the thermometers never get truly clean. You have to watch the milk more closely. In all of my time at the Lake store no one overflowed milk, but at my new store it happens daily. And to good baristas. A customer falls down or there is a commotion and the milk is burned and overflowing.

Traditional machine lovers will tell you to just to listen to the milk froth, but really you have to watch because listening to milk froth is hard in a chaotic morning rush. Traditional machine lovers will tell you it's faster. It's not. If you think that it is, you are a dummy. Traditional machine lovers will also tell you the espresso tastes better, and in California, they only allow traditional machines. Do they have nothing else to fucking worry about in

California? The espresso can taste different, but it's a crapshoot. People come into a Caribou or Starbucks for the caffeine and the quickness. The espresso tastes don't matter much, I have found out. The number one complaint about Caribou by customers? It takes too long to make their drink. These fucking machines aren't helping! More on 'Coffee Asshole Dickhead Snobs' and their complaints later!

The store was basically a clusterfuck. I was leaving the store in the hands of people who could barely make a drink and ring it up correctly. Christian asked me later if I was stressed out during those times? Yes. They were lean times. Things got better, but just not as quickly as I portray it here.

I would take the weekend off and there would be complaints on OSAT (the results of printed surveys given to random customers.) I would work one morning and we would clear $1,000 by noon and I would take the next day off and they would barely clear $500. It is amazing how having the right people in place truly makes a difference in the coffee business. You might think you are getting a cup of coffee, but truly at Caribou we will get more out of you. Little by little I rooted the bad people out. Truly though, they didn't like me. I asked them to do things they never had to do before such as asking a customer if they want a large or a cup of oatmeal. I know, I'm such a fucking dickhead!

Larry was moving to Minneapolis and told me he was transferring and I was really relieved. Larry said there was a real negative energy about the store.

"What do mean?"

"That's what people tell me."

"Who?"

"Everyone."

"Well it's best we all part ways then." Larry showed up at another store at 8 a.m. during rush time, unannounced, and stood at the end of the bar until the store manager asked if he was all right. He was not hired. Larry entered the service industry limbo where he hasn't been fired, but doesn't get any hours.

Vanessa gives me her two-week notice saying she doesn't like the direction the store is going. I had been scheduling Vanessa about four hours a week and I couldn't believe it took her so long to quit. I cover Vanessa's remaining three shifts with Jake in case she doesn't show up. Vanessa calls me and says she is offended I covered her shifts. I pretend to take Jake off the schedule, but tell him to still show up. Of course Vanessa calls last minute and says her new job is more important. She doesn't show up for her last two shifts.

I finally work Neil off the schedule and it was the greatest day of my life! I encouraged him to transfer somewhere else, but he is shy and lazy. I make the schedule two weeks out, so he knew he wasn't on it. I feel bad for Neil for a moment, but I quickly envision him somehow not selling one piece of bakery on a Sunday morning. Not one fucking piece! Did he tell people it wasn't for sale?

He ends up transferring down the road and I tell the store manager Elizabeth not to take him. "I literally can't let him work here anymore. That's how bad he is. He literally can't do anything and has somehow gotten worse." But Elizabeth needs people badly, so she takes Neil. A few weeks later Neil doesn't show up for a Saturday shift. Elizabeth wants to kill him, but Neil never shows up again. I don't say I told you so because I feel bad for her. It sucks when the store owns you.

CHAPTER 17
FEED THE MONSTER

Dear applicants to Caribou,
Do not tell me in your interview you want to work at a coffee shop because it is so chill and relaxed. It's not. Don't tell me you want to work in a coffee shop because it looks really easy. It's not. Don't tell me you want to work in a coffee shop because it's just serving coffee. It isn't.

There are three phases to hiring. Phase one is reviewing the online applications. It's the first thing I do when I walk in every day. Each applicant can apply at as many Caribou coffees as they want, so other Caribou store managers are looking at many of the same applicants. It's first come, first served. Most applicants apply at more than just one Caribou if they are looking for a job.

Phase two is the phone interview and figuring out if they have a pulse and a personality. Phase three is the actual interview. It seems so easy on paper, but the sheer logistics of calling an applicant, getting a hold of them, getting them into the store for an interview in a timely manner, then making a decision and getting their background check completed and having them set up for training can be a job in itself.

The payoff for all this hard work is easy to understand. Sometimes just a few great employees can dramatically change a store. And a few bad hires can destroy the store and the store manager's life! Christian believes that two or three truly engaged people can drive sales, increase customer satisfaction, and make the store manager's life so much easier. He is right, but finding engaged people is truly difficult when we are paying $8 an hour and the job is fucking tough. The job sucks. And as I interview people, I sometimes feel like Huck Finn trying to get people to whitewash our fence. For the fun of it.

Phase One: Reviewing applications

1. The first thing I look for is how long does the person want to work for Caribou? Each applicant has to pick a timeframe they envision working for Caribou: seasonal or a few weeks, under three months, over six months to a year, a year to two years , or make a career out of Caribou.

   I will not select anyone looking for seasonal employment. So no students for the summer, no students home the holidays, no people looking for a holiday job for extra money. I do not have the need to hire someone, teach them everything I know, and have them leave. I wouldn't think about anyone unless they wanted minimum of six months work, but honestly I want someone who at least thought they'd be with me over a year.

2. The next most important piece of the application is the day-to-day availability. I need people who are available all the time and are flexible, or can at least work mornings Monday, Friday, Saturday and Sunday. Those are our busiest times. If the applicant said they could work 8 a.m. to 4 p.m. and no weekends they would never be hired. They would never be called. Obviously, at least to me, I wouldn't hire an idiot even if they had open availability. But being able to work whenever I need them certainly helps.

3. What is the wage they are expecting? If they said $20 and over I won't call them. They are already unrealistic about what the job is or they have no idea how the real world works. If they requested between $10 and $12, I might call and say the position starts at $8 for regular employees and $9 for shift supervisors, plus tips and the extra free drinks and coffee. If I like an applicant's resume I will call them and that would be the intro to the phone screening. I won't pull any punches because I don't have time. "You wrote down you wanted $12, but it pays $8. Let's not waste each other's time." Typically these do not pan out.

4. What's on their résumé? Because I was so caught off-guard with the pace of Caribou, I put probably too much importance on service industry experience. Have they faced a rush before? Do they have food service experience? There were literally thousands of applications from former engineers, business people, marketing people–basically people that think it looks fun to work in a coffee shop. Ugh! I feel bad too because knew many had been laid off and were out of work. If you've worked in an office for a long time, this is no place for you. Trust me. If you've never had to give a cup of coffee to a total dick without saying anything, this is not for you.

5. I also avoid job hoppers. Did the applicant leave a job without another? Not a great sign. I don't have time to train someone who is just going to up and leave. The real trick of looking at résumés and applicants in general, is finding someone who is good enough to help, but not necessarily good enough to leave. If you are super smart, energetic, outgoing, and a go-getter you probably aren't going to be working for $8 an hour very long. I need people who are staying for a while. But are good. It's not easy.

Phase Two: The phone screening

The next part is a phone interview, or really a short conversation to see if they have one thing: personality. If they don't say, "Hey, how are you?" or have a semi friendly voice message it says a lot about who they are. I called countless people who when I introduced myself would say...nothing.

"Oh hey. Are you still interested in interviewing?"

"Um yeah. Definitely." We'll I'm not interested in you now because this conversation is so awkward.

I won't say that I have hired someone because of a great phone screening, but I definitely have decided "no" on applicants during my phone screening. I'm looking for courtesy and a little personality. I have called literally countless awkward applicants and it goes something like this:

Me: "Hey, this is Ben, the store manger at Caribou."

Kris: Silence.

Me: "Is Kris available?"

Kris: "This is Kris."

Me.: Hi. How is it going?

Kris: "Fine."

Silence.

Me: "Are you still interested in working for Caribou?"

Kris: "Yes."

There are a couple things I consider during these conversations. First, they might not recognize the phone number and be a little cautious about strange calls so they are a little hesitant. But if they are truly applying for jobs they have to pick up the phone with some professionalism and personality. Plus, once I say I'm with Caribou you should be a little interested to hear from me if you want to work here.

Now compare this to an applicant named Liz who I later hired. Liz showcased her personality on her answering machine, which is another decent indicator of personality and sense of humor–two things that I'm looking for. Liz's answering machine said she was out was not available but to have a great day. Simple but good.

Me: "Hi, this is Ben the store manager at Caribou Coffee."

Liz: "Hi Ben, I'm so glad you called!"

Me: "So you're still interested in interviewing?"

Liz: "Of course! I've always wanted to work in a coffee shop and I just moved to the city, so I thought it would be a great job and fit my schedule."

Liz and I were off to the races.

The awkward part of a bad phone interview is letting them know they didn't get the interview. Usually I say, "Well I'm just making a few calls to see if people are interested and someone will give you a call back if you are selected for an interview." I know I'm a wuss.

One applicant's wife or girlfriend answered and she called to him, "Mike" in a sweet voice. "What the fuck do you want?" he replied. That seemed like a red flag. Most bad applicants are just quiet and give short answers. They just aren't for me.

But the worst of the worst, are way too eager. Stalker applicants call back a lot and are creepy in general. One guy said he had such a good phone conversation with me he was now a customer for life. "If I disappear, someone should check that guy's basement," I tell Jake.

Another applicant had a great phone screening, but in real life she was nuts. On the outside she appeared normal, but there was just something off on the inside. And worst of all, just giving her the interview made her fall in love with me. The interview was horrible from the get-go, so I knew I wasn't going to hire her, but I just asked some random questions to make the interview stretch into a reasonable time. Liz watched the whole thing and then told me she had the feeling the girl wanted to eat my hair.

Another red flag is people who give too much detail about what's going on in their lives way too soon.

"Well, my son got tripped up with aggravated sexual assault stuff, so I had to quit my last job. But we all live in the same house with his girlfriend and sons. Boy are they hellions. But I'm real eager to work and my son could help out too whenever you need."

"That's good to know."

The résumé liars are fun. "So you were a store manager at Bed, Bath and Beyond?"

"Yup."

"What were some of your duties there?"

"Uh, you know, uh, registers and hiring and, uh, selling most things there."

"So what did you look for when you hired someone?"

"Uh, someone who could do the registers and sell most things."

"Okay well you're lying and maybe crazy, so I'm going to pass." No, I didn't say that but I wanted to!

Or people will quickly ask odd questions over the phone.

"Now do you do a drug and background test?"

"Um…yeah. Typically. Why do you ask?"

"Oh, I guess, uh. No reason." Okay good, that's normal to ask.

"Now, do we deal with people a lot?"

"Why do you ask?"

"I guess sometimes I could just take or leave people."

"Well the job is kind of dealing and working with people all day, every day."

"I can do that."

Some applicants keep calling and calling and do not take a hint or a straight out no. One woman thought she would be so great for the job that I just couldn't pass her up. I was pretty straightforward with on the phone after realizing she was crazy, and said I could not meet her salary demands of $16 an hour. That wasn't the end, though. She called at 8 a.m. on Saturdays to see if I had changed my mind or had more openings. "There is no worse time to call me than right now. 8 a.m. at a coffee shop is a little busy."

Phase Three: The Interview

Things I look for but aren't deal makers or deal breakers.

1. What are they wearing? I understand it's an $8-an-hour job, but still, bring it a little clothing wise. I don't expect a three-piece suit.

2. Timeliness is important, because nothing is more annoying then getting there 30 minutes early.

3. Do they like coffee? Or have someone in their life who likes coffee? It adds to the average hourly rate if they appreciate free coffee.

4. Does the applicant smile, laugh, laugh at my jokes, make self-deprecating comments about themselves and, show they can make a mistake and laugh about it?

   Are they crazy? Are they good crazy? Do they have self-awareness? Having little to no self-awareness is not necessarily a bad thing. It helps to sell if no's don't bother you.

5. Have they worked in the service industry? Do they have a good attitude? If they have a good attitude I can teach them how to make a mocha and a latte. And if they have "rush" experience, even better. "Tell me about a time someone you worked with failed." (Did they help?) Have they had to do a million things at once? Did they have a good attitude about it?

How competitive are they on a scale of one to 10? Many people think competitive is bad, so I have to ask probing questions to see if they are.

6. Would I want to spend eight hours a day with this person? Is this person going to show up every day? How did they leave their last job? Did they just walk out? I go through the Oreo and tree and superhero questions too. But really it comes down to will they show up every day, work hard, and have a great attitude? Sometimes it's hard to figure out in 30 minutes of interview time.

And if I like them I do not wait 24 hours to think about it, I don't have a second person interview them, if I like them and I want them, I offer a job on the spot. The offer is pending the background check, then I will call them, and make a schedule. There are so many outside factors involving job offers from the applicant. If I'm having a bad day, tired, plain don't care, or an applicant fools me, it leads to a bad hire. Hiring is not a science.

JENN:

Jenn was my first hire but sixth interview at my new store. Jenn had worked at D'Amico and Sons and talked about the lunch rush. Her favorite part of the job was making espresso drinks, so she wanted try a coffee shop. Jenn wasn't exactly bubbly, but she was sarcastic in an outgoing way and she made me laugh at the interview. Her only drawback as a candidate was she was a college student.

"I have to take off a semester to save some money," she explained. She went to college at a small liberal arts school in Iowa. Can't afford college? That was perfect for me. She had a very, very outside shot at a music scholarship, but she blushed as talked about it, "I'll never get it, I don't even know why I mentioned it." I hired her on the spot. Jenn was half Vietnamese and immediately I had diversified the store.

On Jenn' first day, a Tuesday morning, I scheduled her, myself, Anthony and Arnold, and my plan was to train Jenn the right way by shadowing me. We started out with Anthony at the register, Jenn and I at the bar, and Arnold as Super Glue. My head was going to explode hearing Anthony not upsell, not ask about bakery, and at one point make a guy wait for coffee to brew and the whole line stopped. Fortunately Jenn was unbelievable.

"How many shots for larges in hot drinks?" Jenn had a paint pen and was writing the drink combinations on the bar. Genius. Jenn knew the game. She asked a few procedural questions, like how many shots, how much sugar, how many chocolate chips, etc. I taught her our milk standards, how to do our whip, just kind of Caribou specific ideals. I was amazed by her.

"Wow," Arnold commented to me. "Jenn already has legs on the bar."

"I know! Pretty fucking good hire, huh?" I was mocking Arnold and he didn't know it. I wanted to hug her and tell her she was the savior of my life. And over the morning Jenn got better and better and handled a mini rush on her own.

"Are you okay to do this by yourself?"

"Yeah. I'm fine. Do what you need to do." I liked Jenn even more because she could read my mind. She was normal. She was hard-working. I want to call her a genius because she could do the bar in hours. She was calm and efficient.

"Hey, you two can take off for the day," I said to Arnold and Anthony.

"What do you mean?" Arnold looked confused.

"I mean you two can go home. Jenn and I can handle it. Have a great day."

"It's her first day, bro." Anthony must have seen the writing on the wall. I couldn't point to the writing, but I was standing right in front of the writing.

"I know!" I was giddy. "I know it's only her first day!"

They walked puppy eyed out of the store. "Oh the times they are a changin," I almost called out. My first hires would define me as a manager to the other employees. If they sucked and didn't care it was a representation of me. I hit it out of the park. Jenn instantly allowed me to have her cover the bar on busy days and allow me to be greeter. Because very few people in the store could do either.

DETERMAN:

My second hire was the same week as Jenn, but was not quite the home run hire. Jenn became a phase three barista in a couple of weeks. Determan might not be a phase one barista...to this day.

Determan was a local kid who had recently graduated from a small liberal arts college and had a perfect résumé. Caribou encourages hiring a few local people, usually high schoolers, but Determan is even better because he is local, not going anywhere, and wants hours! I envisioned him entering the management program and being a shining star of my review. Getting people ready for the next level was a big deal in Christian's eyes.

Determan reminded me of me when I started the coffee game, even though he worked at Dairy Queen and the state fair concessions booths. I was happy he had worked the service industry before. As I look back, there were a couple red flags in his interview, but I overlooked them because I was excited by the management potential (I told this once to Liz and she laughed so hard she started hyperventilating) and because of the local angle.

Determan worked at the french fry booth at the state fair for three weeks and he had worked at Dairy Queen for about two weeks. These were his only two jobs. Ever. He was now 22 and a college graduate.

"Why did you leave Dairy Queen?"

"My grandpa had got me the job, but they said after two weeks they didn't have any more hours."

Hmm....

In his interview he admitted he makes mistakes and I tell him that's okay. Just don't make the same mistake over again. But it's not that simple for Determan.

If my life were a movie, Determan would be the comic interlude. He screws up constantly, but he has a good heart, so I give him chance after chance after chance. He is the loveable kid brother who you want to kill then hug then kill then hug daily after he screws up. I truly live my coffee shop life with the mantra, 'make tons of mistakes, but never make the same mistake twice and you will be okay.' Determan's ability to forget the simple task is what makes his mistakes just so fucking impressively idiotic and entertaining. Instead of the three shifts as barista, I kept Determan with me for about two weeks. I make him constantly do things over and over again. Determan worked the bar in the morning once. Once. Determan worked the greeter spot in the morning once. Once. It was too much, too fast, and that when I decided Determan might not be management material. Maybe not even coffee shop material.

Determan forgets to put the lid on the blender and it sprays cooler all over the wall and himself and usually Jenn or Emily. Determan! You forget the lid once, Okay. Twice? Okay time to remember. Three times and more? Goddamnit Determan! After spilling some of the blended drink out of the top the cooler, the batch is now incomplete. Determan fills up the cup and it's short about two inches. I watch his mind turn, debating if he should serve the drink.

"Make another one, Determan." Now Determan decides he is not going to make another full drink, that would be wasteful when he only needs a couple of inches. The problem is we only know the recipe for a full batch. Determan guesstimates what the ingredients for two inches of a mocha cooler should be. After blending it has the consistency of glue somehow. He shakes it out in the cup and it looks like two different drinks mixed together. And disgusting.

"Start over." A mocha cooler that usually takes about 30 seconds to make has taken Determan about six minutes. And I wish I had video taped it!

"Um, can I get a lid?" I hear a customer ask. Determan had not put a lid on a large iced coffee.

"Sure can." And he jovially puts a lid on.

"You can go ahead and put a lid on everything. Unless it's a house cup." Later, I see Determan trying to bring a large hot coffee to a customer, balancing it so it doesn't spill over. I do a double take, "Lid, Determan!"

The worst is when Determan tries to be helpful to the barista and taps off drinks on the screen when he is greeter, thinking he took care of a cold drink. But he taps off the wrong drink and screws up the whole process. "Did you just Determan my screen?" becomes part of our jargon.

"Don't you touch that screen!" I hear Liz yell like an older sister shooing away her little brother.

Determan would disappear into the bathroom for long stretches. "Maybe you should talk to him about it?" Liz asked. "I don't want to know what he's doing in there, but he is gone too long sometimes."

I respond with, "Maybe you could have that talk with him? Kind of a growth opportunity type thing for you? Management stuff." Liz says no.

Determan would drink a large espresso with an extra shot and than have to go pee every 20 minutes in the Saturday afternoon rush. He would start hopping around and I'd sigh, a very Kirsten-like sigh. "Go quick so you don't wet your pants."

The sign of a horrible greeter is when the barista is helping them. The greeter should be making the barista's life easier. I watch Determan as the greeter and I think his instinct is somehow the exact opposite of what should be done. He takes an order of a large coffee, blueberry muffin, and yogurt. As soon as he hears coffee he should get that first. Determan gets the yogurt. Pours the coffee halfway, then puts the muffin on a plate. The customer is obviously ordering to go. He finishes the coffee and hands the customer his food and starts addressing the next customer. He never took the customer's money.

I try to walk Determan through his routine at greeter. Determan complains he gets dizzy from walking to the coffee, then to the bakery, and then to the register. I think about all the people in the world toiling in mines, and tar pits, and horrible jobs and how they would react to Determan getting dizzy in a three-foot space. I feel like they would choke him to death. Determan does gets better though. Kind of.

Determan without a doubt cannot work the bar. And I thought he would eventually get it. It took me a long time too. So Determan becomes the late morning/afternoon greeter because it's slow and he is okay at upselling. I need people to work in the slowest time who do not mind getting literally no tips. Determan has no options, so he's perfect.

I will come into the shop at 4 p.m. and Determan will have forgotten to switch full batch to half batch. We haven't done full batches since t10 a.m., so for six hours we had been giving watered down coffee! Even at the slowest of times, Determan runs out of coffee, just completely forgetting.

When a whipped cream can is not properly emptied of the air but opened to be washed out, it explodes whipped cream everywhere. This is called a "Determan" because Determan has done it so many times. On one famous whipped cream blow-up, Determan somehow dropped the whipped cream lid down the sink drain. Literally a one-in-ten-billion shot! Everyone who hears about it looks at the hole and the canister lid and shakes their head in disbelief. Somehow though Determan manages to blow the whipped cream out of the canister every time he changes it. We all watch him. It's a joke you know is coming and can't help watching.

Determan has also hit himself in the nuts while mopping. Numerous times. He forgets to close the bakery door or will forget to get a bakery item for the customer. Determan making a tea is hilarious because he never has learned the lesson of putting the sleeve on 200-degree water. He completely drops the cup often and it's such a waste of time and profits, but just so fucking funny. Physical comedy at its rawest. He struggles with making change, and when I am on bar, I help him on the greeter spot. Sometimes he will ask me, "where is the vanilla latte button again?" There isn't one, we build the drinks. *"I wrote a whole chapter on it!"* I want to scream. Determan will write the trivia and give the wrong answer. "Are you sure Shakespeare didn't write that?" a customer asks me while pointing at the trivia. "Uh...." *Determan!* Or misspells a bunch of words, so that the trivia looks like a 3rd grader wrote it. "You were an English major," I remind him. He shrugs. In downtimes at night, which is a lot of the time, Determan writes in a journal and one day he leaves it out. I decide, however, that I don't want to know Determan's inner thoughts.

In spite of everything I wanted Determan to be a shift supervisor, but he says he gets too tired when he works so many hours. I thought eventually he would get the hang of everything. There are only so many things to know at Caribou, so eventually you have done every little task a million times.

"You worked 36 last week." Determan works 4 p.m. to close most every day of the week.

"That was the most hours I've ever worked in my life!" The next day he calls in sick. I don't fire Determan because I have fun with him. He has a good personality and a good attitude, except for getting tired if he works over 30 hours a week. He knows tons of people in the neighborhood and they all love to chitchat with him. We talk in British accents for shifts, and Determan loves sports, and I decide to keep Determan but have him just work the boring nights. Determan is good to eat up hours in the coffee shop though when we only have three or four customers an hour.

And so the guy I hired to be a store manager, with the fancy degree, and the fancy city pedigree, can't handle much and gets sick if he works over 36 hours a week. I smile though. Determan. Although we all joke, we come back years from now and Determan will be the vice president of operations.

LIZ:

I vividly remember interviewing Liz and not being blown away by her as an applicant. She was a college graduate who moved to the area from New York. She was young and was living in different cities for awhile to see what fit her. People give me a lot of stories when I interview them, so I guess I didn't believe her or not believe her. She wanted to work in a coffee shop though. I hired her and remember thinking she would probably call me some Sunday morning and say she was on a boat to Russia and wouldn't be back.

Liz is the romanticized vision of a barista working in a coffee shop. She is funny and smart, hard-working and witty, and she has those heroine-like qualities romantic comedies love. In the movie of my life, we see a working montage of Liz to Rusted Root's, "Send Me On My Way."

The first time I worked with Liz she made a funny voice like the Target Lady (Kirsten Weig) on "Saturday Night Live." I start dying of laughter.

"What?"

"You sound just like the Target Lady!"

"Who?" But the next day she has perfected it and anytime I look like I'm going to get mad she breaks into the voice! Liz's father is a DJ in her hometown in Ohio, so she met various celebrities growing up. Sometimes she will imitate Cindy Lauper while she's on the bar and I start dying of laughter again.

Liz picks up the bar incredibly fast and not only can work the morning rush, but can keep a conversation with me and the customers, and will play music trivia with me. The first person to yell the name of the band and song playing on the radio gets a point. Liz keeps track with the paint pen on the bar. It doesn't mean Liz is a pushover, far from it. When customers ask her how she is doing she answers honestly. "I'm kind of crabby today. A weird guy tried to hit on me." Liz lives in a shitty apartment downtown, but loves getting to know different cities.

"It's not the most dangerous place I've lived, but close." Her other job is at the Build-A-Bear Factory in the Mall of America and they want her to be a manager. I want her to be a manager too, but she wants to work both places.

The Liz's of the world are hard to find and the Bear Factory figured it out as quick as I did. The Bear Factory is pushing her, but I do not and I knows it's why she stays. The Bear Factory also uses bear jargon, which we love to talk. Beartacular, den leaders, pawsome, customers look at us strange and we laugh.

We work hard and have fun. Conversations between Liz and me have included questions like have we served a serial killer, have we served a murderer, and has the Brady Bunch mom had sex with all three of the Brady boys? Customers chime in like it's all normal conversation. One customer said they knew for a fact we had served a murderer. Spooky!

Liz is curious about life and is spending her twenties like many people wished they had, which is what she wants. She is always on the lookout for great new drinks to try as her shift drink. She imitates the black guys hitting on her and that spawns both of us trying to talk black. "Sup baby," we imitate. The customers stare on and we upsell, make drinks, and have fun.

I stare through the window creepily at the Bruegger's employees who are busy throughout the dinner hours. I don't really know them well enough to stare that way, but it makes me laugh. I back away when they notice. Then Liz is there instantly staring creepily too.

Liz is saving $5 every week for a trip to Iceland, and one day a customer over-hears and gives her $5. Another day a customer says she is so nice, and asks if she is huggable. He's an old man.

She thinks for a moment. "Uh, no. I'm not huggable."

"Uh, actually if a customer asks for a hug you have to do it." As much as I get to know Liz she still cannot tell when I'm being serious. I erupt laughing.

"Quit asking people for hugs!" I shoo the guy out.

Later, Liz takes a long pull of her shift drink.

"Did you put cinnamon or something in that? It tastes good today."

Liz's face tells me two things. That she knows I tasted her drink, which Liz does like. Also, she now knows that I have tasted her drink before. Her face is angry. A cloud of hate!

I erupt laughing again. Liz composes herself. Liz is laughing, but still has to pour out her drink and make a new one.

"I know you didn't drink it, but I still have to throw it away. I have a problem, I know."

Liz talks to every kid who comes through the line and just about every customer. We make the trivia question something 80's related, whether movies or music or pop culture, and just plain have fun in the mornings. The customers in line guess and laugh at our shenanigans. It is like a party inside a coffee shop in the most uptight and quiet neighborhood in the world.

EMILY and KENZIE:

Emily had been an assistant store manager for Caribou at a busy drive-thru location. She needed a change of scenery, so I brought her on because I didn't have many options. I knew she worked for a knowledge-hoarding manager who sounded really rude. Emily was about five feet tall and was an ultra athlete. She did triathlons and marathons. Christian said we could give it a few weeks and if it wasn't working for everyone we could move her. Emily was, in a word, unbelievable. She was so nice and folksy with every customer, she upsold, she had fun, she did the little things, she got customer compliments, and she kept an eye on things when I was gone. Hell she ran things all the time. On July 4th weekend the ice machine broke down. I had the weekend off and didn't even know anything about it until I got back.

"So the ice machine broke down and you got it fixed? All on a hugely busy weekend?" I quizzed Emily.

"Yes. Is that okay? Did you want me to call you?"

"Not if you had it handled." I don't tell Emily that Neil and Noreen would call me if we ran out of nickels.

"That Emily is really great," a customer told me one day.

"Yeah, I'm lucky." And I made sure Emily knew that.

Then I found Kenzie, who had been an alcohol substance abuse counselor and had worked at Caribou during college. She was going back to graduate school and for God knows what reason she wanted to work in a coffee shop again. I was worried she would want to leave for a bigger store because our tips were lower in the afternoons. She hit it off with Emily and Liz and Determan. I knew she would stay. Ninety percent of the time life was great.

Once the new team was in place, sales had never been better. Our customer count was down because of the economy, but sales were growing. In every e-mail Christian sent out to the market, our store was mentioned for unbelievable sales. Christian would ask how I was doing it. It was easy if you put your best people as greeter, not as barista.

The most important part of the shop is the greeter, even though the barista is the most famous part of the coffee shop. One might have visions of a sexy Tom Cruise type, whipping up drinks and dancing, while making the perfect latte. There are romance novels about baristas, not the greeter. But the greeter is the most important spot not only because of the interaction before and after the sale, like upselling and bakery add-on, but also because the greeter also handles 99% of the coffee questions like the difference between light and dark and where coffees come from.

The most important part of the greeter is controlling the crowd and maintaining the pace for the barista. You see an overworked barista in the weeds and I'll show a shitty greeter. Does the coffee shop crowd need to be controlled? Hell yes! These idiots don't order quick enough, make "cute" funny comments, can't decide what they want, try to take orders over the phone, stand too far away from the register so they get butted in front of, or order and then don't move down to the end of the bar.

If you want to see the greatest greeter ever head over to Ivars Fish and Chips on the waterfront in Seattle. Twenty people in line all the time, half are idiot tourists, the other half grumpy locals, but the greeter controls everyone. To be a great greeter you have to be firm sometimes, even if you come off as a jerk. Making one person upset by being too firm is better than pissing off 20 people off became their caffeine is slow. Or their fish and chips.

I trained people my way, not the typical Caribou way, meaning for their first three buddy shifts they were strictly on bar. On the fourth shift? Welcome to the bar! I only allowed myself, Emily and Liz, and eventually Kenzie on morning greeter where we dominated selling.

The biggest complaint about me was that people felt thrown into the bar too quickly. Absolutely. I couldn't afford having people not pull their weight quickly. I would prefer one bad day getting in the weeds and learning from it, than being scared of the bar their whole career. There were some rough moments for sure.

MARGE:

Marge was in her late 40's and life had not bounced her way. She was eager to work at Caribou because we had health benefits, but she was not supervisor material. She was quiet and folksy and Minnesota nice. She was a perfect employee because she was going to stick around, yet not want to go anywhere with the company. She'd be a lifer! Marge had worked at Starbucks, but never with the traditional espresso machine. Also, there were only two of us during a mad morning rushes, not the six or seven employees like Starbucks. You have to multi-task more with only two people.

I might have put Marge on the bar alone too early, but she had to learn. We had a bad rush and I was frustrated she wasn't helping more. I felt like I was doing the work of three people. I realized I sounded like Kirsten. I didn't say that to Marge, but she felt my anger and began to cry. Now it was awkward, she was crying and I was trying to pretend I didn't notice her crying. And I was still angry and frustrated.

"I made Marge cry," I texted Kirsten.

"It happens," she replied.

"I just wish she put that anger into working faster."

"YES!" Kirsten replied. I was too hard on Kirsten in the beginning and now I feel like we are one and the same. Kirsten's not worried about anything except getting customers their caffeine quickly. People's feelings be damned because the customers' business comes first.

Jake and Determan screwed up a rush so bad I had to give a woman a gift card. We had days we got in the weeds and that night it would be on the OSAT. Little by little things didn't just get good, they got really great. It was still a hellish job of never ending tasks, but at least our numbers showed we were doing the best we could.

In fact our numbers were so high Christian thought maybe I was cooking the books.

"Are these accurate?" he asked after an impressive bean promotion. We donated bags of coffee to the Wounded Warrior program. I had Jake wear his ROTC fatigues. Our little store was number one in the company for awhile in selling beans. People donated like crazy! Genius!

"They are dead on accurate," I told Christian. Christian would later credit our store with pushing the bigger Caribou store to believe they could sell more beans. Caribou is big into believing and whatnot!

When I took over the store, I envisioned Christian visiting every few days to check up on me, but he only visited at scheduled times which wasn't very often. We talked about family and life, and went over each employee and how many more I needed to hire.

"How are things going?" he asked me earnestly.

"I never feel like they are going great, but our numbers keep me motivated. I know we are a huge improvement over the last team. I know it. I guess just keeping the store going is a daily grind."

"It's tougher than it looks," Christian says.

"It is. I think about Kirsten a lot."

Christian gave me a knowing nod. "How so?"

"She was tough and not easy. I might be more like her than I thought I ever would be. She would be talking to me an inch from my face telling me what to do. And I was like, who do you think you are?"

"There is a reason I send every trainee to Kirsten. She tells me everything straight and is the same way with most people. She can tell me who will cut it and who is going to have a rough time."

"What did she say about me? I was a mess."

"She told me from the first day you would be good."

"Really?" I am shocked. And happy. And a little embarrassed.

"If you have drive Kirsten will make you prove it. I hired you because on your interview you told me about your family's trash-talking Scrabble and ping pong games. I had a feeling no matter how wild the situation got, your competiveness would not allow you to be the one to bring everything to a crashing halt. Billy told me about how you did at the drive-thru and I had the same training."

"Really?"

"Every executive in the company does the same training so we know what it truly entails. My training manager told me on my last week I would be left side of the bar. He said, 'today is the day for you and it comes for everyone.'"

"Were you scared?"

"I was panicking. But I wasn't going to let the whole store come to a grinding halt because of me. You can't teach that. You have to find it in people. Kirsten does that. Some of your peers have been much harder than you on her. And there were people who were good, but just couldn't handle the rushes."

Talking to Christian, I realize why Kirsten is so loyal to Caribou. The people. Christian is a good man.

Everything at the store was going solid except for a few hiccups. AJ was a college student who lived in the neighborhood. She interviewed great, and she had a good work history of being a supervisor at a movie theatre, so I hired her. But something was just off. I couldn't quite put my finger on it. She would ask for too many refills, she would buy drinks at other stores, but refill them at ours. She would be a little bit late for her shifts. She called in a couple times, but nothing over the top. I was thinking about making her a shift supervisor until Liz, Emily and I were discussing her.

"There is something off about her," Liz casually said. Liz had hardly a mean bone in her body and I knew I was picking up the same vibe as Liz. Zoe will spend a day doing training videos downstairs and then walk upstairs and ask to split tips. She screws up on drinks and asks if she can drink them. She asks to keep a lot of stuff, which is weird.

On a big weekend, Zoe called Determan and Liz to see if they could work for her. They couldn't, but she never said anything to me. I overstaffed because I thought the store would be wildly busy. At 2 a.m. on the night before our busiest planned weekend of the year, Zoe texted and said she was in the hospital and "so sick." Liar! I was going to give her a special cup of coffee and fire her, but I never got the opportunity! She was the special cup that got away.

My worst mistake though wasn't hiring anyone; it was promoting someone. Harold. I shake my head as I type Harold. Harold will go down in infamy as the person who changed the rules for a very special cup of coffee. Harold was so awful, but he owned me.

CHAPTER 18
HAROLD AND THE LIST

Dear crotchety, old customer who is offended we even offer you anything
besides a plain cup of coffee,
    We are a business. I'm sorry that you do not realize that, but we are just
doing our job. Do you feel like my last name is Caribou and I'm the one
making the decision to have bakery and packaged coffee and all these
merchandise trinkets? Did you think the guy making all these decisions would
be working the register at 7 a.m. on a Tuesday in this store? Then you must
feel super lucky to have found the company decision maker on such a lark!
Good for you! So feel free to complain about everything!

Harold wanted to talk to me. Alone. At this point in our relationship I
knew Harold was a little odd though I didn't mind him, except for the kissy-
wissy with his girlfriend. Harold acted like a ladies man to Jake, Determan
and me, but when his older, ugly, girlfriend came in they hugged and made
kissy face. For like literally 10 minutes. "I missed you so much!" he would
yell! They hug and snuggle for minutes and then talk about their days.
    "How was your day?"
    "Awful I didn't get to see you!"
    It is disgusting and an affront to men and women everywhere. I felt bad
for him because he was obviously a late bloomer type who met this older
woman and now she controlled him. Actually, Harold hadn't really
bloomed yet. He was weird, but I didn't mind weird because even though he
was shitty at selling he wanted what was best for the store. He could do the
bar too, so we didn't get in the weeds with him. I made Harold shift
supervisor because of these things and it was the worst mistake I made at
Caribou. Maybe the worst mistake I ever made in my hiring career.
    Harold had worked for Caribou for 3 three years and his kissy-wissy
girlfriend had been the shift supervisor with Brennan and Tori. She wanted
to be store manager, but Westin got it so she began to bitch and complain
and be a pain in the ass. She had left Caribou not too long before I got there.

Harold had never been a shift supervisor because he was going to school. He was told that he had to have open availability.

"Who told you that?" I asked.

"They did." Harold blamed a lot of things on "they." I promoted him to shift supervisor and he wanted $1 an hour more than he should have gotten because he said he thought he was worth it. So there were a few red flags, but he was a million times better then Noreen or Neil.

Harold and I sat in Bruegger's as he pulled out "the list," as it became known amongst the store employees. Harold proceeded to bring up a list of things that weren't getting done:

- The window shade was not pulled up at night.
  (*I don't give a shit. Pull it up then?*)

- The front of the refrigerators are not wiped down every day.
  (*I don't give a shit.*)

- The inside of the refrigerators are not wiped down every day.
  (*I really don't give a shit.*)

- The chairs are not wiped down. (As long as the tables are wiped and the chairs don't have shit on them...then I don't give a shit.)

- The inside of the tea cans are not emptied and cleaned out.
  (*Wow, I really don't give a shit.*)

- The extra register drawers are not counted nightly. ("If no one used them then they don't need to be counted. So I don't give a shit.")

- "I know you disagree with giving the extra espresso, but I really feel like people have come to expect it. And it's wasteful." I sigh. The traditional machine makes two shots of espresso for every shot, so often there is an extra shot. Arnold and Harold ask the customer if they want it. Many have come to expect it and Caribou Coffee specifically says in training 'don't fucking do that.' They should be paying for extra espresso. So they are charging for a medium but giving a large. "It's not our decision to make. Charge for the large and quit giving away the extra shot."

- Jenn has been giving him attitude and he doesn't know if she is right for Caribou. (*Jenn didn't take his shit and I liked her even more now.*)

- The dishes aren't done at shift change on some mornings. (On Friday, Saturday and Sunday mornings there was no time to be off the floor. It was packed until 1 p.m. and then it was a ghost town. Ghost towns are good for doing cleaning chores.)

- The trivia is too easy for customers. (The trivia is not meant to stump people. It's meant to be a conversation starter to engage people. This complaint really proved to me that Harold does not get what we are trying to do at Caribou.)

- "We have typically wrapped up the donated bakery individually." I sigh. At the end of each day the expired bakery is donated to a local foodshelf. I throw the bakery in a plastic box with plastic wrap over the top. It takes about one minute. Harold wraps up each piece individually at the end of the night. It can take up to 25 minutes or more because he is so fucking precise.

I monitor our payroll incessantly, paying particular attention to shift changes and closing times. This is where we waste time. Harold wasn't getting out until 30 minutes past closing. I would leave about five to 10 minutes past closing time. We were ready to leave right at closing because we rarely had any customers in the last hour. Or last two hours. And now Harold wants everyone wrapping every piece of bakery.

"I just feel like its important for those people to have the freshest bakery possible." Harold says in his indignant voice.

"We need to concentrate our resources on better things," I tell him. Now you reading this book might think I am an asshole and don't care about the unfortunate. I do. To a point. The bottom line, which I try not to yell at Harold, is those precious minutes after closing are not making us any money. That time could be better used adding a third person to the morning shifts. Where you, dear reader, want your caffeine fast.

"Quit wasting payroll when the store is closed. Not to mention our bakery case was built in 1985. The bakery is as hard as a rock after being out almost two days. I'm trying to save payroll to make everyone's busy mornings easier. Do you understand?"

"We've always done it that way in the past." I sigh.

"You seem upset?" Harold asks me.

"I just wish you would be this passionate about selling the bakery and upselling," I tell him.

"Yeah, we don't like to upsell–it eats away at our tips." Harold stares at me innocently enough. My head didn't explode, but I was worried it would.

I had heard this theory from Beck at the Lake store at the beginning of my Caribou career when I didn't know any better. So I watched how people tipped if I didn't upsell or offer anything versus if I upsold and offered everything. I would chitchat and then I wouldn't say a thing. I would say a joke, I would say something serious, I would compliment their clothes, I would make fun of them in a slight way. I would comment on their kids, I would ask what they had planned for the day, or I would try not to say anything the whole order. Everything was based around adding to their order. Busy day at work? You need an extra shot of espresso. Out with your kid? You two should share a healthy carrot cake. Feeling stressed? Treat yourself to a large!

It wasn't even close. People love attention. I found that people tipped, and tipped way more, when I spent time with them offering different things. People appreciate the effort. I tell Harold I have found the opposite to be true. I've tested it. It's not even an argument.

"Well just by the fact most people throw in change it's getting closer to that next dollar." He replies.

What Harold means is that if a hypothetical tab is $4.74, the customer often leave us the change we hand back from the $5 bill or just the coin change from a $10 or $20. This is true, but if you give the best service they are more likely to throw in another dollar if the change was less than 25 cents. But Harold really assumes a lot about money and ordering without any evidence.

"Are you assuming that upselling is leading to the next whole dollar?"

"That's typically the way it happens."

"And that's why you don't upsell?"

"Yes."

I think about firing Harold right than and there. I start to calculate in my head if I could cover his hours. It would be brutal on me if I fired him. Harold will not upsell or offer bakery because he thinks if a customer adds on something, the purchase price will get closer to a whole number and the customer will put the change in the tip cup. This is not true. First of all, 60% of our customers pay with a credit card. Harold is in a sense getting himself fewer tips, our store fewer sales, our store fewer hours, and more work for him, just because he won't fucking offer a piece of fucking banana bread!

"That's what Caribou wants. It is the expectation of the job. What else do you have?" I motion to his list.

"I think only certain people should be allowed to clean the bar at the end of the night." Another reason why Harold stays so fucking late wasting our payroll is he will only clean the espresso machine after the store is closed. We rarely have any customers in the last hour.

"Caribou does not need the machine cleaned after hours, just a full cleansing once a day. There are three spouts. Clean them separately and then if a customer comes in you are set."

"I just think it really affects the quality of the espresso."

It doesn't. One week I didn't clean the espresso machine just to see if anyone would notice. They didn't! Not even Harold or Arnold who fancy themselves coffee assholes dickhead snobs. What does cleaning the espresso machine after hours mean to you the customer? Slower service in the busy times!

"Typically that's how we've done it. I guess now that I look at the list it seems kind of petty," he said. I nod.

"When Harold says 'typically' it is just so aggravating," Liz comments to me one day. When Harold says "typically" it makes me want to punch him. But I can't tell her that.

"Do you have anything else you wanted to discuss?" I ask him, hoping there is no more.

"We typically make the cold press in the gallon pitchers." Ah, the cold press. My head almost exploded in sheer wonderment/frustration/anger–everything under the sun. The store had been making cold press, or iced coffee, and putting it into one-gallon pitchers every night. When a customer ordered cold press the barista had to open the small fridge, poor the drink, return the jug to the fridge. When empty the jugs had to be cleaned, and they are not easy to clean. So I changed the whole process by making the cold press in a five-gallon bucket with a spigot on the bottom. The greeter could swing around and handle the drink so it was one less task for the barista, plus no jugs to wash. So I cut out five steps. Harold wasn't happy. Why not?

"That's just the way we've always done it."

"But this way is better and easier. Unless you can come up with a better reason than that's the way we've always done it, I don't really know what to tell you." Harold raised his hands up and shrugged. I cannot tell him that he is a dumb idiot.

"Well, I guess it's not a bad list for extra cleaning, but in the big scheme of things I kind of don't care about any of this. I need people to sell. Not do extra cleaning. I guess I just don't really care about any of these things."

Harold nods to me. "It's hard for us because you care about things we have never really thought about." I agree.

"Who is us?" And at that moment I'm pretty sure I planted the seed in Harold's head that everyone who does not have the goals that I have, is on their way out. It's hard to see seed planting in heads, but he got the jist.

As much as I wanted to fire Harold right then and there, I couldn't. Because Harold owned me. Noreen was gone and Neil was on the way out, and I had accepted a transfer shift supervisor named Adam as temporary fix. I needed Harold or I would be working 80 hours a week. Maybe more.

The list was the beginning of the end for Harold and the store. Harold was shift supervisor and now wanted things done his way, but no one cared. His girlfriend hated the company and tried to start trouble. Harold was weird with the new employees and tried to defend the old ones.

Harold knew he was one of the few shift supervisors and he also knew he was the only one besides me who could do the bar on busy Friday, Saturday, Sunday and Monday mornings. It fucking sucked, but Harold owned me. And my every waking thought was to get hired up so I could get rid of Harold. But times move slowly in the hiring world. And Harold became opinionated on odd topics.

Harold texted me he didn't like the way I was treating Larry. Larry said he was going to transfer, so I took him off the schedule. Yeah, that turned out to be a lot harder than Larry thought. No one was hiring someone who can't do the bar or the register. I scheduled Harold and Larry together for a few shifts and the store was a fucking disaster! So I quit scheduling Larry and Harold never said a thing.

Harold walked into the shop on a busy Saturday morning, waited in line, and then told me he needed next weekend, which he was already scheduled to work, off.

"I already paid for the hotel and everything." Oh you paid for it, then of course you can have it off! You fucking idiot! And he's telling me this with fucking customers around!

"Do you know how the request-off log works?"

"Yes, I'm really sorry. I paid for it already." But Harold owns me and knows it. If I don't give him the days off he might just not show up and I'm fucked either way. Even if he didn't show up and I did fire him, it wouldn't help me in the service industry world. Because either I or a shift supervisor has to here.

Another time Harold comes in on a busy Saturday morning, and waits in line, and asks us to get him his half-pound of free beans. *Are you fucking kidding me? Bush league!*

"You can get that yourself like every one else." Harold comes around the back, grabs a new bag of beans, pours his, then like a douche leaves the bag on the counter. He doesn't date it and doesn't put it away. I literally had to hold Jake back from going to kick his ass in the parking lot.

All of these complaints were compounded because the whole store knew about the list. Harold told everyone about the list, too.

But Harold owned me.

Harold would not train Determan or Zoe or Jenn on the bar. "I'm very protective of my bar." This phrase was uttered countless times when mocking Harold.

In the grand scheme of things someone like Harold would be perfect for me. Someone who is passionate about cleaning and equipment care, and would meld great with my selling focus. But Harold would not teach people what he knew. So yeah, Jenn stood up to him so Harold didn't like her.

"I don't know if Jenn has the right personality to work here," he complains to me. I want to fire him for not letting people work the bar! How the hell are they going to learn?

Harold was passionate about the opposite of everything I was passionate about. He cared about everything I didn't give a shit about. But Harold owned me.

After Harold's note, he was put on notice and it turned out not only was Harold not great at selling, but he was also not as great as he thought with cleaning and organization. One night he forgot to close the icemaker top. I almost lost my shit. If the ice machine motor burned out we would have been fucked without ice that idiot! Harold owned me though.

Another night he left the garbage in the hallway. You can clean the inside of the fridge out all you want, but what does it matter if you leave the garbage out? Harold owned me.

I talked to Harold about his screw-ups, which were non-negotiables, without any sort of discipline. In hindsight, I should have written him up. I felt like if I did he would leave I would be in a worse situation. Anytime Harold screwed up or forgot something, his excuse was he was cleaning something that someone else forgot. Harold then went way, way overboard on Sunday soak. Every Sunday night we soak some different metal pieces that don't get cleaned well enough during the week in a special solution. Harold took literally every piece of metal in the store and soaked it! *The fucker!* It took us two hours to put the store back together on a fucking Sunday rush morning. Harold owned me though.

Each Caribou has a "red book," which is a communication log between the shifts and manager. All the coffee and bakery waste is documented, including espresso bar timing and proper taste of the espresso shots, and any customer orders the morning shift needs to prepare. A typical note is "Joe-To-Go of light–9 a.m. Paid." This means a customer wants a Joe-To-Go, which is a canteen of roughly 10 cups of coffee, and they want any light roast. It says it was already paid for and they will be arriving at 9 a.m. to pick it up.

This allows the morning greeter to have it ready for the customer and plan ahead for it. There is nothing worse than an unannounced Joe-To-Go order because it's an extra full batch of coffee to brew. The Joe-To-Go takes time and can get us in the weeds quickly. Joe-To-Gos do help our sales. *Call ahead when you what them, people!*

I peruse through the red book one day and notice a lot of orders for five gallons of coffee, sometimes multiple orders for five gallons of coffee. And I notice the word paid by all of them. If someone had bought all this coffee our sales would have spiked in the last few days historically. They did not spike. I would also need a heads-up to order more whole bean coffee on my weekly order. I did not receive a heads-up. I notice all the notes are from Harold.

When I ask him about it, Harold says, "Oh actually that is donated coffee. I think it's really good to give back to the community."

"Do you know what our donation budget is Harold?"

"Uh no."

"Zero. All donations are through the home office."

"I just thought it was good to give back to the community."

"Right." Harold will call me to ask me about the last time the wheels of the freezer were cleaned because he can't find a log for it, but does not ask me about giving away hundreds of dollars worth of coffee?

First off, coffee is expensive. Caribou is trying to limit our coffee waste because it's expensive. Brewing less in the slow times, brewing on demand, reusing coffee for coolers, anything to reduce waste and expenses.

Secondly, I order coffee every week for what we need. We don't want extra coffee because Caribou doesn't want us using expired coffee. I don't have extra 20 pounds of coffee to brew to donate! Particularly when they want five gallons of decaf! *I always forget to order decaf anyways!*

Lastly, we live in one of the richest places in the world. We are not giving coffee to needy kids or football teams that don't have jerseys or a field. We are giving away free coffee to literally some of the richest people in the world for their events. My God! No more fucking donations! I wrote it in the red book. Now I'm the neighborhood asshole.

"We need to set up a coffee for an event. For about 50 people."

"Okay, great."

"Can we get that donated?"

"We are out of our donation budget. Sorry."

"You did it for the marching band!"

Or a customer would say, "You did it for Northwest High School! You're not going to do it for us too?" Does she think I donated to those people because I like them better?

Harold also didn't plan for the fact that we only have four five-gallon coffee containers. So when the event is done, they need to return it for the next day. Of course they don't remember. Now I'm spending my time tracking down these fucking containers! *Harold!* I wanted to make Harold do it but he was never around when his mistakes made life at the store awful.

One snooty booster member calls the store in the morning. They ran out of their donated coffee.

"We are going to need two more containers refilled."

"We can do that, but you will have to pay for it."

"But it was donated."

"It's not an unlimited donation." Go pick up a can of fucking Folgers! Harold still owns me. But not for long.

Everyone hated Harold but he owned me because I didn't have enough supervisors. I would lay in bed at night dreaming of the day Harold was out of my life.

"He's the villain in your movie life," Gisele comments. But I don't even want to give him that much credit.

After I hired Emily, Liz and Kenzie, Harold saw the writing on the wall. Week by week I needed Harold less and less. So Harold decided to be really helpful and work shifts at the Caribou down the road that was understaffed. *Oh Harold, what a great guy!* When Liz asked him why he was working at the other store he told her that store was because managed. I love Liz because she started laughing uncontrollably and hyperventilated. Classic!

On a Saturday at 12:55 p.m., Harold called me and said he couldn't come in because he told the other store he could work. "Well, you are on the schedule here at 1. And I can't stay. So tell that store no."

"Uh, okay," he says. I call the store to see if the manager needs help finding people. Harold answers.

"Oh you're already there." I couldn't fucking believe he was there already! What an asshole.

"Uh, yeah. I kind of overcommitted."

"He really pushes the limits of what an asshole is," comments Liz, who overhears the phone conversation.

"He gives assholes a bad name," I comment.

What a fucking dickhead idiot. The women he had promised to cover for also has to leave and is forced to leave the store unmanned and close it down. That's a big deal at Caribou and most restaurants/retailers. She is fired. All because Harold didn't read the schedule and didn't call me until five minutes before his shift. He knew about it all day! If he had brought it up earlier I would have had time to get it filled or change my plans.

The last straw was when I came in to check e-mail at night and found Harold eating bakery while he was doing the nightly bakery pull. It would have been a write-up, maybe a termination, but really what it meant was I would have to cover his shifts. So I decided to break the rules. I would let Harold stay, but he would get a very special cup of coffee. It was only fair. Instead of spending time daydreaming about Harold being off the schedule, I now spent my time planning Harold's special cup of coffee.

I knew Harold drank out of the in-store mugs a lot. Making a special cup out of those wouldn't work because what if a customer asked for a mug and accidentally got a very special cup of coffee? That is against the rules. I had to be very careful. Harold made it easy by being an idiot and asking whoever worked after him to make his shift drink for him. Everyone else made their own because they are not an asshole.

He would then watch the drink being made very carefully and complain a little if it wasn't just perfect. And his drink was really pretentious too! What a dick. I started scheduling myself right after Harold was done with his shift, and I raced to get the bar spot just so I could be the one to make his drink. And I had to get the cup out of my bag and near, without Harold or other employees seeing. It was never coming together so I scheduled Harold and I together his last half-hour. I was able to sneak the cup I had so lovingly peed and pooped in and dried out! Double whammy for Harold!

I put the large cold drink cup and a hot one on the top of the stacks just in case he switched his order. He didn't and I even casually asked what he wanted me to make him today! I was trying to conceal my giddiness!

I quickly grabbed the large iced cup as Harold watched me very carefully as I made his half cafe, iced, cubano, whole milk latte. What a douche bag drink. (I later gave him the hot cup for his tips!)

Harold watched as I delicately did the cubano part and mixed everything according to company policy. Harold took a sip through his straw. I could have sworn he noticed. His head did a little double take. *Justice.*

"That's pretty good. Actually."

"Enjoy Harold! You have a great rest of your day!" I wanted to tell the world! I wanted to sing and dance and live and laugh and love!

A few days later, Harold comes into the store again during a rush and says he cannot work one of his scheduled shifts.

"Are you serious?" Are we seriously fucking going through this again. Harold has bought a couples cooking class for his girlfriend. Movie villains eventually learn their lesson and change their ways. But not in real life.

"Yeah I'm really sorry, but we paid and I am taking my girlfriend." God damn does he own me! I can't do anything but give Harold another special cup of coffee. Harold also created the rule that a special cup of coffee must be given for each incident. Meaning we know Harold is a dick, but he doesn't get a special cup for every drink. It must be given each time he is a dick. But I never see Harold again.

Liz, Emily and Kenzie are all promoted to shift supervisors. And when he doesn't own me anymore, Harold doesn't show up ever again. And that's when life gets a little better. I wanted to fire Harold in a blaze of glory and let him know what I thought! But the service industry world is not the best place for revenge. Harold was just gone. *Oh, except for drinking my pee and poo! Justice!*

The last thing Harold ever texted to me was that everyone thought I was a bully and I was mean, and that was my impact on their life. He is kind of right though. To successfully run a coffee shop or any service establishment, you have to get people to do things your way even when they don't want to, or they disagree with your goals. It's never easy, it's overly demanding work, it is complicated, and it can be embarrassing if you screw up when serving customers.

I lament over texts to Kirsten how hard it is to man the morning rushes, keep hiring and staffing, keep a high OSAT score, and simply make everyone happy.

"Why do we do it?" she replies.

I don't know. I really don't know.

CHAPTER 19
EVERY DAY I NEED ATTENTION

Dear customer who asks for a "skinny" drink,
I now realize "skinny" means sugarfree. I was just using skim milk, but not sugarfree flavoring. I imagine you thinking, "holy shit, is Caribou's sugarfree shit tasty!" Skinny is a Starbucks term, not a Caribou's. We learn about the Starbucks menu so customers will get what they want. Caribou makes macchiatos differently, and a Caramel High Rise cooler is like a caramel frappuccino. To be honest, I can barely learn Caribou drinks, much less a different menu. Sorry!

She walked in wearing a white, wife-beater tank top and those sunglasses that are really glasses. They never go back to normal lens all the way, so they look creepy. She was short and chubby, with dirty blond hair. She was in her late fifties, loud and abrasive. She started yelling out something as she walked in. It was a lazy afternoon and I had never met this woman.

"Short and Spunky! Short and Spunky!" She threw a gift card on the counter and walked off towards the newspapers.

Leslie was on the bar and I looked to her and she shrugged.

"Ah what?" I was confused.

"Short and Spunky! " She looked at me and obviously didn't recognize me. "What! Are you new?"

"Yes. What would you like?"

"What happened to Westin?"

"He got a job selling vacuums," I say cordially.

"They can't keep anyone here after Tori left. This place has really gone downhill."

I was a little stunned. "Well I'm here now. What would you like?"

"Now you're going to need to learn my drink. It's three shots of espresso, in a medium cup, three Sweet and Lows mixed in and with a little water and light ice."

Sigh. "Short and Spunky" did the classic "taste it in front of us to see if she approved" move. I would learn Short and Spunky's drink could never be made perfect. That's why Short and Spunky ordered it. It would either be too much ice, too little ice, too little water, the Sweet and Lows not mixed in right or some shit.

"Did you add the Sweet and Low?" She would ask, smacking her lips.
"Yup."

"Three shots of espresso?" *Why are you doing this to us?*

She came in most days and yelled out "Short and Spunky!" and threw her card on the counter and walked away.

"Now what did you get again?" It wasn't like she was the only customer. She seemed put off by the question, sighing and telling me, "Boy, you have a lot of turnover here. They can't keep anyone here since Tori left." *Yeah you mention that every day.*

"Well, it is a service industry. I'd love to pay everyone $50 an hour, but it's not in the cards." I should point out that Short and Spunky never tipped and always paid with a gift card. Short and Spunky was named by Tori because she really was short and spunky. So cute! I hate her! She walked in and yelled out her order, even if someone was already in line and ordering. She wouldn't wait for the person ahead of her to finish ordering. Almost unbelievably rude. And if anyone new was working she made a big deal of there being more new people, even though they were great workers. Can you tell how much I hate this person? A lot. I don't point out to her that Paul and Larry were idiots. And Jenn is way better and Determan is nice. It didn't help morale for the store when she points out every visit that we aren't as good as the old crew. And if she wanted people to stay she should have tipped!

It wasn't one thing she did, but many awful acts that grated on me that convinced me Short and Spunky deserved a special cup.

A guy walked into the store one day and said he was supposed to order the "Short and Spunky," and that we would know what that meant. I guess she thought we really liked her and this was all some cute game? Special cup! On the house too! I was a lot nicer to Short and Spunky after having her drink a glass with my pee in it. She started asking about my family and I thought things were going better. The store was obviously running way better and I had great people in position. Until I got an OSAT comment that I knew was from her. Same old shit. Not the same as Tori, too much turnover, not enough for the community. Bullshit. So on her next trip I asked her if she wrote the harsh comments.

"Well things have really gone downhill since Tori left."

"We have a better staff. We donated 150 pounds of coffee to the Wounded Warriors. We are faster and better and have more fun. What else are you looking for beside fast and fun service?"

"Tori would sing and dance around."

"That's not us." Short and Spunky asks Liz if she put in the Sweet and Low.

"Yes," Liz replies icily. Short and Spunky was the first to get two special cups of coffee. And then a lot more.

Short and Spunky drank so much of my pee and poop I began to wonder if her drink would still taste right to her after I'm gone?

A 30-something Asian woman always ordered a coffee cooler, and would always ask, "Is the espresso good today?"

"Uh yeah. It's top notch." She didn't come in every day, but a lot, and always asked if the espresso was good.

"It's good every day." What a weird question, I thought. Did she think there was some code coffee shop lingo or that I would tell her it was bad and she would not get a drink today?

One day she started hanging out at the end of the bar, which was weird and in my bubble. Apparently the woman hung out at the end of the bar a lot when Harold or Arnold would work.

"I used to work for Caribou years ago," she told me. She dressed normally and she looked normal, but why was she always here alone? Talking to us?

"Really?"

"Are you surprised?"

"Why do you ask if the espresso is good every day?"

"You know, because some days the espresso is bad."

"It is?"

"Yeah, if you don't clean it and stuff."

"Whoever is on bar tests the espresso in the morning and at shift change. So it's at least consistent. And you get a coffee cooler every day. You don't even taste espresso, just sugar." I couldn't tell her sometimes I don't clean the bar to see if affects taste, which it does not to me. And no one has brought it up. I didn't know if the woman was lying or a weirdo, but I didn't like her. And the fact that Harold and Arnold seemed to like her made me like her even less.

Sometimes she would make comments that irked me. "You didn't tap and swirl much there." "Do you ever schedule a Super Glue?" "Doesn't an iced medium have six shots?" I would stop to think about what she was asking and screw up.

I ignored her, but she stood at the end of the bar, just watching me. Our coffee shop is small and having her stand there was annoying in rushes. And awkward in slow times. She tried to talk to me and to customers, and it was awkward. One day she asked me if I thought it was weird she hung out so much at the shop.

"A little."

"Oh why is that?"

"Well, I have a family that I don't see as much as I want. A son and a wife and friends too. I have to be here 50 hours a week, so I guess it's weird to me because I can think of a million other things I'd rather be doing outside of this coffee shop."

I never saw her again.

One particular regular doesn't even order a drink. She rushes into the shop and wants two lemon poppyseed breads….from the freezer. Which is downstairs. So it's annoying because someone has to run downstairs. I follow the woman outside one day and she gets into a cab. She drives around town in a cab. "I'm in a hurry too." Oh you're in a hurry! Well no one else is in a hurry beside you. *Oh no-wait.* She has frizzy blond hair, her clothes are always rumpled, and her makeup a little too bright, or smudged, or none at all. Her whole life is an unorganized, hurried mess.

Another regular is nice and chatty, but has developed the habit of asking for extra chocolate-covered espresso beans. She flips apartments in the area, rides her motorcycle around the neighborhood, and gets a mocha in her own mug every weekday. So we are the nice Caribou folks we are supposed to be and give her a bunch of free beans. So I'm ordering fucking extra espresso beans every week because we are giving away what now stands at about 15 extra at a time. I should note we sell these chocolate-covered espresso beans. So she's a regular and she's nice, but she expects more because she is a regular and it is costing me money.

Some semi-regulars love Harold and Arnold because they just cover the entire cooler in whipped cream and chocolate chips and more whipped cream and more chocolate chips. Which is good once and awhile, but the semi-regular will make a rude comment if the barista doesn't do it. It's annoying more than anything.

The owner of the shoe store next door is nice and always orders a large coffee. Now the Caribou rule is you get one free refill if you stay in the store. He leaves. Comes back. I give him the refill and he always tips a dollar. But technically he is taking advantage of us. The rule is if you leave you have to buy another coffee. Another regular from the rug store across the street does the same thing, but I like him eventually because he always gives us perfect scores on the extra OSAT surveys I give him. With the dollar off and his free refill he gets two cups of coffee for about 54 cents a day.

A waitress at the hamburger place near by comes in often and I can always upsell her a piece of bakery. A waiter from the Chatterbox restaurant comes in and caffeinates up and always tips about $5. I give him a free drink, a large cold press with white chocolate, whenever he looks like he's had a rough day. A rough day means shitty neighborhood customers being rude. "Sometimes the whole dining room thinks they are the only ones there," he laments.

There is Seinfeld Guy, who ALWAYS re-enacts the Seinfeld episode about George placing the dollar in the tip jar. "I always take care of my Pisano." It was funny the first 50 times, but the last 200 times have been not quite as funny. But then I think maybe that is the genius of this guy, saying it every time. And then it's really funny!

Sal is a regular who sticks his head in the door and says hello even if he isn't getting anything. Then there is Iced Soy Latte, who is bald and partly deaf, and brings his two huge mastiffs one day. "You guys want to meet my dogs?" I'm running a coffee shop at 8 in the morning, but sure I'll go look at your dogs out the window because I feel like you will be offended if I do not.

There is "Crazy, Rich Lady," who parks her fancy car sideways across the parking lot, and wants her drink made this way and that. How annoying. In an annoying turn of events, everyone tells me she now only will come in when I'm working because "Ben is the only one who knows how to make them right." When I started at the store I remember wanting to punch a customer in the face when she said Brennan was the only one who knew how to make smoothies right while she sipped mine.

The Bruegger's employees are the nicest people I have ever met and they are always working hard. Chad, the manager, sees me looking at day-old bagels in packages of 12 one day. Matt is in a bagel phase.

"Take as many you want." It turns out they give us anything we want for free! So I'm torn a little. Do we break Caribou Coffee's loss prevention policy of giving away food for free? I could be fired! I could be arrested! I watch Bruegger's and they are in the same industry as us and have it just as bad. Rushes, customers, more rushes, more cleaning, more tasks, and for the same pay as us. Not awful, but not worth the abuse and the constant hard work. Whenever we screw up a drink, I send them over. Or if I'm doing training for new team members, I'll take the Bruegger's employees' orders and that will be the test. Sometimes after a hard Saturday or Sunday morning, I just send them what I know they like. I guess I'm sticking it to the man, but really it's just giving people who have shitty jobs something nice in their life.

My sister tells me about the great underbelly of the food exchange world. "When I was at Jimmy Johns we were always trading food. The drivers run it all around the city." I don't know if I believe her, but I try it.

I called Dominos Pizza. "Hey this is Ben at Caribou. Do you guys want anything?" A pause. I hear in the background. "It's Caribou." Another pause.

"Yeah, we'll have three mochas..." It worked.

"What do you want?" he asked me.

"How about a large pepperoni?"

"Okay, any breadsticks?"

"What the hell, sure."

"Okay. Driver will be over in about 10 minutes." This is awesome!

It didn't work at some places though, like the Chinese restaurant down the road.

"What you mean? What you mean?" Jake and I quickly hang up giggling.

My employees make like $10 an hour with tips. The least Caribou can do is pay for our dinner! For a few moments life at Caribou can be great. Until...

"What kind of a man would marry Anne?" two customers discuss after an Anne sighting. Anne is kind of a bitch mainstay in the neighborhood and the ladies certainly had crossed paths with her outside our friendly coffee shop.

The first time I met Anne she walked into the store with mirrored sunglasses. I have never seen her without them. She sighed when she saw me, a new guy sigh.

"Large coffee of the day with steamed skim, almond, no froth. They never get it right."

"Would you like a piece of banana bread with that?"

"No!" Anne gasps incredulously. This is how I meet the ultimate bitch.

Anne is a great study in bitchiness because she has to know she is a bitch. She HAS to! But she seems to think the world will tolerate her behavior with no repercussions. Anne's whole life is set up so she can be a bitch and create moments that don't meet her expectations. These moments allow her to unleash her bitchiness and meanness. Let's take her drink for example. Large coffee of the day with steamed skim, almond, no froth. The drink itself gets in the way of a coffee shop's flow because the greeter has to get the almond, then the coffee, and then leave it for the steamed skim. And the barista has to make special milk with no froth. No froth? Anne doesn't want any fucking bubbles! Well, it's milk and it's being boiled, so there is going to be an occasional bubble. And, Anne likes it with a nice dark blend, which we don't always have every day. And the amount of almond isn't always to her liking, even though it's the same amount of pumps every fucking time!

"This tastes really almondy today." *Is almondy a word?*

"I guess I can test the pump on the bottle? See if it's coming out accurately." She harrumphs and walks out.

The best part of making Anne's drink, according to Jenn, is that she peers over the bar and watches like a hawk the entire time. Then when she notices something she doesn't like, she sighs, crosses her arm, and shakes her head. She won't say anything and sometimes nothing is even fucking wrong. We see Anne walking across the street and we make the drink before she even walks in the door. Too many bubbles. Which coffee did you use? I used the dark because that's what you usually get. She wants light roast today. One day I hand her the drink as she walks up to the line.

"Actually today I wanted a cold press, but thanks for trying." Why? Why would this one day you fucking get another drink? We both know you wanted that drink!

One day Anne tells me a mother asked her if she was pregnant. And it felt like the whole store was holding in a laugh. I thought about that moment later. Why would Anne share a story like that with me? Does she think we are friends? Can't she feel the hatred? Is she truly so unaware of her monstrous bitchiness? *Anne!*

After giving Anne a special cup of coffee on the house, I wanted to tell Liz. Liz took pride in her job and became really upset when customers were upset.

"Some people are just not very nice. You can't let them get to you. You know you did your best," I try to console her.

"It's just I made it perfect and she still complains." Liz holds back tears.

"We make drinks for thousands of people a month. Maybe one or two complain. And it's their fault because that's what they love to do." I want to tell Liz so badly that I just gave Anne a cup of pee coffee. I want to make Liz laugh and feel better. I broach the subject of getting back at the rude customers if they deserve it, in a joking fashion.

"Caribou does a lot of tests before they hire us so they know we wouldn't do anything like that."

I don't point out to Liz that I hired her after one interview.

Becklynn is another former employee of Caribou and Bruegger's who stops by four or five times a day. Not buying anything mind you, but just to talk us. Becklynn works at the movie theatre about two miles away and wears a heavy looking backpack. She doesn't go to school anywhere, but walks the neighborhood with the backpack. She is nice but odd, and I guess if it were any other neighborhood I would worry about someone taking advantage of her. She loves Harold and often stops by to tell me to say hi to Harold for her. *Yeah right I'm gonna do that.* I realize later that Becklynn isn't just stopping by, but she is looking for yet another former Caribou employee, Sam.

Sam would come into the shop and sit for hours upon hours, either reading or playing his Nintendo DS. He had no job and didn't go to school. He was friends with Harold, and they played Magic the Gathering together after Harold's shifts. I asked Sam about his no job, no school, no nothing going on situation one day, and wondered why he came to Caribou so often.

"If you worked somewhere for over two years, you would come back every day too." Actually I've worked a lot of places for over two years and I didn't go back to sit at JC Penney every day, all day. I needed help and Sam was trained, but I didn't know why he wasn't with Caribou anymore. Harold started getting pushy about why I wouldn't hire Sam. I asked Tori about Sam after he put in an online application and used Tori as a reference. Sam had been fired by Tori, which tells you how many times he must have fucked up. Tori didn't fire Larry or Anthony or Paul or Arnold! It turned out that Sam had a quite a rough run at Caribou, and the next time he asked me for a job I had some questions for him.

"You were fired for not showing up. I can't have that."

"Yeah my alarm didn't go off a couple off times."

"So you should have been late, not a no show."

"Yeah, I read the schedule wrong a couple of times."

"If you loved it here so much, why didn't you show up?"

He shrugs. He was on top of the world when he thought I thought he could be a great help. Now he's pathetically slumping over.

"When you don't show up you don't just hurt Caribou, you hurt the rest of your teammates who have to pick the slack or change their plans and come in to work."

I think he's had enough as he looks like he's going to cry.

"That is why I won't hire you. And just to let you know, Tori told me you were not rehirable because you were fired. You should know that in case other places call her for your reference."

Sam spent probably four to five hours a day at the store when I was there, and Jake told me he spent the whole shift there when Harold worked. Sam was a lonely nerd and I wanted to like him, but he was annoying. He wasn't one of those likable TV nerds, but a real life nerd that is a little dangerous. Anyone who hangs out at the coffee shop for the entire day is annoying to me. I would watch Sam Google the trivia question and then act like he was guessing the answer. He ordered an iced white chocolate turtle mocha, even though we don't put on the whip or Snickers, because it is cheaper than iced white chocolate mocha. *So clever!*

Every day, no matter what the question is on the Chalk Thought board, Sam writes Batman. What is your favorite fall drink? Batman. What animal scares you? Batman. What is a great location for ice cream in Minneapolis? Batman. It's his nerdy, coffee shop calling card of sorts.

Our coffee shop is often empty except for Sam and Becklynn. Sometimes Sam is reading or playing his Nintendo and Becklynn just stares at him. I wish they'd start dating! They'd be the perfect couple because they are both such hopeless losers. They could protect each other in this big, crazy world. One afternoon they sit in the shop complaining to each other that they are bored. While I'm stuck there, they complain about being there!

"It's 80 degrees out. It's literally one of the nicest days of the year. And you're at a coffee shop." They stare at me. "Go to the lake and go for a walk. The Art Fair is less than a mile away." They go back to complaining. I get more upset. Really more annoyed.

"Why you are not only sitting at a coffee shop, but the slowest coffee shop in the city, is a mystery to me. Ten blocks in either direction are Caribous that at least have a dining room where you can people watch." And not look like such losers, I do not add.

They don't move. Regulars!

Sam leaves for school in the fall after his parents intervene. Becklynn still walks the neighborhood. Every morning she walks by with her backpack, going nowhere in particular, lost in her fantasy world. She quietly walks in and writes Batman on the Chalk Thought board. On some days I find it sad and sweet, and on other days I find it pathetic. Regulars can be a little bit of both.

CHAPTER 20
WHAT IS THE LONGEST RIVER IN CHINA?

Dear customer who waits until I have given their change back to yell out the trivia answer,

You don't seriously want 10 cents back, do you? You aren't moving. You have taken this beautiful Caribou concept, fun trivia in the morning, and completely destroyed it. Now I'm the dick because I can't believe you want the fucking 10 cents back! It's not about the 10 cents off! It's about us creating a fun moment. That you wrecked. Here is 10 cents from my own pocket.

I am an Internet review site junkie. At no time in the history of the world could consumers tell the world about what they think better than right now. It's also when we are reminded how many idiots are out there too. It's not a great way to start off my day because most of the time, reading what people think about their coffee shop experience pisses me off. But I do love to torture myself.

OSAT is an acronym in the Caribou world for overall customer satisfaction. Roughly every 25 transactions a customer survey pops out of the register on the receipt paper. If the customer fills out the survey online they are given a little code to receive $1 off their next purchase. They must to take the survey within three days and complete the survey to receive their dollar off.

I have the OSAT score on an IPhone app and I check it roughly every 10 minutes to see if a new survey has popped in. One a day is a good response, as that would equal about 30 a month, which is the total Christian would like. After completing the survey, the customer's answers and comments pop into the system within moments. Christian monitors these scores too and we want an overall satisfaction of above 75% for the month. I keep track in my head of who got a survey that morning and if any scores come back. My OSAT information will tell me what the customer ordered and what time they were at the coffee shop.

For a while Caribou made the OSAT scores a part of the store managers' review process, but then they had to fire too many managers because they would fill out surveys to raise their scores. Now it doesn't affect my review, but Christian still emails the scores daily with words of encouragement or re-energized focus. He gets all bent out of shape if the scores dip below 78%, which is the company's goal. Caribou takes the scores very seriously, and they want the customer to be extremely satisfied on every visit. (Which we all know is impossible.) You cannot make everyone happy, and we all know that pissed-off people are more likely to say something. An upset person will tell 10 people, but a happy person will not tell anyone. The dollar off is a nice gesture, but it is not enough incentive for everyone.

One of the biggest problems at my store is that no one will fill the survey out, regardless of whether their experience was good or bad. Christian wants 30 replies a month. The service is good, but our neighborhood people don't care about a dollar off. Kirsten's philosophy was she wasn't going to worry about a good OSAT or a bad OSAT and her scores showed it. They were bad. Some people loved her and some people hated her and she didn't give a shit. She wasn't going to play the OSAT game as she called it. I, however, fell in love with the OSAT process and manipulating the survey. By manipulating the survey I mean manipulating idiots, the customers. Maybe you. From Wal-Mart to JC Penney to Chipotle to Children's Palace, companies push out the surveys in hopes of hearing what their customers think.

First off, how the survey is presented to the customer is important. I realized after awhile that how the OSAT survey was presented directly related to the score. The drink could be shitty and the store a mess, but if it the survey was presented right the customer might give a good score.

A "normal" bad Caribou greeter presents the survey like this: "You can take a survey and you can get a dollar off." Or a really bad greeter like Anthony presents it like: "Yo bro, like take this quiz and get prizes." *It isn't a quiz, there are no prizes and quit calling women Bro!*

Here is how a good greeter would present the survey: "You qualified for a survey to tell our home office how your service was today. My name is Ben and we would love to hear what you think." Obviously mine is longer and wordier and more professional and it does take a moment of time to tell the customer about it, when I know all we are really about is caffeine and speed. The survey presented the first way allows the customer to vent about all things Caribou. There is no Caribou in Atlanta, so they aren't highly satisfied. The prices are too high, so they aren't satisfied. There is no viable organic milk alternative. I don't like the bakery options. These are viable concerns for Caribou, but it has nothing to do with my service and my score. Presenting the survey the second way tells the customer this score needs to be about my service today. So when they take the survey they have me in mind, not the fact that Caribou is heavily invested in by an Iranian. They are also less likely to complain about store-specific things that are out of my control like our location, lack of parking, or the slow wifi speed.

There is a reason Caribou employees don't want to present it the second way and that's because you are now on the radar for great service. You tell someone your name, ask him or her to take a survey about how you did today, you better fucking kill it. It's a service industry. When I started at my store, Noreen and Neil would throw the surveys away as soon as they popped out. I didn't say anything because their service was shitty and I didn't want the customer to vent.

The actual online survey process for the customer is a meandering, choose your own-adventure odyssey that collects information about what store you were at, the time, what you ordered, speed of service, cleanliness, community, friendliness and connection. In all areas the score was five for extremely satisfied and one for "call or email me, I had a horrible experience."

I would challenge Christian as I began monitoring the OSAT scores (by the minute) about what the scores represented. Often the survey numbers didn't make sense, because the customers scored us weird. Customers would score us 100% satisfaction for cleanliness, speed of service, friendliness and connection, but than only 85% for overall satisfaction. Or the customer was 100% satisfied overall with their visit, but they scored us very low on the individual areas. Or the customer was a complete dumbshit and scored us all ones, thinking that was the best score. That customer wrote in the comments section, "Sorry, I thought ones were the best."

A red alert is when a customer has a bad experience, and either we try to contact them, or they ask to be contacted.

Out of all the complaints on the OSAT for varying degrees of problems, I only had two people who wanted me to call them. One didn't give a phone number or email, but wanted to be contacted. *What a jackass.* Caribou wanted to me to contact them immediately! *There is no phone or e-mail though? The age of information!*

The other ordered a Café Canela, but it was too spicy. I realized why, since the spicy mocha container is next the Canela container. Otherwise, I read lots of complaints but most people didn't want to be contacted.

My biggest complaint in the survey was the "connection" area of scoring. I would be in the 90's for speed and friendliness, and connection would be in the 50's. I was okay with that, but some stores had connection in the 90's and speed in the toilet. Sometimes I just don't hit it off with a customer. They don't want to answer the trivia, they don't want to be upsold, they just want their coffee, and they are crabby at me for the whole experience. And then a survey pops out. Or a joke I make will go horribly awry as I realize the person has no sense of humor.

Some customers threaten us with the survey. Sometimes we make the wrong drink, or a customer takes the wrong drink, or the drink is just not to their expectations for whatever reason, and sometimes we get in the weeds. We are human. "I'll be sure to note this in my survey," one dickhead proclaims after Marge screwed up his mocha. He didn't actually do the survey. Lazy dickhead. The hardest part of the OSAT game is sometimes the customers are fucking idiots. Their opinions shouldn't matter, but do. *You've been reading this book and you know what I mean now!* But worse than that, they complain about issues that literally are not issues. And I am punished for it.

When I am on the greeter spot, which is most mornings because I am a god at upselling, I prepare all of the cold drinks because it frees up a lot of time for the barista to make hot drinks in the early morning rush. We hit a stretch where Liz and I got 58 people through in an hour! That might not seem like a lot to you, but a good morning is 40, a super busy morning is 50, and the record was 58. We still had fun, upsold, and played trivia with the customers. I had a really good experience with a particular woman at the greeter spot, laughing, cajoling, she loved the Mathew Modine 80's trivia I had written for the day. She ordered a vanilla latte and there were a few other hot drinks ahead of hers. Right after her order were a few cold drinks, which I knocked out. (Cold drinks like cold press or coolers take about 10 seconds to make, but it's 10 seconds Liz has to stop frothing milk on the stupid traditional machine.)

"Am I ever getting my drink?!" she screams at Liz after I serve the cold drinks.

"It's a latte?" Liz asks calmly. The little coffee shop had gone quiet.

"Yes! And I've been waiting here while all these other people get served!"

"Your drink is up next. I'm making it right now." The woman obviously is not going to understand that I made those drinks so hers would be made faster. I really couldn't explain it either because I had more customers. I tried to say I make the cold drinks so Liz can better focus on the espresso machine, but it is a lot to explain.

As Liz served her drink she was still harrumphing. "I'll be sure to note this service in my survey." She waves the survey in the air as she runs out. The coffee shop is dead quiet. The customers are not used to someone being so publicly upset.

"Well that sucked," I say and it breaks the ice. Liz gets in a giggling fit and we try to explain to the other customers what just happened.

Christian points out that between the mean and nice and stupid customers it usually all evens out pretty fairly and he is right. One customer scored us perfectly and commented how we do not use vanilla soy like Starbucks. We do use vanilla soy. Another said he loved our breakfast sandwiches. I actually don't have an oven nor breakfast sandwiches at our location.

Another customer complains that our drinks are big and have a lot more espresso than Starbucks drinks. YES! That very comment that could be written on a customer's survey as a compliment.

Some complaints are so rampant I want to put up a sign that says I cannot control this complaint. Wifi complaints are daily on OSAT for all Caribous. We have wifi, but I can't really control it. I don't turn on a signal that makes it stronger. It's the same one that's at your house. And I'm certainly not withholding it from you specifically if you think I have that power.

"The wifi password doesn't work."

"We don't have a wifi password."

"It's Caribou," she says with a sorority girl sigh.

"I'm not lying to you, the password isn't Caribou because we don't have a password." *Why the fuck would I lie to you?*

One OSAT at the Lake store read in all caps, "I'M OFFENDED THEY HAVE LOCKS ON THE BATHROOM DOORS. THAT IS A HUGE INCONVIENCE AND IT SPEAKS POORLY ON YOUR ABILITY TO CONTROL CUSTOMERS AND IT'S A BAD REFLECTION OF THE AREA." I agree, but there's one thing though: we don't have a key for our fucking bathroom!

"Can I get the bathroom key?" A customer says impatiently while I'm the middle of a huge rush.

"We don't have a key to the bathroom."

"Well it's locked!" Do they think I'm hiding the key from them? Maybe I'm trying to make them wet their pants? Or do they think I'm such a fucking idiot I forgot the door has a key?

"That's because someone is in there," I reply. I like to think it has dawned on them they are a fucking idiot. But I doubt it.

"It's too busy on Saturday morning!" "There is not enough parking!" "Why isn't the Internet faster?" "There are not enough places to sit." There are endless complaints that I can't explain to a fool. These are general coffee shop complaints, but in the areas of online reviews, sometimes the comments are about me and my fellow coffee shop workers. This is a new phenomenon not only with the OSAT, but Google and Yahoo reviews and websites like Yelp. People see our nametags in the store every day and are watching us and commenting, and it can hurt.

I remember the first time I was mentioned in the OSAT comments. "A gentleman explained the difference between white, dark and milk chocolate to my son. We have gone there for years and never knew. Those two are a great team!" He was referring to me and Stephen. I remembered the guy and his son immediately and smiled.

I remember the bad comments more than the good ones. There are fewer good, and I never get used to the sting of a bad comment. They hurt when you are doing your best and it's not good enough. When someone calls you out by name to embarrass you and shame you, it's a hurtful experience. I got an OSAT comment at the Lake store that was something to the effect of "Ben sucks at making drinks." More than angry, I was embarrassed. Every boss in the world knows their employees screw up, but with OSAT and the Internet, I am now called out by name to Christian and Kirsten. I feel like a professional athlete now, except I don't get paid 10 million dollars. I used my OSAT anger to make drinks faster and better than everyone. A mix of anger, shame, and the possibility of being called out on the Internet was a great motivator.

Another comment about me was a complaint that I made no eye contact with the customer throughout the order. I was new, I was still figuring out the register, and I wanted to scream "Do you want your caffeine fast or fucking eye contact?" If you get your caffeine in under two minutes and it's made perfectly do you always need contact? Especially in a fucking morning rush? But that is the world we have created with the Internet rating system and it's easy complaint procedures. Everything is perfect, but you know there was not much eye contact. *I'll fucking work on that!*

"Don't worry about it, Ben," Kirsten told me. Criticism seemed to melt off her. "You win some, you lose some. Do your best and be yourself and that's all you can do." Now she sounded like a seasoned professional athlete. I didn't tell her this review was on Yelp about the Lake store:

"The GM can be really moody, and downright rude if she's having a bad day. I understand we all have our days, but I find it particularly deplorable when those in managerial customer service positions can't act professionally. Moreover, I've also had fair interactions with her, and great ones with the rest of the staff. Unfortunately, however, the negative few have superseded the good ones in my eyes."

The funniest stuff is always true! But I now find myself defending Kirsten and I take umbrage to the jackaninny commenting on shit he doesn't understand. I was just as rough on Kirsten until I was in her shoes. It's a customer service industry, but really it's service industry at an incredible rate. Burnout is a factor and Kirsten has been doing it for nine years. The average turnover rate for regular coffee seller is six months. *Yikes!* The difference between Kirsten and me is I serve the dickheads with a smile, but give a special cup to the deserving ones. Kirsten has no such outlet for justice. At least that I know about, and then I blow my own mind wondering if that's why Kirsten is always on bar–is she serving a little justice?

Sometimes the OSAT comments sting because I can't defend what I am doing. At my neighborhood store of course I am turning over the staff because they are slow and dumb. The OSAT comments reflect what I am doing.

"Is this a training store?" "There is so much turnover." "The old staff seemed more local." *They fucking sucked, I yell at the computer!*

It's creepy how personal some of the OSAT messages are. "Another new manager?" It was weird to me someone noticed I was new at the store. They were watching. And for the most part I can't fight back. You might have liked Paul, but Paul sucked at what you want: Caffeine and speed! The store is better off without him.

Not only did I review the OSAT scores and comments almost hourly, but I set up a Google alert for Caribou Coffee. I read every comment I can find to figure out how customers think. The comments have lots of themes, lots of complaints, a few praises, and lots of everything else. In the end I quit reading all of those comments because they all contradict each other. You can't make everyone happy. And some people are only happy when they are complaining.

"On a day when the temp outside was 95+ degrees, I am not sure why the door was wide open, making the restaurant warm and bringing in the noise off the street." *We open both doors for a cross breeze. The air conditioner can't keep up with the people and the heat. Wind is good.*

"Tables are crammed in – the woman sitting on the hightop behind me kept bumping me, making it rather difficult to work." *A Saturday morning at a ridiculously busy coffee shop might not be the place to hunker down and try to get some work done.*

"My soy caramel latte was okay, but it was served in a tall coffee mug with an inordinate amount of foam. Where are the latte cups?!" *I have no idea what a latte cup is! You coffee asshole dickhead snobs are nodding your heads. The foam on soy drinks is tricky, remember, so it doesn't come out like normal milk.*

"Also, no artistry when making my latte = no tip. If I'm paying $5 to get a coffee drink, I expect a bit more." Comments like these blow me the fuck away! Did they want a rose or a goose in milk? Artistry? What? Speed and caffeine, people! And I call bullshit on the tip. I don't think this person ever tips. Our tip jar is by the greeter, at the front of the line, because that's when people have their money out. People are going to tip or not tip, and in all my time at Caribou I never saw someone not tip, sip their drink, and return with a tip. I never even saw anyone wait and say, "I'm going to wait and see what this drink turns out like. That will decide the size of my tip." Never seen it.

"Staff doesn't seem to be listening to customers so my 'for here' orders almost always become 'to go', wrong drinks are served, etc. In short, the only reason this place has any business is because there are no other coffee shops around."

I'm not listening huh? I have made literally 300 drinks today, but you are consistently not getting your drink in a "for here" cup? More than once? Constantly? But that's my fault? Are we sure you aren't a fucking idiot? How can you not communicate to someone whose job is to make you happy what you want? It's not us ...it's you.

And there are no other coffee shops around? I can't throw a rock in our city without hitting two or three coffee shops.

The great thing about Caribou is that the Caribou culture is no joke. And the Caribou culture fever catches a hold of me, not in the name of the OSAT, but in the name of creating an extraordinary experience. I've always wanted these comments to show up, but they never do.

One customer was 10 cents short. "You could play the trivia?" I offer.

"Yes that's a good idea." I can tell she won't get it.

"Did you say 'Who was Uncle Joey?'" I gave her the discount already.

"Well thank you." She smiles.

Another customer has a wife and child. I sense this is a treat for them. We have samples of our new teas out. I can tell the guy likes it, but that would be another $3.76

"We also have a promotion that if you bring your receipt back after 2 p.m. you get 50 % off any beverage." Their eyes light up. The guy is back at 2:00 sharp for his green tea lemonade and he is happy. I'm happy. He returns moments later with his wife and an empty cup. He dropped it, the wife tells me, as the guy looks embarrassed and upset.

"Could I get another one at half price?"

"Let me do you one better." I hand the cup to Medora. "Green tea lemonade." If anyone drops their drink I always give them a refill for free. I remember a time when I was about 10 years old and my dad took me to Dairy Queen. As we were walking out of the store I let the door close on him and he dropped his banana milkshake. Dairy Queen never offered to replace it. I felt awful. I never let anyone feel like I felt that day.

Sometimes I consciously just blow a customer's experience out of the water. I give the kids some gifts, or I make a big deal about their drink, and I go all fucking out. I hand them an OSAT survey I keep on hand under the register, just to see if they'll fill it out. Not very often.

On a conference call Christian explains how he searched "love" on OSAT comments and found 10 pages of customer comments with the words love. This is not something we would have done at any other place I've worked.

Another district manager tells a story about a woman who was at the Social Security office because her husband died. The Social Security office put her through the ringer to get any money. The woman later wandered into a Caribou and mentioned her husband had died. The cashier said coffee is on us today. Kirsten began to cry listening to this on the conference call. This isn't lip service or trying to pull one over on the media. This is a fucking conference call. This is what we are spending time to talk about with 90 store managers on the call. Not numbers, not cutting costs, not anything but love. Literally love.

But mostly I use the OSAT to truly figure what people want out of their Caribou experience. The number one OSAT complaint is speed of service. I had an idea that's what people cared about, but OSAT proved that people only truly care about speed of service and caffeine. Not latte cups! The usual customer complaints are about how they only have 10 minutes before work to stop and get a cup of coffee and the line was too long. Or they only have 15 minutes on their break and the Caribou line was long and it wasn't moving fast enough.

We absolutely know baristas and greeters mess up. We are humans, and there can be new employees. But usually, and by that I mean 99 percent of the time, it's the customer's fault. So why don't the managers work at the register when they know it would help the store? I'll tell you why—the barista isn't the highest turnover position at the coffee shop, it's the greeter. The greeter has to deal with the customers. The horrible ordering, the rude people, the nuts, the coffee asshole dickhead snobs, the bitches, and the regulars. Plus hearing no all of the time when upselling and doing add-ons. Lots of "no", lots of dickheads, lots of bitches, lots of all the in-betweens.

My store almost leads the Twin Cities in larges sold per 100 customers, which means almost 40 larges sold per 100 customers. The market average is about 25 and our market has about 50 stores. So 15 more people at my store get larges. Why? Because we fucking ask everyone. Forty larges out of 100 is monumental and Christian loves it, but 40 larges still equals 60 nos. So over a five hour morning, that means we get over 200 no's, fuck you's, hell no's, and smart ass comments, and people who think they are funny but are just dickheads. And that's just from offering larges.

I also offer bakery or to "moose" drinks, or to add a shot of vanilla or anything that pops into my mind. In one transaction I can get four no's, and the average person can't handle it day to day. Every "yes" energizes me, and they add up. I get on a roll. It's infectious. But the average person wilts like a flower with all of the no's that add up. They come to dread the no's worse than the rush at the bar and they turn into a Wal-Mart register person, a conveyor belt, and they don't interact with the customer at all.

That is why in a roomful of 26 Caribou store managers, only myself and one other worked the register daily. Our numbers were off the charts. We led every top statistic. My average ticket was twice what it was the year before. I was killing sales goals and I had fewer customers than a year before.

We were the two newest store managers. And we found out burnout is a bitch. And it's real.

OSAT and online complaints basically are either slow service or some other fucking idiotic complaint I have no control over. I wish I could tell everyone who has ever complained about the speed of their caffeine delivery in a coffee shop that 99% of the time it's the customers fault! Think about this. The next time you are at Caribou and you are about to bitch about how slow the line is and yell at the poor greeter or manager or send a passionate poignant letter or email, think about this...

Dear customer, woman customer I should say, who spends a good minute rearranging your wallet while the people behind you are waiting impatiently, but politely, for you to get the fuck out of the way,

They do not blame you, they fucking blame me! They blame Caribou, they complain to corporate, they tell their friends this fucking Caribou is so slow. All because of you are fucking re-ahfucking-ranging your fucking wallet while 10 people stand behind you. You fold your cash up so nice and neat and organized. Isn't that sweet and cute? Fucking get the fuck out of the fucking way! People are behind you in the fucking line! You are the reason people have to wait! But they fucking blame me when you are the fucking idiot!!

Dear customer who wants to know why we don't have more than one milk alternative,

Because we aren't a fucking school cafeteria that has cater to everyone. We are a fucking business. We are here to make money, so just because one person in the world wants soy or organic or natural does not mean we have to get it. And I don't know how to tell you that this bullshit complaint to me, the guy at the register at 9 a.m. on a Tuesday, isn't going to do much good. I don't know how to break this to you, but I don't do the ordering and milk decision s for all 250 Caribous! Do you think I am the fucking CEO working the cash register? But we both know if I was the CEO you wouldn't say shit.

Dear customer who asks if we have a tea list,

You mean like a list of teas that we put up so everyone can see it so they know what to buy? Like the menu that is fucking right behind me? Yes, we do. And we conveniently put the prices near them too. It's that big sign that says "Tea."

Dear customer who starts shaking their head exaggeratedly NO! when I start to explain the survey,
     You are really passionate about not wanting to hear about this survey. Either way it takes about four seconds for me to explain it. You could probably just take it and throw it away or say no thank you.

Dear customer who asks the fucking ingredients of the new pumpkin mix, the Chai, the soy, or wants to know if we have a milk alternative, who holds up the fucking line,
     Maybe if you are allergic to everything in the world you shouldn't be here. Or maybe just grow a pair.

Dear doctor's office secretary that comes in with a 30-drink order,
     First off, thank you for your business. Second off, make sure the drinks are legibly written, and are actual drinks, a mocha-latte-cappuccino iced doesn't exist. And send someone to order the drinks with half a brain, and probably two people because we can't walk over and help you bring them out.

Dear families with intricate orders,
     One medium, iced breve latte, with two Splenda, and one large smoothie in three small cups, and another large iced breve latte, decaf. This order takes a lot longer. Putting it into extra cups, the decaf, and the breve part. An order like this gets us in the weeds.

Dear customer whose credit card swipe part is now invisible or worn off,
     Get a fucking new one. Having to hand enter this is killing our time in line. My bank is Wells Fargo and they automatically send me a new card every year or so. Or you can ask for one. You tell me you need a new card every fucking day and think it's funny and cute. It's not. Get a fucking new card!

Dear customer who slaps their book bag, purse, laptop case and newspaper on the counter and than takes five minutes to order, then after the order spends another five minutes cleaning up and organizing their gear,
     You are killing me on the inside. You are creating an ulcer in my stomach. You are the cause of cancer!

Dear customer who is right-handed but tries to get the change back with their left hand,
    I'm going to slap you.

Dear customer who hands me their credit card and then puts their wallet away, then when I hand the card back they have to pull their wallet out again,
    You dumbass! Have you ever bought anything before? Did you think your credit card was a gift card? Your stupidity is holding up the fucking line! Keep your wallet out until I hand the card back, dumbass!

Dear customer who requests whole milk,
    I now have to add Half and Half and two percent for the same exact tasting beverage and more calories and it takes you and everyone else longer to get your drinks. So enjoy.

Dear customer who wants to know all about the Rainforest Alliance,
    I know you want brochures and information and that's great but there are people waiting to get coffee. That's totally great you want to know more about that, but I'm FUCKING WORKING AND TRYING TO GET PEOPLE THEIR CAFFEINE. Have you ever heard of the Internet?

Dear customer who asks for tape,
    Here is a piece of Scotch tape off a dispenser, now get out. You need more than that? You can try Target, Wal-Mart, Walgreens, or Whole Foods. You want free tape? So you came into a coffee shop? I don't have any tape. Could I go look in back? I can after I help all these other customers. You know, the people buying coffee. How long will that take? Just a few minutes. What do we have here? Lots of good stuff.
    Have a very special cup of coffee on the house while you wait? I know, we are very nice.

Dear customer who makes up drinks like hot chocolate, froth milk, and coffee and a shot of espresso, with a little brown sugar on top,
    Every time you make up a drink it slows down the line for everyone behind you. There is not button for that drink. There is no way to make that drink on the register without me making three pages worth of notes. You may think you're cute or unique, but you are a fucking pretentious asshole.

Dear customer who waits until I hand them their coffee, and apple fritter, and then starts pulling their money out after I tell them the total,
    Have you ever bought anything in your whole fucking life? Do you think this is for free today? Have it fucking ready and hurry the fuck up! If I could

put a "Have your money ready" sign up, I would. I can't though, because we're classy!

Dear customer who complains there is "not enough parking,"
   If you want a coffee shop with more parking then you are going to have to move to the suburbs. It's really that simple. City stores are not going to magically create more parking spots.

Dear customer who asks what alcohol we have and when I say none you spin around staring at the sky wondering where you are,
   I don't have time to explain to you what a dumbass you are.

Dear customer who complains they have to listen to commercials when we have the radio on,
   You are really running out of things to complain about in your life.

Dear customer who, after being given a survey, asks, "Do I have to take it?",
   Wow. Yes.

Dear customer who asks if we are owned by terrorists and have to follow Islamic rules,
   Sigh.

Dear customer who does not say simply "No thank you" when I offer beans, food, an upsell or drink recommendation,
   We live in the age of Capitalism. Maybe you haven't realized this, but we are all out to make money and that includes Caribou Coffee. So in some crazy scheme to make more money we offer different products. When I say, "Would you like a triple berry muffin" that's not my idea. That's my company's idea. Being rude to me instead of just "No thank you" is not appreciated. When I say would you like to try a sparkling juice or tea? You can just say, "No thank you." I'm not trying to change your caffeine fueled latte to an iced tea. I'm trying to give you a sample so you'll come back later.

Dear customer who gets butted in front of in line,
   Don't fucking get mad at me that you can't navigate a fucking coffee shop line. Step up when it is your turn because if you hesitate, people will go ahead of you. Don't get mad at us, be mad at yourself because you are weak and have no self-esteem. If you walk into the shop and can't get your drink, then It's on you. Not us.

Dear customer who replies "He's no longer with us" when I ask if you need gift cards for Father's Day,
    Everyone dies. Get over it. And I'm fucking doing my job!

Dear customer who complains there are so many choices,
    Hot chocolate and mochas and coolers get white, dark or milk chocolate. Do not say to me, "so many choices." Not everyone gets the same fucking thing. Caribou, in some crazy scheme to make money, decided to offer some different combinations.

Dear customer who orders in the quietest inside voice whisper in the world,
    Get some balls! Because your order is going to get screwed up and then you'll find the voice to complain. So when I repeat your order back to you don't get that pissy face because I'm fucking doing this for you and every fucking one behind you!

Dear customer who literally has to shake your daughter to get her order because she is texting,
    You should be the parent of the year. And don't even fucking give me shit when it's not the chocolate she wanted!

Dear customer who can't get the change out of her purse because she keeps hitting refresh on her Facebook,
    Wow! I love Facebook, but come on! You're not talking to anyone, I'm just watching you hit refresh. You have a problem. And you are so inconceivably rude I want to spit in your coffee while you watch me spit in it and then hand it to you.

Dear gabby customers who are so busy gabbing you don't move,
    Let me explain the concept of the coffee shop. You order at the register and you walk down to the end of the barista bar and your drink will be ready in a couple of minutes. It's a pretty basic idea that has been made popular in like 20,000 coffee shops in the country. The one flaw? When someone orders and doesn't fucking move! Then when I say your drink will be ready at the end of the bar you give me a look like how rude? But if I didn't speak up then you'd stand there and the 10 people behind you would get madder and madder. But they wouldn't blame you. They would blame me and Caribou. So get the hell out of the way and get your drink!

Dear woman who orders hot chocolate and argues about how many scoops of chocolate she wants and the drink is supposed to get,

Tell me how many scoops you want, you annoying bitch! Why are you putting us through this? You lean on your tiptoes watching how many scoops of chocolate I put in the pitcher. Has Caribou just been adding so much fucking chocolate to your hot chocolate it just bothers the shit out of you? And then you don't tell me you did not want whipped cream because you were obsessed with the chocolate chip scoop total! Now I have to do the whole thing over again with you staring at me! Argh!

Dear customer who argues with me when I tell him we are out of blueberry muffins,

We run out of bakery as huge groups buy more than we have thawed. I know I have bins of muffins out but those have not thawed yet. Do you think I have muffins to sell and am just not selling any to you? Why are you wasting my and everyone else's time arguing with me?

Dear customer whose kid just lost their shit because we are out of blueberry muffins,

You are not helping your kid in any way by asking me if I can get one out of "the back." There is no fucking "back." And we are a coffee shop not a bakery. And my dad would slap the shit out me if I did that even today, and it would still be better parenting than yours. You are ruining your kid and embarrassing yourself. It pains me to watch this.

Dear old-ass fucking woman who pulls out the coin purse to pay for her coffee,

You are killing me you are so fucking slow. Do you have any awareness at all, as the line swells, of the glares, the comments, the eye rolls, the uh-hums, the hurry the fuck up glares? Is that what happens when you get old? You lose all self-awareness? Oh, you can FINALLY get rid of some change? Have you ever heard of a fucking bank? They'll cash it all in for you! You're killing me! Why do you think a coffee shop wants a register full of change? Why? Coffee is not 10 cents any fucking more!

Dear customer who does not have their money ready when I'm ready to take it,

Have your fucking money ready! I feel like I need to say that again, so everyone can hear. HAVE YOUR FUCKING MONEY READY! Those "Have money ready" signs at the drive-thru now make sense to me, but I can't hang one up because it would insult your intelligence. It kills our time in line when you idiots are not getting exact change, but just getting money out. Then you realize you have only four dollars so then you pull out a credit card, and I can't decide who I would shoot if I had a gun? You, or me.

Dear customer who is getting a bunch of drinks for the office,
    I appreciate what you are doing but you need to get some details on what they want or be prepared to make a decision. You can't text or call them all on every option. You just can't. Luckily for you, I happen to be in the coffee business and could probably tell you what are the popular options. You are holding up the entire fucking line and I hate you right now.

Dear customer who wants oatmeal without the dairy powder,
    They've done it before, you say? We may have done it, but should we do it? Our oatmeals are premade so now I have to grab an empty cup and the oatmeal and make one from scratch in a morning rush, just so I make one guy happy. But the 20 people behind you are going to get pissed. But no one is going to blame you, they are going to fucking blame me! It would be nice if just once another customer realized the idiot making a special order was the cause of the delay, not me. Just once a customer would yell, "Hey dickwad! Quit ordering like a fuck-up and just get what's on the menu so we can all get out of here quickly!" That's my dream. But no one ever says a thing. Even if the customer is a dick or a bitch or orders some ridiculous order no customer has ever stood up for us. It will get very quiet, but nothing more than that. Thank God I piss and shit in the cups of these customers or I would really lose it.

Dear dickhead customer who pretentiously asks for cheddar cheese on his sandwich,
    They are pre-made, dick fuck. Oh, then you want a ham and cheese? We don't have that, dick fuck. We don't have a fucking deli back there, you jack-off.

Dear female customer who calls during a busy time and asks if a darker man is sitting across from our counter,
    I thought it was going to be a stalker complaint. You want me to give him your number? I'll do it. Who am I to get in the way of fate?

CHAPTER 21
COFFEE SHOCK

Dear Starbucks employee who wants to know what the fuck "moosed" means
because his customers say it to him like he should know,
  We are brothers now! We know each other's pain! Hold me!

On everyone's first day at Caribou Coffee, a "coffee talk" is performed. I did mine with Kirsten and Christian before we filled out my tax forms. We sampled the light roast, the dark roast and the decaf of the day. I was not an experienced coffee drinker and Christian told me it would take a few months to pick up the nuances of coffee. He encouraged me to taste everything. Christian hired me to be a good manager more than a seasoned coffee person. Some Caribou managers didn't like coffee or caffeine at all. And that's okay.

Every shift, not just every day, but every shift, a coffee talk is to be performed. A coffee talk is sampling the coffee of the day and talking about what it tastes like, what we feel, how it smells, and what it reminds us of. There are no wrong answers and it's okay not to like every coffee. Caribou is big on coffee bean origins, so during a coffee talk we would find out where the coffee was from, if it is a single bean or a blend. We had a big, beautiful glossy coffee book that told us everything there was to know about the bean. Caribou wants every employee to sample every coffee every day. Of course it gets so busy we don't have time some days, but in a world of shareholders, and profits, and cutting costs, Caribou pushes every employee to try every coffee. And when Caribou introduces a new drink or pastry, each employee must complete a "make it, taste it" to know how to make something new and to see what it tastes like. All so we can talk to customers.

When I met Regional Manager Helen at the home office, the first thing we did was a coffee talk. Caribou is not shitting you about coffee knowledge. And the customers eat it up. Every coffee is assigned a three-word indicator of the nuances of flavor, like a fine wine. The hints of flavor can sometimes be misconstrued as the flavors being added to the coffee. It's like wine, even though I don't drink wine, I would tell customers. A hint of cherry or dark chocolate.

Customers want to know if a coffee is dark roast or light roast, letting their roast define them. Customers don't want any Robusta coffee beans, and I confidently assure them that all of Caribou coffee is Arabica, meaning it was grown above 3,000 feet.

Christian and Helen had shown me hundreds of pictures of their trips to different coffee plantations. Helen told me about how the owner would dive into a coffee bean pit if she saw one green bean. One green been would destroy the quality. She took it seriously, Helen assured. Quality coffee beans were their passion.

Christian showed me a picture of sacks of beans for Caribou that were lush brown, a sack for Starbucks that looked like beans that hadn't been watered, and a sack for McDonalds that looked like rocks and sand. At Caribou, from the farm to the store we deliver quality! I visited Caribou's home office and spent time with the roast masters. These three guys "cup" every batch of coffee that is sent to the warehouse. They pour hot water over grounds and do the largest, wettest, slurp I've ever heard. Why do they slurp? To coat their mouth with coffee. They explain to me that you have taste buds all over your mouth and the coffee coating each different taste bud releases different flavors.

They spit out the coffee because they do this about three times a day, and they like to sleep at night. They blind taste the different cups and rank the three and compare notes. If anyone feels the coffee isn't great, they don't roast it or ship it to the stores. They taste every fucking batch. They slurp unbelievably loud and spit it out into a souvenir cup. It's gross and cool all at the same time. What a job!

I asked the head guy if we would run out of better beans for our coffee. Would Caribou get so big like Starbucks and have shitty beans? "Starbucks chooses to have shitty beans. We don't." But he did agree at some point that quality may suffer if Caribou went global, but he said it won't in the foreseeable future. A bigger concern is the climate changes in South America. It is raining longer and there is not a long enough dry period for the coffee to grow properly. They work with the farmers to spread out the coffee trees, the beans come out in a cherry.

This is why coffee is "fresher" at Caribou. Starbucks could never do this or at least they don't want to invest time into it. The coffee is roasted and then shipped to the stores. The coffee expires in three weeks, or earlier if opened. Once opened, the coffee has 10 days to be brewed and seven days to be sold to a customer. It hasn't been ground yet either, as that is all done at the Caribou store. If the coffee is not used in 21 days from when it's roasted, something really amazing happens: it's thrown away. *You read that right!*

Not used for Coolers, not shipped back to sell in bulk, not ground up and sold to customers, not anything like that because Caribou truly believes in what they preach. This means the coffee is ridiculously fresh. It may have all been harvested at the same time, but Caribou tries to get the best bean and serve it to customers quickly after roasting. They preach great coffee, and great coffee is fresh, so they throw out what they consider old. Compare this to Starbucks who mostly ships coffee already ground up, and the espresso beans are whole and need to be used in 13 months.

Thirteen months compared to three fucking weeks.

So when someone says to me, "I really like Caribou's coffee better than Starbucks, I think, *NO FUCKING SHIT*. It's not really even comparable. Starbucks 'coffee of the day' is taken from expiring prepacks almost a year old, and in some cases older.

Three weeks for Caribou.

This makes for fresher, better tasting coffee, but at the end of the day it doesn't pay the bills. Do you realize how much coffee they throw away in the name of serving the best cup of coffee in the world? A ridiculous amount! Only until recently did Caribou begin saving the hourly brewed coffee waste for Cooler mix. For years they just threw away unused coffee because it wasn't fresh enough.

Behind the scenes at Caribou is a labyrinth of people trying to get the best bean to their customers. My question is why?

I worked for JC Penney for many years and the new CEO at the time was Myron "Mike" Ullman. He was one of the CEO's you hear speak for a few minutes and you wonder how the hell this guy is running the company and you aren't.

My first pet peeve with Mike was he liked to be called Mike, even though he wrote Myron on everything. He rode a Segway around the store on visits because he had a bad back, but on a promotional video in the store said he enjoyed being dropped out of a helicopter to go skiing. Yeah. At any rate, Mike spoke via teleconference once and said a lasting comment and I wasn't even in the coffee business at that point.

Mike had been on the board of directors of Starbucks through the glory days. Mike joked about how growth is hard and Starbucks "had a product that was addictive." I have never forgot that statement. And it held true through my time with Caribou. People do not go to Caribou and Starbucks for coffee or lattes or service or ambiance. They go for caffeine, or more to the point, they are addicted to caffeine.

People want caffeine and they want it fast. This would also explain why Starbucks is everywhere. They serve caffeine quickly. Better than anyone. Here is a dirty little secret about coffee and espresso: People are very passionate about their coffee and espresso when they KNOW it's their coffee and espresso. How do I know this? Because I fucked up brewing coffee every which way possible! Brewing coffee on the fly during a morning rush is harder than you think.

First thing you do is lay out the coffee for the next shift. We usually do one light roast, one dark roast, and one deaf. You pull the coffee bags out and weigh out half batches and full batches. That way you know what batch to brew the coffee on and you make sure the right amount of water is used.

In the beginning I was constantly forgetting which coffee was which because while laying out these coffee measurements, I was still on the floor working. I'd wait for lulls to do side jobs as most people in the service industry know. However I didn't focus on remembering where I was in the process.

Light on left, dark on right? Or was it?

I didn't measure that, was that a full?

I'd forget to switch the batch to half, so full water was going over a half batch of beans. Oh fuck, I forgot to grind that! And this process happened before having to brew the coffee every hour. I would pour the beans into the grinder and then a customer or 10 would come in. When I returned to the grinder I would forget what flavor beans were in it or I would pour another batch of beans into it. *Shit.* I was making and serving coffee that wasn't even a flavor, or I would simply forget which coffee was dark and which was light after it was brewed. Kirsten's system had green for light roast and blue for dark roast and I was constantly forgetting which was which in a rush. I imagined a customer taking a sip and throwing it at my feet.

"What the fuck is this shit?" I imagined getting fired for just not serving the right coffee because it is Caribou's thing. I would watch customers walk away with their cups of coffee, knowing I had fucked up in some way and I'd wait anxiously for their reaction. But it never came. No one has ever said a thing about any coffee I've made, except a few complaints like it's too hot or there are grounds in the coffee. I've had no flavor or strength complaints. Not one OSAT comment, not one weird look. Not shit. Nothing. Guys who drank dark roast for 30 years were given a cup of light roast and didn't bat an eye.

You might think maybe they were just too polite to say anything. I wouldn't be writing this book if people were too polite.

So I started experimenting with the coffee just to see if anyone at all would notice anything.

This pompous ass would walk into the store and decide if he'd buy a cup based on what we were brewing that day. He'd make a big show of staring at our sign with the light and dark roast of the day and then say, "Nope I'm going somewhere else."

I instinctively hated the guy of course, so then I was curious if he really knew his stuff. The next time he came in and I learned his favorite was Guatemala.

"I'll have Guatemala tomorrow!" I feigned excitement to get this asshole what he wanted. "What time are you coming?" So the next day I put the sign up for Guatemala. And brewed Starlight.

"Hmmm now that's a good cup of Joe."

"Absolutely." You pompous idiot jack ass.

One particular regular we called Tennis Outfit because she wore a tennis outfit every day. All day. Even at night. Weird. She wanted Mahogany to be served every day and would stomp her feet if we weren't serving it. Literally, walk into the store and stomp her feet like a five-year-old. Did she know she could purchase it and make it herself? Yes. She said it tasted different. She was not a favorite of mine, but Liz felt bad for her.

I roasted some shitty coffee from Africa that Caribou forced us to sell, a blend, a mid roast, and threw up the sign for Mahogany. She didn't bat a fucking eye. She didn't flinch. She didn't raise a brow. She put in her cream, a little sugar, and she drank and went on with her life. The power of positive thinking!

A lot of people at my store ordered the dark roast. Sometimes people would complain that I had the Caribou Blend as dark roast. So I tested it even more. The most prestigious suburb in maybe the world, rich palates, and distinct flavor connoisseurs, conspirers of coffee essences had no clue they were drinking Guatemala instead of Obsidian.

Caribou allows Caribou Blend to be used in a pinch if you run out of espresso beans. So I used everything in the espresso machine. No one said a thing. No one said a thing and these are people who complain about fucking everything. No one called me on it, no one tasted the difference. *You are reading this screaming, "I can, I can! I know my coffee and every blend and every aroma! I can!"*

Well you can't.

"I belong to coffeenerd.com and I get my latte every day and I blend my own coffee and blah blah blah." You didn't know. You don't know shit. I was trying weird stuff just to see if anyone would say anything. There is an entire coffee industry built on principles I was ignoring, mocking, and no one was saying a thing.

I would use coffee beans in the espresso machine. I would always roast Starlight, the lightest roast, for the whole week. I would switch the light and dark roast signs. I would brew espresso beans and serve them as Caribou. I would use any and every bean in the espresso machine and no one said a thing. I would switch two larges of two different flavors in one order, on purpose. No one has ever said shit.

And because I had unlimited resources, I tested just about every concoction I could think of or that idiot people would order. Can you taste difference between a large latte with skim milk and a latte with one Splenda? Nope. Can you taste the difference between a mocha with skim or whole or 2%? Not really. How about the difference between three pumps of vanilla and five? Or one pump and four pumps? A little. I would pick some drinks and have Jake make them and I'd do my own little taste tests.

I never had anyone say, "Hey this isn't my fucking coffee. What are you trying to pull?" Not one. They had caffeine and they got it quickly. And if they were bitching because it wasn't a pick-me-up, that there wasn't enough caffeine, or any caffeine, I would become indignant. *I usually forget to order decaf for the store. So that sign that says decaf? HA!*

CHAPTER 22
IF YOU DRINK DECAF I MIGHT HATE YOU

I'm not saying I hate everyone who drinks decaf, but I pretty much hate everyone who drinks decaf because is it just such a fucking waste of time. My time, your time, everyone's time.

I began to hate decaf drinkers after becoming a phase three barista. The key to being a great barista in the Caribou environment is using your ears. Listening to the next person's drink before it is on the board. When I was in the Zen, crazy-making-drinks-before-they-are-ordered, synergy moment, I found I kept making mistakes on one type of drink. Fucking decaf drinks. I just didn't hear that word consistently.

"I'll have a Caramel High Rise, medium with skim milk." I would already have started the shots and maybe even frothing the milk. "And make it decaf." "Oh, decaf too." "Better make that decaf."

I probably didn't hear because it's just such a ridiculous waste of time and energy to make or drink. And decaf drinkers are obnoxious and passionate about not having caffeine, but buying expensive drinks centered around covering up the espresso flavor.

"This is decaf right?" the rudest woman wearing a mink coat asks. Fuck, I think. I look at the board and fucking realize it was decaf. "ah…" I stammer.

"Because I can't have caffeine." My thoughts are pure hatred as I remake this woman's fucking decaf Mint Condition while the drinks pile up on the order board. As I remake the woman's drink she comments to the next customer about how she thinks she "has gotten caffeine in her drink before."

Well, idiot decaf drinkers, here is a dirty little secret: It's not completely decaffeinated. Nope, they can't get it all out. So all of you idiots who say you can't have any caffeine and caffeine is bad for you and you are allergic to caffeine and the world will stop if you have caffeine, you people are drinking caffeine. So when you have that cup of decaf at Thanksgiving because if you have any caffeine you'll be up all night, well you are dumb. Because that there coffee has caffeine in it.

The real question is why would someone who is either allergic to caffeine or doesn't handle caffeine well be in a fucking coffee shop? These people are out in droves slowing down the whole operation for their decaf nonsense.

The bitchy woman in the mink coat taught me one of the best barista lessons of all. When you're in a huge rush and you may have screwed up the drink, sell it confidently. Announce the drink loudly and proudly.

"Now that's decaf right?" a customer asks. "Absolutely! Have a great day." You may call me a dick and awful at what I do, but it all goes back to the only thing you care about: speed and caffeine. At the end of the day one person getting caffeine is better than 10 people not getting their drinks quick enough.

At the beginning I hated decaf drinkers because they overcomplicated the drink order by simply being decaf. I had to find the decaf button on the register. I had to remember to make decaf, I had to remember to fill the decaf espresso beans, and in a rush I would pump shots of espressos, and when some idiot orders decaf it ruined my flow. And my flow ruined equals a slower drink time for the customer.

I realized decaf drinkers were dumb too. One day this idiot decaf drinker ordered a large decaf Mint Condition with milk chocolate with an extra shot. "Whoa, whoa," I said. "You want to add an extra shot of decaf espresso to a decaf drink?"

"Yes," he replied. "Can you do that?"

That makes absolutely no sense paying more money for that but absolutely!

"You better believe it!" I didn't hate decaf drinkers as much, but I mocked used them endlessly for my financial gain while mocking them in my head. And they fell for it hook, line and sinker. You want a decaf iced latte? Would you like to moose that? How about double moose it?

You want a large decaf coffee? How about make it a Depth Charge today and add a shot of espresso? Cha-ching! I can upsell the idiot decaf drinkers all day. Let's add dirty hot water to more dirty hot water. Oh wait, I forgot that's the annoying decaf tea drinkers! They are almost the worst.

"What do have that's herbal?" I was caught off-guard. Caribou never told me what herbal tea meant.

"What do mean?"

"Does not have caffeine?"

I stared at the woman wondering what the point of drinking flavored hot water was that tastes like warmed-up cat water? She got impatient.

"How much caffeine does the Mint Verbena have?" Again I stare at her. We don't have caffeine charts or anything. It's either caffeinated or not caffeinated. Even though it's all truly caffeinated.

"I don't know, to be honest. Some, I guess."

She seems upset at my honesty and naiveté on all things tea.

"I'll have a medium decaf Earl Gray I guess."

"Do you want to make that a large for 30 cents more?"

"Oh, okay."

Yes get the large, I say to myself in my Dr. Evil voice. Get the large glass of hot water with dirtier cat water flavoring.

Each morning I prepare decaf (when I haven't forgotten to order it) and each morning I think of Matt's dirty diaper. That's what decaf coffee smells like to me.

"A large decaf milk-chocolate mocha."

"Yes." How about I give you a cup full of lard. Same calories.

I argue with my dad because he says he likes a decaf vanilla latte because he likes the flavor. If you love the flavor of coffee so much, why the fuck are you adding a huge amount of milk and vanilla flavoring to it? Very few people like the taste of espresso by itself. This is same reason we add Coke to Jack Daniels. That's why there is this billion-dollar industry of caffeine plus milk, chocolate and different flavorings. So don't tell me you like the fucking flavor.

I hate and pretty much forget about decaf in all facets of life. I think about taking it off the menu, but Caribou would freak out and so would a few customers. I forget to order decaf coffee and espresso quite often. A regular comes in most every morning and orders a large decaf. We don't brew decaf coffee the same as our dark and light roast because not as many people drink it. So we do a quarter pour-over. I usually forget about it or don't make it. The woman complains the decaf isn't as hot. I want to tell her to go fucking somewhere else then. I obviously do not care about the decaf so why do you keep coming here? There are two other Caribou's and a Starbucks a few blocks down.

I make a two-shot small decaf latte. The old woman says, "Now this is decaf right? I don't want to be up all night and have to hunt you down." Kind of joking, but kind of not joking. Kind of trying to be tough guy in front of her friend.

"Yes decaf skim latte."

"Because I got decaf here once awhile ago and it wasn't decaf."

"Here?"

"No, another Caribou."

"How long ago?"

"I don't know. Maybe a few years ago."

"So you got a latte, maybe with caffeine, a few years ago at another coffee shop? But it wasn't here?"

"Yes."

"Let me remake that for you just so I'm sure."

I smile as I pour two regular shots. No need for a special cup. Have fun sleeping tonight.

You know after thinking about it more...I do fucking hate everyone who drinks decaf.

CHAPTER 23
COFFEE SNOB ASSHOLE
DICKHEADS (CSADs)

Dear coffee snob asshole dickhead barista at snooty coffee shop,
I'm fucking with you when I order a frappuccino thing with extra caramel and sugar and lots of whipped cream and sprinkles and a big cherry on top. Get over yourself.

My uncle and dad proudly call themselves coffee snobs. Like a badge of honor they buy expensive coffee, have a Keurig machine, went through the buying a home espresso machine phase, returned to coffee shop coffee, and in general believe they like better coffee better than the average person. But they are not Coffee Snob Asshole Dickheads because of a few reasons. The definition of a CSAD is one who realizes Caribou and Starbucks do not serve what they want or how they want it served, but they still frequent Caribous and Starbucks and demand drinks and procedures that are not common nor normal. A CSAD mocks the world of Starbucks and Caribou drinks.

I recognize CSADs pretty quick. Why do these Coffee Snobs come to a Caribou looking for a straight espresso with the machine cranked a quarter inch for better taste when they know I can't do it? Because they are dickhead assholes. Do they go into Applebee's and ask for filet mignon? Do they go to In and Out Burger and ask for a medium rare burger? Do they go to Cub Foods and want the organic, locally grown watermelon department? In Minnesota? They are want-to-be elitist dickheads who look down upon the masses who enjoy caffeine with taste. *Oh poor us who like chocolate to mask the taste of espresso! We are so less than you.*

I have learned to pick out the smarmy asshole ordering a drink in front of a girl or his buddy. "One shot of espresso and in a clear cup please. They always forget the cup." He says to the girl.

"Uh…we don't have clear cups."

He laughs smugly and shakes his head. He knows Caribou does not have clear cups, but he continues to ask for clear cups. That's the fun part for coffee snob asshole dickheads.

Two guys walk in and ask me if this is a coffee shop? Sigh. "I'll have a double shot and a seltzer water on the side if that's not included." It's not. I watch the guy take a sip of his espresso in our house cup and he's such a fucking faker. He is acting like a Coffee Snob, but the Asshole Dickhead part is real. He asks for a to-go cup and fills it with cream and sugar.

CSADs think it is an affront to espresso to add sugar or milk. And they order like a creepy weirdo Eastern European spy that James Bond or Jason Bourne is about to kill. They try to tell the world they are better than everyone by a smug grin and ordering something we don't serve. If you are such a connoisseur of espresso why the fuck are you in this Caribou? Is there no other coffee shop open on a Saturday morning? They act like they were forced to come in order to be a great guy to their friend. Now they have the arduous task of finding something drinkable on this childlike menu. Their espresso palate is so refined, so delicate, that drinking caffeine is more art than habit.

CSADs love to complain about the taste of the Super Automatic machine! They love the traditional machine because the taste is so incredibly great. Let me tell you, it's not that big of a difference. Sometimes no difference at all and if there is a difference it's usually because the barista fucked up the process on the traditional machine. Coffee Snob Asshole Dickheads love to complain, though, and synonymous with Caribou and Starbucks is the fast machine. And that's my point. Caffeine and speed are what people want! You want some minimum wage coffee idiot messing with the espresso machine? Trust me, you don't. They can hardly get the drinks the right way without adding 10 steps with the espresso preparation. And that's what Starbucks and Caribou have evolved to. Fewer movable parts so the drinks are made consistently and quickly every time. It's actually a good idea and if you have ever been in a rush you want to hug and kiss the Super Automatic. And if you hate the Super Automatic so much, why do you frequent our Caribou? Because you are a dickhead asshole.

CSADs have a great presence on Internet review sites and they love to complain when a greeter at Caribou doesn't know their Italian or fancy term for something fancy. Why do you still frequent Caribou if they know we don't know their terminology and they don't like the service? They wouldn't have anyone to look down upon. Just like the bitchy regulars who order an impossible to make perfect drink, CSADs frequent Caribou to give themselves something to complain about. And they know their caffeine will be served fast, unlike the fancy coffee shop French bakery across the street. From a Google review of a Caribou:

"I ask for "café au lait." She has no clue what I am talking about. The girl, barely old enough to drive it looked like, called over the "manager." They still couldn't figure out what is was!"

This dickhead could have solved the whole incident by saying, "coffee with steamed milk." That's not the way of the CSADs! They love to mock and humiliate a poor high school girl trying to make some money.

I have had this very situation occur and we didn't know what the guy wanted. CSAD are above explaining what is in a drink. This particular asshole just kept shaking his head at poor Leslie, not telling us what this mysterious Italian sounding concoction had in it. "What exactly is in it?" I ask.

"If you have to ask, you don't know and you don't know how to prepare it. Which is kind of important." The smug laugh follows. And he eye rolls to the woman with him. I have to stop myself from asking the woman if that impresses her? I weep for our future if it does.

"How about a large Americano on the house?" Special cup!

CSADs complain about the workers in Caribou and Starbucks. The workers are too young, or too new, or too old and slow, or don't know enough about the history of coffee and espresso, or are just plain someone they don't like because they don't know their coffee asshole lingo. Let me tell you CSADs elitist swine, we are working here for money and a livelihood. A small percentage of us love people, love coffee, love coffee shops, and some realize they are good at the whole multi-tasking thing. Some of us like people and some us do like the customer service people interaction. But does it look like we studied for years and years in Italy to perfect our craft? Do you think we have PhD's in espresso and this is our life's work? Do you think we make $500,000 a year to do this?

The last telltale sign of CSADs is no tip no matter how far we went to make what they wanted. We just can't ever deserve it! They really are just people who are unhappy with their lives and want to torture the people who are forced to interact with them.

After I started working at Caribou, I started reading and watching anything I could to find out about coffee at my local Barnes and Noble and Netflix. What I found, and pains me to no end, is that CSADs are the defining voice in books and movies about anything coffee related. It pissed me off to no end! The basic argument of the coffee snob dickhead asshole is the world is ending because Starbucks is taking over. The world isn't ending. Americans want their caffeine fast and tasting good.

Starbucked: A Double Tall Tale of Caffeine, Commerce, and Culture by Taylor Clark is my favorite coffee book about the history of Howard Schultz and Starbucks. I almost didn't read the book when I realized in Taylor's book dedication he is a Coffee Snob Asshole Dickhead. "To Gina, my little sister, a great lover of coffee–even if she drowns it in vanilla syrup." *Yes, that awful tasting vanilla!*

Mr. Clark has two points that help my argument that customers only care about caffeine and speed of service. One, Starbucks opens new Starbucks across the street from each other constantly and it increases business. Why? People want their caffeine and they want it quick.

Taylor also writes in 1989 there were 585 coffee houses in America. Now how many do you guess there are? 24,000! Fifty-seven percent of these are what Clark calls "mom and pops." "Paradoxically," he writes, "the surest way to boost sales at your mom-and-pop cafe may be to have a Starbucks move in next door."[1] My point is that there are plenty of fucking places for you CSADs to go! Leave us alone in a morning rush asking for a handcrafted espresso in a house cup on trienta setting! Three reasons CSADs keep coming back to Caribou and Starbucks are speed of service, caffeine, and it gives them something to bitch about!

Starbucks has 18,000 stores and Caribou has roughly 600 and Peete's Coffee has 200ish. The real competition to Starbucks, and all coffee houses, are gas stations and McDonalds. Holidays and Super Americas are getting better at packaging up caffeine quickly. Many gas stations have coffee for just $1 for a large and you can add chocolate or any mix-in you want for free. McDonalds already has the infrastructure in place. Fast, easy, built in drive-thru, and a million stores. I asked Christian if he was worried about all the competition. Caribou doesn't have drive-thru's in older stores. Christian felt the quality of our service and the fact that our coffee was the freshest would keep us going. I knew that customers liked our service, but at the end of the day, they only cared about caffeine and speed of service. I worried about Caribou and its employees.

The New York Times reviewed <u>Starbucked</u> and it was very surreal experience for me because a Coffee Snob Asshole Dickhead wrote the book and it was reviewed by a Coffee Snob Asshole Dickhead named PJ O'Rourke. PJ dices up <u>Starbucked</u> because it's the cool thing for a reviewer to do, and he also doesn't think it is very well written. He mocks Mr. Clark's similes. PJ may be exposing himself as the worst of the worst Coffee Snob Asshole Dickheads:

---

[1] Taylor Clark, *Starbucked: A Double Tall Tale of Caffeine, Culture and Commerce* (Little, Brown and Company: 2007), 314

"After that, Clark discusses rumors that Starbucks deliberately sells bitter, burnt-tasting coffee so that customers will order its more expensive syrupy, milky concoctions (which I think are truly undrinkable)."[2]

Really, PJ? You think warm milk, espresso, and a little vanilla, or chocolate is truly undrinkable. Truly undrinkable? Bullshit! My dream is to have PJ drink a straight shot of espresso and a mocha while hooked up to a lie detector. Get over yourself, you ruling elitist dickhead. Why the fuck would you not want a Mint Condition over a cup of coffee? At least say it's because of the calories but don't say it's because you hate flavor. You are an idiot, PJ, and probably not that cool to hang out with. Straight espresso drinkers are altogether weird. PJ seems pretty normal though:

"He (referring to Mr. Clark) both appreciates the 'Starbucks experience' (whose advantages elude many of us 60-year-olds)"[3]

PJ just can't wrap his head around why someone would want the "Starbucks experience"? How about great-tasting caffeine, convenient locations, fast and friendly service, and a place to hang out with friends for awhile? PJ probably can't be bothered with the masses. I envision the delicate genius' assistant being forced to get the Starbucks drink, and hide it in a fancy coffee mug. PJ complains it's a little cold and asks for the change back. Sixteen cents, as his assistant sighs.

How Starbucks Saved My Life: A Son of Privilege Learns to Live Like Everyone Else by Michael Gates Gill was reviewed by the Minneapolis Star Tribune as "A wake-up call." After reading it I wonder if they got their books mixed up? I was interested in reading the book because I was going through the process of becoming coffee shop trained. I wanted to know if everyone thought it was as awful as me. I wanted to know how someone else saw the whole thing. The writer Michael Gates Gill, son of the New Yorker critic Brendan Gill, (whoever the hell that is), lost his high paying job as an advertising executive. He was sitting in a Starbucks while they were doing a career fair–the same cattle call for interviews as I went through. He is noticed by the store manager and later hired. From there Michael's story gets....weird. As I read the book a few observations jumped out at me from a coffee shop barista/greeter/manager point of view. I tried not to judge

---

[2] O'Rourke, P.J. (2007, December 16). Venti Capitalists. New York Times. Retrieved from http://www.nytimes.com/2007/12/16/books/review/O-Rourke-t.html?pagewanted=all

[3] O'Rourke, P.J. (2007, December 16). Venti Capitalists. New York Times. Retrieved from http://www.nytimes.com/2007/12/16/books/review/O-Rourke-t.html?pagewanted=all

Michael as a parent because he seems to be a pretty awful one. He has four adult kids and recently had a baby with a woman. And doesn't seem to have much interest in any of them.

First off, Michael refers to his mom as "mother," which is a huge red flag for weirdness.

Michael says he had worked at Starbucks for two months and hadn't worked the register. He'd been cleaning all the time? His training was a failure and the manager should have been fired. Or something altogether weird was going on.

He claims all he did for two months was clean, and he was in charge of cleaning! He is so proud he has a place at Starbucks. But clean what for 20 hours a week? He would at least be filling cups, filling coffee, cleaning the bar. He doesn't say that though. He is afraid to go anywhere near the register or the bar.

Michael goes to a tax accountant who has to point out that he is eating at a fancy restaurant called "Oyster Bar" on his American Express. I don't get lunch. Nor have time nor money to eat at restaurants for lunch. And if you need to go to a tax accountant to be told not to eat at restaurants on your American Express credit card you are a fucking idiot. I laugh at the title of the book thinking about his meeting with his accountant. "A Son of Privilege Learns to Live Like Everyone Else" my ass! In the book he is finally forced to be greeter.

Michael describes his first days as greeter and EVERYONE orders correctly. He also says they introduce themselves to him. I had maybe two people my whole career introduce themselves by name and those were both managers of stores nearby. And they both later asked me to donate free coffee or give a discount on coffee.

"Here at Starbucks both the partners and guests seemed to agree tacitly that everyone should be treated with respect and dignity."[4] I laughed out loud reading that and thought about throwing the book away.

Then he describes three greeters and one barista, Crystal, the heroine of his novel. In a morning rush in New York City? One barista? And he said he got a 10-minute break? In a morning rush your only break is to get a quick piss in. But often there is no time for that.

"I had the realization that Starbucks was giving people not only unique health benefits but also encouragement to make sure they took care of themselves."[5] I have worked for numerous companies and can't remember when I was encouraged to take care of myself. Except maybe to get dollars

---

[4] Michael Gates Gill, How Starbucks Saved My Life (Gotham Books: 2007), 138
[5] Michael Gates Gill, How Starbucks Saved My Life (Gotham Books: 2007), 140

off my health coverage if I belonged to a club. Maybe in a HR pamphlet that no one reads. And then I think, is this a Starbucks propaganda pamphlet?

Soon Michael commits his first act of theft–eating a raspberry scone with coworker Joann. Christian's wife worked for Starbucks and she has some fun horror stories that oddly enough are the exact opposite of Michael's experience. She was working and heard a voice through the speaker on the bar wondering why she was putting some chocolate chips in a bag. They were watching. Not at Michael's Starbucks, though.

It is now September/October and Michael describes learning to close the store at night. Um, what? He hasn't fucking closed yet? Nor has he been on the bar? Are they giving him preferential treatment because he is white? What the hell is going on? He hasn't closed the store nor has been on the bar, but he is working at least 20 hours a week? What the hell is he doing the whole time?

Michael says that the partners (other employees) "made no special allowances for him."[6] Except of course he hadn't been on the bar or closed the store. Or done anything really, but clean and run the register.

Michael writes he, "noticed that many of our guests treated partners with extra courtesy. It was as if they wanted to make sure we weren't working too hard."[7] Bwahahahahahahaha. That's me laughing a lot.

Michael is asked by a customer, "How are they treatin' ya?" He replies, "Great people, great coffee and great benefits!" Later in the paragraph he adds, "If I or any other partners had replied in the negative, I got the sense that they were ready to do battle on our behalf."[8]

Let me clear one thing up with you, Michael: They were not. The guy was being folksy. Second, this is where I officially suspected this book is an advertising gig by Starbucks. This guy's story is not adding up. Although, it makes Starbucks come off as a bunch of idiots so you would think some lawyer somewhere would be like, "This book is probably a really bad idea for our rep."

On page 176 he writes on his first store closing a guy pulls a knife on him. Not to rob him but because he asked him to leave as it was past 12:30 p.m. And what do Michael and his co-worker do after a knife is pulled? Keep closing of course! Not a call to the police, not a call to the home office, not a call to the district manager, not a call even to the store manager. Business as usual. Michael blames himself for trying to take control of the

[6] Michael Gates Gill, How Starbucks Saved My Life (Gotham Books: 2007), 146
[7] Michael Gates Gill, How Starbucks Saved My Life (Gotham Books: 2007), 157
[8] Michael Gates Gill, How Starbucks Saved My Life (Gotham Books: 2007), 158

situation. A guy pulled a fucking knife on you dude! Review the cameras, anything? What if the guy killed someone later? He just keeps working.

A few years ago, a group went around the Lake store area early in the morning holding up Caribous, Starbucks, and other service industry places. Beck was on with a assistant store manager at the time. Right when they unlocked the doors the guys came around the side of the building and forced them in back. The burglar tied Beck to a chair with duct tape and she was worried about dying, getting raped, and never seeing her boyfriend again. The new manager couldn't remember the safe code because he was new and he was nervous. Beck was worried the guy was going to shoot him because he was getting upset. They managed to get the safe open, all for about $600 dollars. Beck was fine, but the new manager never recovered. He was nervous and quit a few days later. It's a traumatizing experience when our world is confronted with violence.

However, Michael didn't tell anyone about his violent encounter. Odd.

Months pass and Michael still hasn't been on the bar. This is impossible. The hiring machine of the service industry wouldn't allow it. The service industry has too much turnover. As soon as you hire someone they are on the clock to contribute. Caribou had three buddy shifts then the employee is live in the schedule. Training someone for six months isn't possible.

Turnover hits the service industry quickly; the good and bad employees leave. Michael would be one of the senior members of the store soon. Store Manager Crystal would depend on him to fill out the schedule and work rushes.

We realize Michael is a Coffee Snob Asshole Dickhead. "But believe it or not, Michael, many partners don't like coffee that much," said Crystal.[9] No shit! Why would you drink straight coffee for free if you could drink anything in the store you wanted for free? Store Manager Crystal makes Michael a "coffee master", but he still doesn't make drinks or espresso. Or maybe even coffee?

Michael plans a coffee night and his regular customers arrive to sample and learn about coffee. Uh huh. They came back at night huh? Right.

When Michael meets Abe, the Starbucks district manager. He doesn't mention the knife incident. Nor that he cannot make a drink on the bar.

But Crystal wins manager of the quarter at Starbucks, even though she didn't address a violence free workplace issue, and Michael cannot run the bar.

Throughout the book Michael points he is old and the rest of the world is young. Most coffee shops have old people though. I hired Marge and she was as old as Michael. The service industry spits out everyone and you have

---

[9] Michael Gates Gill, How Starbucks Saved My Life (Gotham Books: 2007), 179

to feed the machine any way you can. Age, sex, race, religion be damned. If you can contribute, there is a place for you.

Finally it is February and Michael starts to learn the bar. The store would have turned over twice already at least. I think it is easy to say that Starbucks wrote the book for publicity, but if they did they really came off like a bunch of assholes. Their hero comes off like an asshole. It really does not paint a picture of the coffee shop experience. It's the coffee shop experience for someone who never worked with real customers. It seems like they would all be nice, but they are not.

Did Caribou save my life? No, but it definitely changed it. Here is what I got out of working at Caribou: The job is hell. It's a neverending list of tasks, constantly repeated. But I got better at it and now nothing can intimidate me. I have stared down a morning rush, understaffed, in the weeds, and battled back. I am a god. I am fucking Superman. I can face anything in my life and know that I have been through much fucking worse. My perspective in any shitty environment is simply that, at least I'm not on the bar with Kirsten at the Lake store! On a fucking sunny Saturday!

I meet people now who have worked in a coffee shop and we give each the knowing nod. I know the hell you've been through and that it didn't break you. I stuck it out for two reasons. My fiancé and my son. I would do anything for them. I needed money and insurance.

And when I think about <u>How Starbucks Saved My Life</u>, I think Michael missed out. He didn't really face his fears, he didn't make any life changes, he really never hit rock bottom. He never took a life inventory. He never made a change. And he didn't show you, the reader, what a coffee shop is truly like. And his book makes me think a lot about how the world truly does not see what a coffee shop is like. Michael didn't do anyone in the service industry any favors. If you recall in my story I had to fight to get time on the bar to learn. Michael's story is the version if I hid from everything I was scared of and had enough people working with me to make it happen. Then I found out Tom Hanks is making the book into a movie! My only hope is David Fincher reads this book.

My favorite CSAD is Howard Schultz of all people! Who I basically am in debt to for my livelihood. From Howard's book <u>Pour Your Heart Into It</u>:

> "Schultz recounts the story of how Starbucks got into the granita business with Frappuccino, in spite of his vehement objections. As with nonfat milk, Schultz's first reaction to the idea of selling cold blended drinks was one of horror. Talk about a lack of authenticity! He was sure the Italians weren't selling milkshake-like concoctions with their fine espresso, and he wasn't interested in going down the

road either. Never mind that customers in California were clamoring for it and some were heading to competitors to get it. But thanks to a determined employee, Schultz did finally see the light. And like virtually all the decisions recounted in <u>Pour Your Heart Into It</u>, this one turned out to have been touched by Midas. The summer it was introduced, the Frappuccino (Starbucks' proprietary version of a granita) "accounted for 11 % of summer sales and the stock price hit a record high." Its first full year on the market it brought in $52 million."

So the biggest CSAD in the world created this whole thing! *Noodle that one.*

If Howard didn't step aside and give the people what they wanted I would be standing next to some asshole in a coffee shop forcing down espresso with no flavor. Thank you, Howard!

You add a little milk, a little cream, some sugar, a little vanilla and the coffee is going to make the caffeine go down real nice. Each American dollar spent is a vote. Starbucks obviously is everywhere, but do you know the number one coffee made at home? Folgers. Add a little Nestles Coffee Mate and boom! You got yourself a nice little caffeinated drink at the right price. It's served as fast as you can make it.

CHAPTER 24
SUPER SIZED CARIBOU

Dear customer who wants to know how many carbs are in every fucking thing on the menu,
   If you cared about your weight that much you would not be having a large Chocolate Cooler and an apple fritter. You're already at like 1400 fucking calories, so what the fuck do some carbs really matter?

You might not know it to look at me, but I'm a killer. I make caffeine drinkers fat. I'm really good at killing people. We call it upselling and add-ons.
   Our focus and key metric at Caribou is how many larges we sell to every 100 customers. I sell roughly 35 to 40 large beverages out of 100, and there certainly is more room for improvement. Upselling, adding on flavor shots, and bakery equals more sales and profit. And more guts and heart attacks too. It leads to more big butts, little pouches, puffy cheeks, and clogged arteries.
   Would you like a large for only 30 cents more? How about a reduced fat banana bread to get you going in the morning? I change my voice for different upsells. My "makes sense" voice: "Would you like a large for only 30 cents more? It has another shot of espresso." My overly cheery voice: "How about a Triple Berry Muffin! Or would you like to treat yourself to a large for only 30 cents more?" That always gets people on days that are going to be rough. Like Mondays, or Tuesdays, or Wednesdays, and definitely Fridays. And Saturday and Sundays always! The customer approaches the register. "Big day today?" Every nugget of information they give me is inside information and helps me deicide what upsell will work.
   Liz and I figure out that about two and half pumps equals 70 to 90 calories. A woman gets a small latte every day and I upsell her to medium and then to large. So if a woman gets a large latte and I say, "would you like to add a shot of vanilla today?" She says yes. That's another 200ish calories. Then she makes that her everyday drink. 200 extra calories a day. Then I

sample the reduced fat banana bread and she makes that the start of her day. She's dying slowly. Add another 420 calories. I've added over 600 calories to this woman's day. It was easy! And probably took 10 years off her life.

Caribou, in a stroke of evil genius, and creating a selling culture to us math idiots, made every medium drink 30 cents less than a large drink. And every large drink 60 cents more than every small drink. No tricky math needed to upsell. Including coolers, which are a slam bang easy upsell on hot days. But for that extra 30 cents you can get a lot more calories. That's not even counting the Caribou bakery upsell. That's where the calories really pack a punch all in the name of healthy, classy, upper crust of society frequenting Caribou customers. Now all fast food is shit, you'll say. But this is sold under the guise of gourmet food and sandwiches. And then the "healthy food" was added. Yes, healthy.

I had never thought about the calories in Caribou drinks and bakery until one day Gisele told me I was getting fat. *I am getting fat.* I ate most of my meals from the shop, but I stayed away from the cookies and brownies. I stuck with the yogurt, oatmeal and the reduced fat menu. Customers asked once in awhile how many calories something or other had, but I'd give my "I can look it up if you truly need it, but we are fucking busy" look. All calories are on the website too! My one indulgence really was I liked a mocha after rush in the morning. I knew coffee didn't have calories, but what about all this other stuff? That's when I realized I was a killer.

Large milk chocolate mocha: 620 calories. Jesus Christ I yelled when I saw that! Some days I'd have two mochas if I worked a long shift. The mochas are 600 calories for white and 580 for dark chocolate. No wonder I'm getting a gut!

So I looked into my delicious healthy alternatives at Caribou:

Apple Cinnamon Oatmeal: 360 calories. 24 grams of sugar, but also 16 grams of protein. Hey workout buffs and health nuts!

Blueberry Almond Oatmeal: 410 calories. One customer told me her vet told her to stop giving her dog our blueberry muffins because the dog was getting fat. That's not a good sign.

Classic Plain Oatmeal: 300 calories. I didn't understand how this little amount of oatmeal could have 300 calories. I'd eaten oatmeal my whole life. Liz reminded me my oatmeal at home doesn't have a tablespoon of sugar added. Oh yeah.

Honey Almond Oatmeal: 360 calories. Ah the nutritious sounding honey and almond oatmeal!

My oatmeal of choice was the Maple Brown Sugar Crunch and it was the most popular oatmeal. I cringed as I looked up the calories. Maple Brown Sugar Crunch: 380 calories. Not that bad! I was prepared for a lot worse. It does have sugar in the title.

Actually, I take that back, the most popular oatmeal is Very Berry oatmeal and another Caribou healthy catch phrase: Very Berry.

Very Berry Oatmeal: 480 calories. The berries include strawberry, shit, and sugar. 34 grams of sugar. Anything is good with 34 grams of sugar.

I remember the first time I made yogurts at the Lake store, I scooped out two scoops of yogurt, then an ice cream spoonful of the topping, then another scoop of yogurt, and Kirsten and Beck fought over who could lick the spoon. I love my yogurt at home, I thought, but the only thing I fight over is the brownie or cake batter spoon. Before I looked up the yogurt calories, I asked Liz how many calories she thought our yogurt might contain.

"Hmm. The standard calories for yogurts at the grocery seems to be 80 to 120 calories." I agreed with her. I knew Gisele bought yogurt that was 100 calories.

"But," Liz added, "they have to make them taste better in the restaurant biz. I'll say 150 calories. That would be fair I think." I agreed.

Blueberry Yogurt: 270 calories. 8 grams of protein, 35 grams of sugar. How can this little cup of yogurt have so many fucking calories?! And why is it my favorite? Because I'm eating healthy?

Apple Cinnamon Yogurt: 270 calories. 6.7 ounces. You could eat three of the Yoplait fatfree yogurts or this one?

Very Berry Yogurt: The most popular yogurt and without a doubt must be the most healthy yogurt. Unnamed berries must be good for us? 320 calories. 48 grams of sugar.

Liz and I stare in shock at each other. Mentally calculating how many Very Berry Yogurts we've eaten in the past. A lot.

Now let's get onto the specialty drinks of Caribou and where every morning I upsell you to a large because it's an extra shot of espresso! The best deal in the house! We only sell larges at Caribou! Our store is ranked daily by how many larges we sell out of 100 customers and I am the best at it. I sell over 50 larges to every 100 customers. The thing that gets in the way the most of selling larges? Goddamn hippies who bring their own cups for fucking sustainability. Those can't be upgraded to larges. Saving the planet and ruining my upsell numbers!

Latte, hot (hot beverage cups are 20 ounces): 240 calories with 2 percent milk. If you add a flavor shot add 90 calories. You like that winter specialty drink the Cafe Canela? That's because it's a latte with spice and sugar and five pumps of vanilla. A large Cafe Canela shoots up to 410 calories.

The Chocolate Latte: I hate people that order chocolate lattes because it's a mocha without the whipped cream and it's annoying to froth milk. It ruins our flow at the greeter and bar. Chocolate latte shoots you up to 600 calories for a large. 460 for a medium.

The Caramel High Rise: 390 calories, and the large has 460 calories. Why? A basic latte but add caramel shots, whipped cream on top, and more caramel drizzle. Caramel is good! The favorite drink of our yoga crowd, no wonder the instructor encourages them to keep coming. Get fat at Caribou and come back to yoga to get skinny.

Chai Tea Latte: The drink of choice for you fucking health nuts. 380 calories for a large.

Pomegranate Vanilla Oolong Tea Latte: Basically all sugar for you hippie wannabe health nuts. 38 grams of sugar and 340 calories. Sugar Milk should be it's real name.

The Hot Apple Blast: Promoted as a fall drink and hints at healthiness. Fall leaves, crisp apples and Grandma's house! Let's go leafing, but when you add the whip and the cinnamon and the Caramel and the drizzle we are at 520 calories.

Caribou is known for their hot chocolate. People come in and say they love the chocolate and it's sooooooo good. That's because a large hot chocolate with milk chocolate has 700 calories. It had better be good for 700 calories! And for you overprotective parents who will not let your kids have caffeine, the kid's hot chocolate has 430 calories and that's for 12 oz. Parent of the year my ass! "Ben, I wouldn't let my kid have that," you are yelling at the page! I order the Reindeer drinks. Kid friendly and healthy.

The Reindeer: Milk and cherry flavor shot. 390 calories and 53 grams of sugar. Jesus fuck! No wonder your kid just swore at Grandma! It was the sugar!

The Mint Condition: Mint flavor shots, white chocolate, whipped cream, and Andes mints on top. It's a favorite! Anything could be a favorite for 830 fucking calories. 700 calories for a medium.

Cold Press with White Chocolate: 340 calories in a large. Everything is a little better with white chocolate! Upsell king!

Remember that Regular Latte for a not-so-bad 240 calories? Guess what season it is? Pumpkin season and here at Caribou we mix the shit out of pumpkin into fucking everything. And do you know what pumpkin is? Sugar, sugar, and some pumpkin flavoring!

Pumpkin Latte: 520 calories for a large!

Pumpkin White Chocolate Mocha: 920 calories. Talk about sugar and caffeine rush! I call it a "cugar" rush! Or caffeine rush. Almost half your daily allotted calories in one 20-ounce drink. We love our fucking pumpkin at Caribou. Everything is better with pumpkin is one of my favorite and cheesiest upsell lines. It works. How about a piece of pumpkin bread? Pumpkin bread: 430 calories.

The Turtle Mocha: The most popular Caribou specialty drink. Here's why: Caramel syrup, milk chocolate, espresso and milk, whipped cream, and not just caramel drizzle on top, but Snickers bits on top too! 810 calories for Caribou's most popular specialty drink.

The Berry White Mocha: This delicious combination of raspberry or cherry flavoring and white chocolate with whipped cream and white chocolate chips runs 570 calories for a medium. So when I suggest a large for 30 cents more? Say hello to 700 calories.

The Campfire Mocha: A super popular drink with marshmallow flavor shots and marshmallow bits and whipped cream on the top! What fun. A medium runs you 590 calories and when I upsell you to a large it's 730 calories. (These estimates are all with milk chocolate as Caribou policy is to make each drink with milk chocolate unless a customer specifies white or dark.)

Vanilla White Chocolate Mocha: Each Caribou employee has their Lex Luthor/Kryptonite drink. A drink you always forget to make correctly and can't find the button for on the register. The Vanilla White Chocolate Mocha is my Lex Luther drink. I remember everyone who has ordered it and my mind thinks they want a white chocolate mocha with a vanilla extra shot. That comes out more expensive than pressing the White Chocolate Mocha button. It made me realize I wasn't smart. A medium has 570 calories and a large has 690. The difference between a White Chocolate Mocha and a Vanilla White Chocolate Mocha? 90 calories of vanilla flavored sugar.

Caribou unveils a sparkling refresher drink selection and it is advertised as a healthy alternative to soda. Caribou envisions their customer getting a latte in the morning and then stopping by again the afternoon for their refresher, or bringing the family on the weekend. So what exactly is this healthy alternative to soda? Healthy? You decide: (Large iced Caribou cups are 24 ounces):

- *Berry Black Tea:* 230 calories in a large. 53 grams of sugar.
- *Very Berry Juice:* 210 calories in a large. 46 grams of sugar.
- *Mint Lime White Tea:* 320 calories in a large. 78 grams of sugar.
- *Green Tea Lemonade:* 280 calories in a large and 69 grams of sugar.

- *Lemon Ginger Pomegranate:* Do you know why you like this one the most and it's the most popular? 350 calories and 77 grams of sugar.

Now how about one of Caribou's delicious and healthy Strawberry Banana Smoothies which are sometimes called Northern Light Smoothies, but are not low sugar or fat.

Strawberry Banana Smoothie: A not-so-crazy 420 calories. Not bad. Although, it contains 96 grams of sugar. That's why your kid just ran through that wall.

Mango Orange Key Lime Smoothie: 540 calories and 123 grams of sugar. Little Susie gets really energized after a smoothie!

If you really want to talk calories that lets talk caribou bakery and the caribou coolers. Two things that people definitely get together. Coolers in the morning are very popular because it is delicious way to mask the flavor of coffee and espresso. It's like caffeine in a birthday cake and ice cream.

Maine Blueberry Muffin: 620 calories. For one fucking muffin! So when you are yelling at your kid to finish his muffin, remember he could have two chocolate chips cookies instead. And Dear customer who asks if they are really from Maine or did they just get here from Maine, shut up.

Carrot Cake: 510 calories. The healthy Carrot Cake!

Triple Berry Muffin: 600 calories. "What do you have that's healthy?" My standard answers are the Triple Berry Muffin and the Reduced Fat Banana Bread.

"Reduced Fat" Banana Bread: 420 calories. You read that right. A Chocolate Chip Cookie is less calories than Reduced Fat Banana Bread. Did they make a 1,000 calories banana bread and then reduced it? Claiming we reduced it!

Monkey Bread: 360 calories. I have no idea how they fit so many calories into something so small. Check one out! They are just so small.

Black and Blueberry Cobbler: I don't know how this has 360 calories because it tastes like paper. It looks so good though! It's an easy upsell to anyone who hasn't bought it before.

Toffee Fudge Brownie: This is really good but looks like shit. At 470 calories, it's easy to taste good. So when you have that cup of coffee and I sweetly say, "How about a brownie to go with it?" 470 calories for one little brownie! Bam!

Milk Chocolate Chip Cookie: 340 calories.

Oatmeal Raisin Cookie: 290.

So how many times have you been to Caribou or your favorite bakery and said, "I'm going to watch my weight today, so I'll have the Chocolate

Chip Cookie?" The cookies have less calories than the muffins. Almost less than the yogurt. And definitely less than the Reduced Fat Banana Bread. So before you give your kid shit for wanting a cookie for breakfast, look to the science!

The three most popular bakery items at Caribou are the Lemon Poppy Seed Bread, Apple Fritter, and the Cinnamon Coffee Cake. Whenever a customer orders a piece, I always ask if they want another piece for later? You bet your ass they do! All three are good size portions, but nothing too huge. You don't look like a fatty eating two at a time. Sometimes I track my upsells for the morning by calories. It adds up quick.

Lemon Poppyseed: 470 calories. It has frosting, but somehow people think it's healthy. Many regular customers get two pieces and it's my go-to sale when someone is standing at the bakery case holding up the fucking line. I've never had anyone complain about it, but then no one knows it has 470 calories.

Apple Fritter: 490 calories. It's apple based, so it must be healthy. So all of you health nuts that I upsell are really not doing your healthy selves any favors.

Cinnamon Coffee Cake: 540! 540 calories packed into this small piece of cake should be illegal. I could eat 10 pieces of the coffee cake it's so good. Jake and I split an entire tray of them one day. And we could have done it again! This shit is like crack for Caribou customers! God I could go for a piece right now!

The easiest upsell in the world is the Caribou Cooler. Caribou's answer to the frappuccino is good on a hot day and a great deal. A large is only 60 cents more than a small. On a hot day that's all I have to say. Mediums to large are so easy too because it's four ounces more for 30 cents. I have upsold more Caribou Coolers than I could ever track. But if I did keep track I know I would have sold literally millions of calories! I said it, millions!

Straight Coffee Cooler: 380 calories. No whip, no nothing. Not unreasonable calorie wise.

The Apple Blast Cooler: 430 calories and 78 grams of sugar. That's the healthy one.

Vanilla Cooler: 610. You're thinking that's not that bad. 610 calories. In one 10-minute span you can drink just under one-third of all the calories you should have all day. And this has no nutrients what-so-ever.

Milk Chocolate Cooler: 780 calories. One of the most popular coolers, it's the classic. It's like a big glass of chocolate milk you remember from your childhood. Except this has seven times the calories.

Dark Chocolate Cooler: 690. Whenever I get the "I don't know about that, "frown" on my Cooler upsells, I suggest dark chocolate. The healthy alternative! "I heard It's good for your heart," I say earnestly.

White Chocolate Cooler: 750. "Oh you don't like dark chocolate? White chocolate is a little better for you than milk chocolate." By 30 calories I don't say.

Caramel Cooler: 610 calories . And you're probably thinking hmm, the caramel is the healthy one! 97 grams of sugar. Sugar, milk, ice, and Caribou's secret Cooler mix that seems just to be more sugar.

Now we are getting to the big boys. Not only were these drinks high in calories, but some cost over $5 a pop. So if I could sell a fancy Cooler it raised our average ticket. Then a bakery item? Home run!

Berry White Mocha Cooler: 920 calories. Make that with milk chocolate and it's 950 calories. Yes, you read that right. You thought Berry and White and you thought healthy? Healthier at least? Nope.

Black Forest Cooler: 770 calories and 127 grams of sugar. It's actually just a Dark Chocolate Cooler with a bunch of pumps of cherry flavoring. More sugar!

Campfire Mocha Cooler: 940. 140 grams of sugar. Yeah! Another big boy with marshmallow flavoring, milk chocolate, and marshmallow bits on top with more chocolate sauce! 940 calories, but this one at least you know is bad for you. I think.

Mint Condition Cooler: This was Jake's shift drink of choice. "Hey did you know that's 920 calories?" He didn't believe me. "Holy shit!" he yelled "No wonder I'm getting fat." And just like that Jake was off the Mint Condition Cooler. 920 extra calories a day does not keep the doctor away.

Turtle Mocha Cooler: 920 calories. 141 grams of sugar. Ka pow! 920 calories. So, you can have two of them and eat nothing else all day. And some people do.

Cookies and Cream Snowdrift: No caffeine for the kid right? Nope. Although it has 920 calories for a large. 114 grams of sugar. Your kid just punched his hand through the back window. Now you now why!

I was making change for a nice guy regular who gets Mint Condition Coolers and I asked him if he had a busy day at work today. He said, "Unfortunately yes," and I said, "Well that can be good and bad, but it's good to be busy." He kind of said yes. I looked up and saw his work name badge and he was a sex offender parole officer. I started laughing and we both laughed. The guy is super nice.

He is pretty big and labors while breathing when he talks. I want to tell him these Coolers are killing him. Almost 1000 calories a pop. I don't want to even mention the bakery to him. That's the last thing he needs to get hooked on. No one believes me when I say Caribou is slowly killing the neighborhood. We mock McDonald's, but McDonald's isn't the trendy do-gooder like Caribou. McDonald's isn't a part of the Rainforest Alliance like Caribou. McDonald has all Spanish speaking people working there. McDonald's stopped the supersize movement because of the supersize movie. Caribou gets a free pass because it's just coffee. It's a lot more than that.

Christian told me that he got so many OSAT comments about how the Triple Berry Muffin were reduced fat and tasted like shit. They switched to the Regular Triple Berry. We still pretend they are healthy and customers are happy. It seems like the whole menu is like that. The moral of the story is rich people are getting fat too.

CHAPTER 25
ON SERVING IN REAL LIFE

Dear customer that tells me I should write a book about all my wacky coffee shop stories,
       That's not that bad of an idea.

What I find fascinating about Barb Ehrenreich's book <u>Nickel and Dimed</u> is that she tried to re-create my life. And then write about it. I was living my life and wrote about it later.

I worked every job Barb wrote about and I also managed most of the positions Barb worked. But she missed millions of little points and details that could not be re-created, but needed to be lived to understand the magnitude of the situations. She was rich, white, and had lived a life of privilege, maybe middle class privilege, but privilege nonetheless. And what I found even more fascinating was that everyone loves the book. It's on Barnes and Noble's must read table, and summer reading lists, and it's taught in schools from high school to college. The book is a part of our culture.

But Barb missed a lot because she could not create the whys of life. We know Barb wrote the story from her perspective, a rich white woman who tries to get by on minimum wage jobs. But she always had something to fall back on; a lot of money and her regular life. She didn't truly know what it's like to not have money or a place to stay. And she definitely didn't know what it took to navigate her way in the workplace with people who have nowhere else to go.

The harshest scorn in her adventures is saved for management. Which is so much fucking harder to do it's depressing. And maybe most importantly Barb did not have to work a shitty job to support kids, which would make her experiences look tame. She didn't have to work two jobs so her son could play an instrument, go on a school trip, and shop at the outlet center instead of the Goodwill, or worry every day that by working a shitty job she was not giving her kids simply an even playing field with other kids.

Barb made funny points and simple arguments that you, sitting in your nice home or school, nodded when you read. She put a face to awful managers and bad corporations, she told the story of nice people not getting a fair break. Barb put a nice face to a name of someone who we thought was getting screwed over. Life is not fair, but sometimes it is, and the world needs its ditch diggers too. And I can say this because I am a ditch digger.

I have been my whole life. Call it fate, bad luck, laziness, or whatever, I am the people Barb writes about. I started out at shitty jobs and now I manage at shitty jobs. Although because she was trying to imitate my life, she had a different mindset or outlook than someone living it. She tried to befriend the people I was, I know, I worked with, and that I hired and fired. And she wanted to try to live like us. And until this writing no one has ever said a thing disputing or giving a different perspective. So from a ditch digger point of view these are my thoughts on her story.

Barb's first chapter "Serving in Florida" is her foray into the service industry. Barb's first task is to find a job.

"My next stop is Winn-Dixie, the supermarket, which turns out to have a particularly onerous application process, featuring a twenty-minute "interview" by computer since, apparently, no human on the premises is deemed capable of representing the corporate point of view."[10]

The computer application/interview process is the first step in weeding out idiots. It's really like a first-first interview. If you can't pass the computer part we don't want you. I know it seems harsh, but it is true. At Caribou applicants would tell me my store was not on the list of stores to apply to. "What's your name, so I can look for your application?" I was getting their names but I knew not to waste an interview on them. Applicants would tell me they didn't have a computer, so how should they apply? You are showing great problem-solving skills, so I'll just hire you on the spot! How does $100,000 a year sound?

The computer application process weeded out people who might have slipped by and wasted my time. Because that's what an interview is that doesn't lead to a hire. A waste of time. There is no extra time given to hiring. It's a part of the job. So every time I have to do an interview you are getting your caffeine slower. Sort of.

Barb questions the strategy of the computer test. "Then, popping up cunningly out of the blue: How many dollars' worth of stolen goods have I

---

[10] Barbara Ehrenreich, *Nickel and Dimed* (Picador: 2001), 13

purchased in the last year? Would I turn in a fellow employee if I caught him stealing? Finally, 'Are you an honest person?'"[11]

Stealing has different levels of importance in different cultures. If you steal you're not the devil, but from a trying-to-make-money position, it's annoying. And guess what? People answer yes to these questions all the time. And I bet Barb wouldn't mind someone stealing to pay for medicine, or food, or something the thief had deemed important–UNLESS IT WAS FROM HER! Then it's different.

While looking for work Barb uses her small funds for lunch. "I lunch at Wendy's, where $4.99 gets you unlimited refills at the Mexican part of the Super-bar, a comforting surfeit of refried beans and cheese sauce. A teenage employee hands me an application which I fill out, though here, too, the pay is just $6 and change an hour."[12]

First off, everyone knows unlimited buffets in no way save you money. You can't eat five days worth of food in one sitting. It might seem like a good deal to the unpoor, but it's not. Barb would be better off buying a loaf of bread and a jar of peanut butter. Secondly, employers do actually pay based on experience even in minimum wage jobs. So how does she know it pays $6? It might have paid $6.50 with her experience. Is the high school kid who gave her the application giving her this information? Maybe he is making $6, but she'd make more with her experience? Did she talk to a manager? Is she eligible to be a supervisor and make more? The drive-thru people usually get more too. Nope, she left without asking questions.

"Only later will I realize that the want ads are not a reliable measure of the actual jobs available at any particular time. They are, as I should have guessed from Max's comment, the employers' insurance policy against the relentless turnover of the low-wage workforce. Most of the big hotels run ads almost continually, if only to build a supply of applicants to replace the current workers as they drift away or are fired, so finding a job is just a matter of being in the right place at the right time and flexible enough to take whatever is being offered that day."[13]

ABSOFUCKINGLUTLEY!!!

Barb hits my hiring strategy on the head while thinking it is a bad thing. Conventional wisdom says if I need a waitress I will post a position. That

---

[11] Barbara Ehrenreich, Nickel and Dimed (Picador: 2001), 14
[12] Barbara Ehrenreich, Nickel and Dimed (Picador: 2001), 14
[13] Barbara Ehrenreich, Nickel and Dimed (Picador: 2001), 15

doesn't work effectively. You only get the best person to apply while the position was posted. You need to continually interview and find good people. Then work them in and start getting them trained up. Barb complains about this strategy and of course later quits in three weeks, because Barb thinks being hired and trained and then leaving fucks over the "home office" or the faceless company that owns the restaurant. Nope. She leaves her fellow employees and management staff out to fucking dry. What Barb doesn't realize, or care about, is that someone has to do her work and pick up her shifts and she left everyone up shit creek. But Barb doesn't see that because Barb perpetuates the very act that the hiring process is over-compromising for. Her. Noodle that one all you <u>Nickel and Dimed</u> fans!

Later in the chapter, Barb is frustrated at the hiring process. "Three days go by like this and, to my chagrin, no one from the approximately 20 places at which I've applied calls."[14]

Good managers realize Barb is not going to stay working for them for very long. And that's why she doesn't get a call back. Her need for a job is sketchy, she has no work history, and probably something just doesn't seem right. Which is because she is a writer, lying, and the management smell her out and don't call her back.

When Barb is eventually hired by Hearthside restaurant it is leads her book down a particularly bad path. Barb is a bad applicant but bad managers do not know it. A manager asks what is your availability? And she says that's basically why she hired. Remember back to my hiring chapter? Never, ever, ever just hire based on availability.

So she is being hired by a bad manager. Inevitably at a bad place to work. How different would Barb's book be if she were hired by a good manager at a good place to work? But it never would have happened. She would not be hired by a good manager.

"She (Gail) dips into her own tip money to buy biscuits and gravy for an out-of-work mechanic who's used up all his money on dental surgery, inspiring me to pick up the tab for his pie and milk."[15]

He used up his money on dental surgery? And he was at a restaurant? And he got dessert? Who gets dessert at a fucking restaurant if you're poor? This guy hustled them, but I don't understand why Barb didn't just give him the milk and pie. Like steal it. And maybe she would have more money for herself if she didn't buy strangers food.

---

[14] Barbara Ehrenreich, Nickel and Dimed (Picador: 2001), 15
[15] Barbara Ehrenreich, Nickel and Dimed (Picador: 2001), 19

"Sometimes I play with the fantasy that I am a princess who, in penance for some tiny transgression, has undertaken to feed each of her subjects by hand. But the nonprincesses working with me are just as indulgent, even when this means flouting management rules—as to, for example, the number of croutons that can go on a salad (six). 'Put on all you want,' Gail whispers, 'as long as Stu isn't looking.'"[16]

Again, Barb and Gail are actually hard workers! Remember Barb wakes up at 4 a.m. in a cold sweat! Except doing a simple thing like not putting six croutons in a salad. The manager said six croutons is the recipe and gets mad if it's less or more so we don't do what he says. But Barb wakes up at night in a cold sweat about being the best.

How about the manager hoping and praying that the two fucking waitresses don't put more croutons on the fucking salads so he has to fucking address it! Because he has a fucking million other fucking things to do! But the manager is the asshole to Barb.

I've run into the "crouton" situation myself. When I arrived at store number one almost everyone was putting four or five spoonfuls of chocolate chips on the mochas. The Caribou recipe calls for only about seven chocolate chips.

"Why so many?" I asked.

"Because customers like it better," Harold told me. Why did Barb put more than six croutons on the salad? Because she thought more was better.

Is it? It depends on the person. But Caribou decided seven chocolate chips was good. It also makes all mochas uniform from store to store. The recipe will make for consistent taste from barista to barista. The seven chocolate chips makes the drink affordable and cost effective. And it also allows customers to request more or less chocolate chips. And I know when I order chocolate chips every week we will have plenty because we uniformly using the same amount.

This is the same situation with the croutons. Is six too many or to few? Hearthside restaurant has said six is good. Customers can ask for more or less and the salads are uniform from restaurant to restaurants. Pretty simple.

Not to Barb who views controlling croutons as a way for management to throw their might and weight around. Why did I decide on seven chocolate chips and Barb's manager decide on six croutons? Because the fucking company said so. And it's their fucking money and their fucking business. And as a manager that's why I came up with those numbers. Those are the rules, the simple expectations. What is so fucking hard for Barb to put six

---

[16] Barbara Ehrenreich, Nickel and Dimed (Picador: 2001), 19

fucking croutons on salads? Because more is better to her? Everyone thinks their way is better. Follow the fucking rules. And her poor manager tells her six croutons, because the company said six croutons. And so she keeps putting more. Why is she so fucking passionate about theses stupid croutons? Why doesn't she either become the manager and argue to change the rule, or open her own fucking salad restaurant and have a bowlful of fucking croutons?

I'm not defending all managers of the world, but this point illustrates what a shitty job it is to mange people doing shitty jobs. So the manager gets fed up with asking politely to put six croutons on the salad. So he becomes an asshole. Because that fucking asshole waitress keeps putting more croutons on the fucking salad. Then one day he runs out of croutons. His district manager finds out. And the manager gets in trouble for running out of croutons because the district manager doesn't think he can run his business correctly. And the manager gets demoted or fired and can't support his family all because Barb couldn't fucking follow crouton directions.

Barb continues on about the evils of managers. "But everyone knows they have crossed over to the other side, which is, crudely put, corporate as opposed to human. Cooks want to prepare tasty meals, servers want to serve them graciously, but managers are there for only one reason—to make sure that money is made for some theoretical entity, the corporation, which exists far away in Chicago or New York, if a corporation can be said to have a physical existence at all. Reflecting on her career, Gail tells me ruefully that she swore, years ago, never to work for a corporation again. "They don't cut you no slack. You give and you give and they take."[17]

This could not be any further from the truth! If everyone loved doing these shitty jobs you wouldn't need managers and you wouldn't have constant turnover. Managers are there to make sure the shitty jobs get done, and therefore makes it the shittiest job. Barb makes it seem like the restaurant would run seamlessly without a manager there. It wouldn't. I'm not sure how she would think that would happen, but I think at some point she needed a slant for her book. And evil management sounds like a good one. Fucking managers who don't let us put as many croutons on the salad as we want!! Yeah! Wait what?

---

[17] Barbara Ehrenreich, Nickel and Dimed (Picador: 2001), 22

Barb is working hard again, but the manager finds her not working. "Freshen cherries; anything to look busy. When, on a particularly dead afternoon, Stu finds me glancing at a USA Today a customer left behind."[18]

Once again our poor hard working waitress gets caught by the evil manager reading the paper. I have also been in that position. And it is a truly awful situation to have to address not reading a paper in front of not only customers but me, the manager. At least fucking do your job when you know I'm watching or around. To Barb, the manager was sneaking around hoping to catch her! That asshole tricked me into reading the newspaper, while on the clock, in front of customers, and her boss.

Barb complains that a manager can sit down whenever they want. Let's get one thing straight that never dawned on Barb. Being a manager of people doing shit work is infinitely worse than doing the shit work. And there is no debate. Because at the end of the day when everything doesn't get done the manager has to stay and do it.

Barb continues about why workers do not want to be managers. "Whose teenage son cooks on the graveyard shift and who once managed a restaurant in Massachusetts but won't try out for management here because she prefers being a "common worker" and not "ordering people around." [19]

That's because it sucks.

Barb never thought about being a manager and none of the great people who worked with her wanted to be the manager. That's because it fucking sucks.

Earlier in the chapter, Barb waxed poetic about doing just the best job ever! Barb waxes poetic about how she's a hard worker and how she always tries to be the best! Ha! "If you're going to do something, do it well, In fact, 'well' isn't good enough by half. Do it better than anyone has ever done it before. Or so said my father, who must have known what he was talking about because he managed to pull himself, and us with him, up from the mile-deep copper mines of Butte to the leafy suburbs of the Northeast, ascending from boiler-makers to martinis before booze beat out ambition. As in most endeavors I have encountered in my life, 'doing it better than anyone' is not a reasonable goal. Still, when I wake up at 4 a.m. in my own cold sweat, I am not thinking about the writing deadlines I'm neglecting; I'm thinking of the table where I screwed up the order and one of the kids didn't get his kiddie meal until the rest of the family was done eating."[20]

---

[18] Barbara Ehrenreich, Nickel and Dimed (Picador: 2001), 23
[19] Barbara Ehrenreich, Nickel and Dimed (Picador: 2001), 36
[20] Barbara Ehrenreich, Nickel and Dimed (Picador: 2001), 18

Barb has this great work ethnic for the three weeks she works there. Then she leaves without giving notice.

"I leave. I don't walk out. I just leave. I don't finish my side work or pick my credit card tips, if any, at the cash register or of course, ask Joy's permission. To go."[21]

Barb doesn't just quit, but quits in the middle of her shift. Again this doesn't fuck over the corporate higher-ups, it fucks over everyone else she is working with her that day and in the next few weeks. So to recap, she set out to write a book about the ditch diggers of the world not getting their fair due and in the process she makes their lives worse.

At the end of the day Barb quits in the middle of her shift simply because she could. She could not recreate getting and doing shitty jobs, but she could recreate one important fact. Because at the end of the day Barb didn't do the job because she didn't HAVE to do the job.

---

[21] Barbara Ehrenreich, Nickel and Dimed (Picador: 2001), 48

CHAPTER 26
DEAR CUSTOMER

Dear customer fretting over a special cup of coffee,
In a class war I do not lead an army of machine gun toting wild men. I
lead an army of cold calculating snipers. Picking off only the deserving.

There are moments I love working at a coffee shop. The fall air allows us to leave the door open and the sounds of crisp leaves blowing by soothes me. I sit in the corner of the shop by the window and realize I'm in one of the nicest suburbs in the world and the first store of an amazing coffee franchise. People do love coming here and not just because they are addicted to caffeine. My staff is so friendly and so fun, even the crotchetiest of people melt.

Sometimes it feels like my coffee shop is the center of the world or at the bottom of a huge skyscraper in New York City. And of all of a sudden it's like I'm the star of a romantic comedy set at a coffee shop. The perfect song comes over the Muzak or radio and the contemplative mood continues. Maybe this isn't such a bad place and a bad job? Maybe I like it here. The people are fun and the job has become pretty manageable.

I stand in the empty coffee shop. The morning rush has ended on a busy Monday morning. The day's horror has ended and I should feel good. But I know tomorrow another rush will come. There is always another rush around the corner. When I know I should be cleaning and filling I just stand there staring out the window. A song plays in the Muzak and one of the reasons I play the radio normally is because Muzak has a lot of depressing songs. Depressing songs make you contemplate. Contemplation is a bad thing for a coffee shop employee. Put the last rush behind you. Put the customers out of your mind.

All around me are familiar faces
Worn out places, worn out faces
Bright and early for the daily races

Going nowhere, going nowhere
Their tears are filling up their glasses
No expression, no expression
Hide my head I wanna drown my sorrow
No tomorrow, no tomorrow

And I find it kind of funny
I find it kind of sad
The dreams in which I'm dying are the best I've ever had
I find it hard to tell you,
I find it hard to take
When people run in circles it's a very, very
Mad world, mad world

Determan comes up from downstairs and asks me if I'm all right?
"I don't know if I am." I'm crying. I dive into the endless tasks to make the day go by faster.

Determan is finishing wrapping the old bakery when a guy walks in. I listen from the back doing the dishes as the guy starts bullying around Determan.

"What do you have that you're throwing way?"
"We donate ours." The shark has found his prey.
"Well I'll buy it half off then."
"Yeah we don't do that." Determan tries to be polite. That is what he is trained to do and the sharks know it.
"Sure you do." What is he using "the force" on Determan? I don't like this guy. "What do you do with it then?"
"We give it to the homeless shelter."
"I'm homeless," he says. I wander in.
"If you're homeless than why did you just buy a $3 cup of coffee?" He doesn't answer.
"Fine, take something," I say. I remember why I hate this job. People. And then I remember why I love it too.
"Sir, because you're down on your luck let me get you a coffee to go on the house. A very special cup of coffee..."

I don't work for Caribou anymore, but I think about it every day. Every morning I think about Caribou when I make my coffee at home. I drop the filter in and dump my coffee in, sometimes spilling it over the edge. And I laugh because I have the same debate in my head as when I started at Caribou. Do I re-start this whole process to eliminate the chance of having grounds in the coffee? And just like then, I wipe off the grounds I can see. If you are going to wipe away coffee grounds then you already missed some. The coffee has grounds in it. I wince the wince I once winced daily with Kirsten.

At one of my local Caribous I giggle again as I watch a new greeter fumble with the coffee grounds. I watch him have the same internal debate I had, whether to re-do the whole process or not. And he diligently dumps it out, and starts over. And the line backs up! Poor guy. Another visit, the greeter is obviously new and cannot find anything on the register. The line backs up and she gets more nervous and in the weeds.

I think about my time at Caribou whenever friends and family complain to me their last Caribou visit was slow or awful. I don't know what to say. Make your own coffee? Don't go there? There is no easy answer for bad service, except that when you run across great service you should reward it. If your Caribou is great, and it usually starts with the manager, tip. Tell them they are doing great.

I wrote an entire book about not being a dick customer and then I find myself at a Caribou in the food court of a mall. They have four people there, two not doing anything, and a barista with no eyebrows. He makes my mocha and forgets the whipped cream and the chocolate-covered espresso bean. So he hands it to me and I remember being in his position and a customer complaining I forgot the whipped cream. *Do you fucking need whip, I raged inside! Who puts whipped cream on their coffee, I raged on more! I hated anyone who even liked whipped cream at that moment.*

And I stood there staring at the no-eye-browed barista, longingly wanting whipped cream. I crunch down on the chocolate-covered espresso bean and take a sip of the mocha, it would combine the chocolate, the whipped cream and the mocha in a glorious combination! Not today. I walked away without saying anything. Gisele teases me that someone could spit on my burger in front of me and I would say thank you, that I am too nice to everyone. But if they forget part of our order or are slow or just plain unengaged, I can't help but think I was there once. I give them the benefit of the doubt, I feel bad for them, I let it go. The job sucks, I tell her. Let it go. Be thankful. Be humble.

More likely than getting spit in my food I will probably be shot by some asshole, because I go well out of my way to say something to customers who are treating workers poorly. I find it effective to swear and point out what the person did to start the rush. "You fucking just ordered two things off menu. Give them a chance." I say it real quiet and real creepy. Their head whips around and then they ignore me, but are much more pleasant. It also helps that I'm 6'3". Or I'll just say, "Easy. They are doing the best they can."

Worse than getting shot, my protection of horrible customers may lead me to divorce. In some cosmic fucked-up irony, I fell in the love with just about the most annoying customer in the world! Gisele! This is the girl who asks what's in every Blizzard at Dairy Queen. Then orders the Chocolate Syrup Blizzard! "There is no Chocolate Syrup Blizzard!" I whisper yell. I whisper yell a lot when I'm out with Gisele.

"I'm so sorry," I say to the guy as the line backs up. This is the girl who asks the cashier if she can merge her rewards accounts on a busy Saturday afternoon. "No!" I say for the poor cashier. A manager has to do that and she is just being nice saying she can try. Now let's go because this line is backing up. This is the girl who asks for a receipt only at places that don't give out receipts. If they give out receipts she throws it away or says she doesn't want it. My head almost explodes. "Why do you need a receipt?" I want to keep track of my spending, she replies. We have fucking IPhones! You can look up your account on your phone! I'm whisper yelling this as the poor cashier has to go back into the register to print a receipt. And the line backs up.

She asks for three sweet and sour sauces at McDonalds with any order at the pick-up window, not at the order station. She also asks for chocolate ice cream and caramel, which are not on the sundae menu.

At the movie theatre Gisele asks for fresh popcorn and every cashier stares at us. "Uh, fresh popcorn?"

"Yeah, dump the popcorn and make new stuff." She says like everyone asks for it. The cashier slowly turns around and tries to comprehend starting the popcorn process over, instead of off and refilling it when it's empty when the alarm goes off.

Gisele continues to stare at the menu at the restaurant after everyone has ordered. I'm so sorry, I say to the waiter. Just pick something. She finally decides, "Oh I'll get a glass of wine too." And the whole process starts over. And the waiter's shoulders slump.

And she goes from zero to bitch when she feels she we are getting bad service. I want to whisper to the server, don't spit on mine. I'm so sorry, I say. She is an epic rush starter and I love her. It is my burden.

I think about the rush. Every time I drive by McDonalds at lunchtimes, I think "those poor bastards." Every Saturday I see the Starbucks and Caribou's line wrapping around outside the door. I feel the anxiety even though I will never have to work the rush again. I drive by Subway and shake my head. Idiots trying to pick 20 different options. I see the Chipotle constantly with a line and I can imagine what dickheads say to the predominately Latino workers. I think about the rush at the movie theatre, when a movie is huge that no one expected, and the theatre concession stand is overrun with only two people working. I want to dive and help them. I want to run to the front of the line and tell people to have their order and money ready. *That's what we can do to help, I want to scream!*

I think about the rush every time I park in front of a Caribou coffee shop. I think thank God I don't have to face the customers and the lines and the pressure. And then I think, but I could. And I would be great. And life is good.

My friend Dave says that all Americans should have to work service industry for two years after college. He believes this would help Americans see the other side. And I think there is something to that. And that is why I told this story. I wanted to give a voice to the other side, not just to coffee shop workers but all service industry workers. To let you see inside that world and how you can make that it a little better. Hopefully, with a few laughs along the way.

Dear customers who are nice, cordial, polite, and realize they not only affect their service but the people's service behind them, and who are normal, and empathetic, and good human beings,
I truly appreciate you.

Dear customer whose order we do not get right,
I have rung up over 2,000 people this week. I know what the fuck I'm doing. If the order is screwed up it's really most likely your fucking fault. You don't talk loud enough. You don't know what you really want. You order the wrong thing. You change your order too many times. You have a complicated order that doesn't make sense so it is always fucked up. You might think screwing up a drink is our fault. It's not. It's your fault. We are here to get you whatever the fuck you want! If you can't communicate that to us, then you are a fucking idiot.

Dear customer who doesn't do shit when another customer is off-the-chart rude,
I can't do something because I need this job. But feel free to speak up and defend us. In my time at Caribou I've met lots of shitty customers, but I've never met another customer who sticks up for us. I've never seen that even if they know the customer is being a dick. It gets very quiet. Don't get all quiet and enable the pricks. Do something. Help us! And if it's you: stop.

Dear customer who has his stuff spread out over a two-person table on a busy Saturday morning,
When I ask you to condense to one table so other guests can have a spot to sit don't be a dick about it! Don't ask me "Well what about those guys?" Like I was only fucking asking you! Is that what you fucking think? That out of this whole room I was just going to ask you to move your shit? Fucking of

course I'm going to ask them too but you happen to be the first one who is closest to me when I walked into the dining room. You fucking dick!

Dear fuckheads who steal from the tip jar,
    Come on! I'm okay with stealing from a faceless corporation and sticking it to the man, but a tip jar of simple coffee servers? Go fuck yourself.

Dear customer whose credit card is declined,
    I feel bad for you I really do. But I have rung up 500 credit card transactions today and this has only happened to this card. It's not the computer? I just tried it three times while we were talking. It's not working. We don't call the credit card company anymore because this isn't a romantic comedy or something from an 80's movie. I know this is embarrassing but you are causing yourself embarrassment. Either give me a new card or get some cash or get out. Those are our only options. Or I could give you a very special cup of coffee if you want to keep standing there.

Dear customer who complains you thought after handling cash I had to wash my hands before handling anything edible,
    If you are that big of a germaphobe you shouldn't be eating or drinking outside of your home. If you want to call the state and complain that I handle cash and then pour a cup of coffee, have fucking at it. If you literally think I can wash my hands for 20 seconds after each transaction you are a fucking idiot. I think I already knew that though and fyi, everyone behind you in line hates you right now.

Dear customer whose drink is made to Caribou specifications, but not your way,
    I have rung up over 2,000 people this week. I know what the fuck I'm doing. If the order is screwed up it's your fucking fault. You don't talk loud enough. You don't know what you really want. You order the wrong thing. You change your order too many times. You have a complicated order that doesn't make sense so it is always fucked up. You might think screwing up a drink is our fault. It's not. It's your fault. We are here to get you whatever the fuck you want! If you cant communicate that to us you are a fucking idiot.

Dear customer who worked in the service industry for 30 years,
    Yes, we screwed up your Caramel High Rise. I will make you another one in about 35 seconds. The employee that screwed up the Caramel High Rise is obviously new. Here is the thing though. I don't think you were a very good waitress if you are rude enough to make this big of a deal out of it. She is so obviously new and you pointing it out even more is plain rude. You had a first day somewhere down the line too. And I bet you screwed up too. You should

have some compassion. But you don't. So go away and quit quoting to everyone your service industry record. Why the fuck did you do it for so long? Are you upset and taking it out on us? Is this revenge for you on some dickhead customer? Because that is what you are.

Dear customer who browbeats Leslie for offering bakery,
    She's doing her job. If you want to browbeat me, go ahead, I'm higher up on the food chain. As you walk away mumbling to yourself I pity you and all sharks who search the world for people to prey upon with embarrassing and insulting rants. I have to hold myself back from calling you a pussy because you back down with your yellow streak showing. Go find more prey, hoping no one is around to tell you to shut the fuck up.

Dear customer who is super skinny, has huge fake tits, and is on the cell phone the whole time and won't tell me what she wants,
    I don't think your husband loves you.

Dear customer who just can't decide what they want,
    Get to the fucking end of the line! You may think you are being cute or adorable, but this is wasting everyone's time and backing up my line. Don't get pissed off when I ask you to step aside until you have decided. You had plenty of time to decide and at this point it's not about the menu. It's about you. And you are a dumbshit.

Dear customer who wants it extra hot then complains it's still not hot enough,
    I just shot it up to past the temp gauge for the 'I need it extra hot crowd.' If you are trying to embarrass us it worked. Good luck drinking that!

Dear two customers who start arguing because one of you was in the other's space,
    If I have to come from behind this counter you will both fucking regret it. I have a lot of pent-up rage. And if you think I'm kidding, try me. Because I would love it! (Channeling my inner George Costanzia.)

Dear unhappy but beautiful and well-dressed couple,
    You sit there in silence looking like fashion models. I feel so bad for you. Then a "birth advisor" shows up and now I feel worse.

Dear customer who is a bitch,
    Why do you act like this? Do you know you act like this? Being rude and saying your drink too fast or too quiet and then sighing audibly and changing the order. Why are you like this? I think you know you are a bitch. But why?

Dear customer who wants ice in their hot coffee,
   You do realize coffee cools down pretty quick? The coffee industry works on keeping coffee hotter for longer but you want it colder. Getting ice slows me down and you do realize the coffee will get cooler? Do you not realize it will get cooler very quickly or do you just like ice in your hot coffee? You drive me crazy!

Dear customer who calls his mom "Mother,"
   As in, "Mother would like her blueberry muffin warmed up." I feel bad for you. I have no oven. Oh put it in the microwave? Oh I'm a dumb shit! I didn't think to use the fucking microwave. You dumb fuck I don't have a microwave either. I feel bad for you and Mother. I really feel bad for your wife.

Dear customer who says they do not like to be looked at while they are making decisions,
   If only one of us could leave this spot and do something about that. Oh fucking wait, I have to stand here to take orders, but maybe you could decide somewhere else? You dumb fucking idiot!

Dear beautiful yuppie couple whose baby is crying and your response is to ask her if she wants Jamba Juice,
   My kid is 15 months and I'm glad he doesn't know what Jamba Juice is. Your kid is going to be really normal. By the way, all the employees and customers talk about how you two won't last as soon you leave.

Dear customer who complains it is so busy with a stern expression,
   Well it's great weather and we are near a lake, the most popular lake in the city, and it's Saturday and did you think it would be dead? Do you want me to kick people out? What do you want from me? Have you ever thought of going to a Caribou not near a summer hot spot so it wouldn't be busy? Do you think you should be the only one allowed here? As you stand here and stare at me waiting to come up with an answer to your annoying complaint, I have no easy answers.

Dear runners and bikers that come in on Saturday mornings all sweaty,
   The moist dollar bills you take out of your crotch areas are really gross. I'm not squeamish, but this is pushing the limits even for me. You are still wearing the spurs to attach to the bike, like a perverse cowboy with wet money. Wet money is not fun to touch.

Dear customer who gives me wet money,
      Why in the fuck is this money wet? You're dressed normally! I'm wincing and cringing on the inside touching this money.

Dear customers who come in and ask for a sample cup of coffee and are clearly not sampling it,
      You are kind of annoying. Once or twice is fine, but every other day is getting annoying. You are taking advantage of my customer service and the customer is always right vibe we have going here at Caribou. And I don't like it.

Dear customer who asks, "What is the wifi password?",
      There is no password. Oh it's not working you say? I see in the dining room I have about 60 people on laptops and iPads and no one seems to be having any trouble but you. You stare at me not comprehending the very simple words coming out of my mouth. Do you think I have a wifi password and am withholding it? Do you think I'm just being a dick? I can't read your mind and you are just staring at me. It's working for sixty other people but not for you, so it must be my fault?

Dear customer who name drops she went to USC every time I wait on her,
      You somehow bring back every trivia question or chalk thought back to USC, but here is the thing. NO ONE FUCKING CARES!

Dear customer who complains the bathroom is a little messy,
      Yeah a store that sells a natural laxative, go figure. How about I quit making drinks for everyone and go tidy it up? Think that would make everyone happy? I'll make your drink first after wiping up pee in that bathroom.

Dear customer who gives me "that look" when I walk out of the women's bathroom,
      First off the door locks so the men's and women's category isn't that big of a deal. Second of all I have like 14 seconds to go to the bathroom in the morning rush. So if the men's is locked I'm going quick! So don't give me any horseshit! At the end of the day me going to the bathroom in the women's room is keeping my speed of service fast and people happy. Don't ask me about washing my hands.

Dear yuppie couple,
      I see your North Face jacket, your huge watch, your Ray Ban sunglasses perfectly set on your $150 haircut. Don't worry, I see all that. I see the $250 pair of True Religion jeans from some fancy Uptown store I have never heard of. I see the perfect cuts and holes on those jeans. Don't worry, I see the gaudy

rings and bracelets and I see you parked across two spots in the front of the store with your bright yellow SUV. Don't worry I see all that. So you do not have to order a large "skinny" sugarfree vanilla with two-thirds of the vanilla, with a one-third shot of cinnamon and extra hot skim milk before the espresso shots are out in and then less hot milk on the top. And with two Splenda and mix in a little maple brown sugar from one of the oatmeal mixes. You don't have to order that because I saw all that other stuff. Be thankful and humble for what you have.

Dear obviously crazy or downtrodden people who are with friends who are obviously better off,
    When they offer to pay for your drink, don't feign hurt over this. Their life path took them to a different place than you. They did not drink so much or smoke so much or do so many drugs. Or maybe they got lucky and weren't crazy from the start. Crazy person....know what you want is all I ask and have your money ready. And don't argue over who is paying because it slows down my line.

Dear crazy lady,
    I know you are crazy because your lipstick is too bright and crooked. Your eye shadow is too blue and you are wearing too much blush. Your hair was dyed reddish by you at home and it didn't come out right. You are bundled up in clothes you think are fancy but are not. I know you are crazy and you know you are crazy. I'm not going to point it out to you, but do me a favor. Have money ready. And know what you want.

Dear ladies at the bank,
    You complain when I don't call in my change order. But when I do call the bank, no one answers. I understand it's busy. When I do reach someone I diligently give my change order. When I arrive at the bank you snarkily ask if I called in my change order? Yes! Yes I did. You then look to the other tellers, did anyone do a change order for Caribou? Which Caribou? Did you do a change order for any Caribou? No. No you fucking didn't do any change orders, so why the fuck are we playing the "which Caribou" game?

Dear two female customers who have met to catch up, but really don't know or like each other,
    This is so brutal to have to listen to. There is probably a reason you two haven't seen each other for months because you are both so narcissistic. You are killing me with this chitchat neither of you two is listening to while trying to brag about great everything is! Kill me!

Dear customer who ask what the minimum charge is to use a credit card,

No minimum and actually I prefer you use credit cards because getting change costs me time. You heard that right. I would prefer you pay with credit card, not cash. If it was up to me we would only accept credit cards, and I would have no cash in the building and everyone would get their coffee lickety split.

Dear customer who needs change for a hundred,

No. I don't have 10 tens and 5 fives for you. We are a fucking coffee shop. And banks are closed on Sunday so our fives and change are needed. Yes, I know you need change to buy something from someone on Craigslist. I'm not against that. I'm just against the change. I need it literally. Yeah, I understand that person from Craigslist is my customer but that doesn't really change anything.

Dear customer who runs into the shop sweaty wearing no shirt and tight little running shorts and demanding water,

Do we look like a fucking water shop? And us getting you water in front of our other guests because you just need a glass of water makes no fucking sense! What fucking planet are you from? And get some longer shorts you look like a pervert. And you don't need to say "I'll be back to get something later" because if you do you will be getting a very special cup of coffee. I'll have it ready for you, I say in my disgustingly nice tone.

Dear customer from Florida that complains our state is so worthless,

My doctor and my son's teacher can read. That's why we live here. Enjoy your special cup of coffee.

Dear woman who frantically comes in needing three canteens of iced coffee, but doesn't really understand what iced coffee is, and then wonders how it will stay cold, then demands 16 cups filled with ice, then is getting impatient and blurts out "it's for a abused woman's group!,"

Is volunteering for this group your penance for being such a bitch to everyone else? It's probably not enough if it is.

Dear customer who snidely remarks she never gets a lid on her Coffee Cooler,

First off I don't work every day. Second off, you don't come in every day and if you do it's probably at a regular time but since I don't work every hour of the day, so I don't know that you don't like a lid on but you are insinuating I should know. So you think I'm purposefully putting a lid on when you think I know I shouldn't? That's more work for me. So why would I do that? Are you *then saying I've waited on you so many times I should know and I'm just a dumbass, I think that's what you are getting at. What are you getting at?*

Dear customer who when I offer bakery says "no, I know how to bake,"
  You know how to make coffee too but you're buying stuff here. You are lucky there are rules to a very special cup of coffee.

Dear bitchy customer who says Caribou should have organic milk,
  I agree. Sure. That'd be great. I don't make the fucking decisions around here. I tell you to call the home office or email and let them know. "Well, you should tell them," you say. "Okay I will." Now you are turning into a bitch as you now ask the customer behind you if they buy organic milk. This is getting ugly. You are mad at people who don't buy organic milk? Well guess fucking what? We don't buy organic milk! So why the fuck are you bothering us. Go away. I'm not Mr. Caribou who runs the whole company!

Dear customer who orders five Joe-To-Go's without calling ahead,
  Do you think coffee magically appears out of the spout? I kind of used to think that. But it going to take about 30 minutes because I don't know if you noticed but you're not the only one here and you sitting at the closet table with your arms crossed and tapping your foot is not going to fucking make it happen faster. Thanks for not tipping too. You are a class act.

Dear customer who complains that the store is "not open late enough,"
  For you maybe, but for the rest of the world having a coffee shop open after 9 p.m., which is fucking late, seems ridiculous. There are millions of bars, restaurants movie theatres, book stores. Literally thousands of places to go. Now you say maybe I don't want your business? First off I have a family I want to see. Secondly, this is a business, you have been the only one here for two hours, and you bought one fucking cup of coffee! So no I don't want your fucking money.

Dear customer who works next door at the shoe store,
  You fucking made us remake your Americano three fucking times then took a coffee and didn't like that either. But seriously, remake your fucking drink three fucking times and you work next door at the shoe shop? Why? Why would you treat someone like this when you are in the same industry? Are you trying to get back at customers through us? You don't fuck with people who handle your food, especially when they know where you work. How about I come in and try 700 pairs of shoes! Justice! Instead, you will be rewarded with a very special coffee.

Dear customer who invites us to his acoustic guitar set Uptown and then is upset at us when we don't show up,
    We are not friends. Not real friends in the real sense of the word. I chitchat with you and ask about your day because it's my job. I don't mind doing that and it's an enjoyable part of my job, getting to interact with people. But please don't confuse me being friendly with us being friends. We are not friends. So don't get all bent out of shape because I didn't come to your show. It makes you seem weirder for inviting the people at the coffee shop to your show. Just remember this, we are like strippers. At the end of the day, we are doing this for the money.

Dear customer who leaves his $2,000 laptop unattended to smoke, pee or make a phone call,
    Don't. It is not my job to guard your stuff and to be honest I'm not even aware what is going on in the dining area. I'm totally focused on busting my ass getting drinks and you should probably realize this is not your home or office.

Dear customer who ask every time you get a fucking drink if you can tip when you pay by a credit card,
    Do you fucking think I don't remember you? Do you think you are being smart or cute? Here's the thing, I don't even fucking care if you give me a tip, but by fucking asking me when you know you can't is pissing me the fuck off.

Dear crazy but somehow rich woman,
    We know you order two large Americanos, one regular but with four shots for your husband, the other extra hot with four Splendas and a free shot of chocolate, because you bitch if we do charge you for it. Then you want a scoop of ice in a cup and cream all the way to the top. Then you taste both drinks right in front of us and bottle up the line. We know your husband died awhile ago and we know you keep ordering it. I will play this game with you because I feel bad for you.

Dear customer who name-drops locations he just got back from for the weekend like St. Johns and Jamaica,
    You seem really great, but you sit in this coffee shop by yourself every time I see you and you read the paper and then you stare out the window. It's sad and creepy. Did you take the vacation by yourself, is what I'm dying to ask! But I don't want to be fired. And are you name-dropping the fabulous vacation destinations to impress me? Because I'm the only one here paying attention. Is that what you're aiming for? To impress me? Because that's sad. I'm just the guy at the coffee shop.

Dear customer who complains there are no free newspapers,
 I don't know how to answer you. The newspaper industry is already in trouble and you want them to give away free newspapers? Oh, no, you want Caribou to give you a free newspaper? No. You can buy one for $1. Or you can go fuck yourself and quit holding up the line because you are complaining about no free newspapers. Get some balls and steal one!

Dear customers who are fooling around in the bathroom,
 Gross!

Dear customer who is "moving and in a hurry,"
 Oh because you're moving gives you the right to be an asshole? You're the only person in the world who is busy. Another bit of advice is write down what the people want who are helping you move, because you are obviously not smart enough to remember. And that's probably why you are continually late in your life and an asshole. Because you take no time to plan things out. I would give you a special cup of coffee but I don't want an innocent drinking my dried piss. Oh you are moving into the neighborhood? Fantastic. You'll have to stop by with your husband!

Dear customer who asks if anything in the bakery is $1,
 Nope. Now get the fuck out of the line because the price isn't changing and we don't haggle for goods in this country. Start walking and quite looking at your pathetic $1 bill. It isn't going to magically turn into a $5. Start fucking walking because the price isn't fucking changing. I would feel worse for you but who fucking walks around with $1? All you are doing now staring at your $1 is making the line get longer. But it's not magic, you're an idiot.

Dear kid who wants lemonade, but finds out it is $3.33 and not $1,
 Well it's not $1, so you can either buy it or get the fuck out of the line. It would probably be a good idea for you to pass on $3.33 glass of lemonade though.

Dear any guys hitting on any girls in my coffee shop,
 Oh you are both thinking of getting your own place? Oh you both might get a job too? You guys are creepy and these lines aren't working.

Dear any guy hitting on a female barista or greeter,
 The women at coffee shops are being nice to you because of the job. Please do not confuse that with any sordid intention on their part.

Dear local business person who wants to get their product in our store,
I understand your plight but this is not how it works. Caribou is a public company with a home office. I imagine you'd have to set up a meeting, make a presentation, and set up costs and distribution. Talking to the guy at the register on a busy Saturday morning is the exact opposite way to get your product in a Caribou. Oh it's healthy! By all means let's sell it right now! Yes I'm kidding you jack ass.

Dear customer who complains to me that a bottle of coke is $2.74,
If only they sold Coke somewhere besides this coffee shop. That's a million dollar idea!

Dear customer who orders seasonal drinks that are not in season or were on the menu like four years ago,
I don't know the exact recipe for the Ho Ho Mocha we had four years ago at Christmas. Caribou, in some crazy scheme to make money, adds drinks for different seasons and if they do not sell well they do not put them on the menu again. I do not have time to explain supply and demand to you.

Dear customer who starts shaking their head exaggeratedly NO! when I start to explain the survey,
You are really passionate about not wanting to hear about this survey. Either way it takes about four seconds for me to explain it. You could probably just take it and throw it away or say no thank you.

Dear customer who orders a French press which takes 10 minutes to make and then fills it full of sugar and cream,
I fucking hate you.

Dear customer who gets one Splenda in their latte, or a half of a Splenda,
You can only taste the difference in a small. Not a large. Does being difficult make you feel good?

Dear customer who asks if we price match Holiday gas station's free coffee of the day because they match ours,
Fucking gas station coffee? Are you fucking high? The oil change place gives free coffee, should we?

Dear customers who order like they are at Starbucks, then point to a picture of a cold mocha, than change the order to a hot mocha, then end up wanting a Turtle Mocha Cooler,

Jesus fucking Christ! Even Stephen is getting upset and he is fucking going to seminary school! Tell us what you want and we will make not for you. We serve about 300 people a day. We have screwed up on four drinks today all related to you and your fellow customer ordering like fucking fools. It's completely your fault, but what stings the most is you probably think I'm the fucking idiot.

Dear customer who wants me to explain what Five Hour Energy is and the difference between it and a cup of coffee and holds up the line getting agitated,
    I have no fucking clue. We don't sell it and why don't you get an 8 ball of coke if you need all this energy?

Dear customer who has only had a cappuccino at a gas station,
    That you just said this isn't like the cappuccino I get at the gas station is not a great way to start off with me and I'm no coffee snob dickhead asshole. But come fucking on! You think that the gas station cappuccino you dispense from a soda machine is anywhere near how it's supposed to be made? A chocolate cappuccino? If I were you I'd get the cappuccino at the gas station then because it's a hell of a lot cheaper and it's what you want. Everything tastes better with chocolate I agree. But Caribou does not put chocolate in a cappuccino unless requested by the customer. No, I don't think the chocolate cappuccino will become a standard thing.

Dear customer who orders Moosed Decaf Vanilla Latte,
    I don't get it. Why do you get decaf? Oh because you like the taste of espresso? Then why the fuck are you adding milk and vanilla? And why are you moosing it??? For decaf? More decaf doesn't make more flavor. You are making my head explode.

Dear customer who orders a decaf, vanilla white chocolate mocha with three Splendas,
    Why not get a good tasting decaf soda. This is all sugar anyways????

Dear customer who asks if I think Caribou is destroying local coffee shops,
    Well we are local, but yes. We do what everyone wants. Fast, consistent and friendly. Local shops are notorious being the exact fucking opposite of those three things were proud of it! And our prices are higher to boot. So yup. Leave the local coffee shops for the coffee snob dickhead assholes to go to, on no wait, they come here and bitch.

Dear customer who orders a Misto from Starbucks, but can't explain what is because his delicate genius is too busy,

It's a fucking coffee with a shot of espresso. Is it that hard to explain?

Dear customer who complains it's a oxymoron you can't smoke in a coffee shop,
    Again I'm the guy that made that decision! Are you a shut-in? Have you been in the biosphere experiment?

Dear customer who complains hot cups are not recyclable,
    Lady there are literally 100 people in this store and I am busting my ass. I realize you need attention and the world is dying a little bit with each cup. You have two choices. Bring your own mug, or get a house cup and shut the fuck up! I didn't invent the fucking cup! I'm not the guy who is planning on destroying the world!

Dear customer who worked as a barista at a coffee snob shop and made rose petals on top of the lattes and seems to be bragging about it,
    That you are here instead of at your shop is why I am right. Speed and caffeine. That's what people care about. Not rose petals on cappuccinos. And don't act like you're better than us. No, we are not hiring either.

Dear customer that complains we are no "Peete's Coffee" in California,
    Are you trying to hurt my feelings? Do you think I own Caribou? Do you think you are motivating me to make better coffee? What exactly is your goal here telling me we are no Peete's Coffee? Because you are coming off like a dick. Also, your dollar is a way to vote for what company you like best, so in a way you spending money here is voting for Caribou. If you love Peete's go to fucking Peete's.

Dear customer who orders a "trienta rod" shot of espresso and than laughs to himself when I don't know what one is,
    99 percent of all people who order straight espresso in any form are men, creepy, and have that Eastern European pedophile vibe going on. And your laugh to yourself is creeping everyone out. You're weird. Do you go into McDonald's and order a medium well-done burger and laugh that sick, desperate laugh?

Dear customer who orders a medium Americano iced in a large cup and then complains it's too watery. And complains every time you order it that it is too watery,
    Let's look at this. A medium Americano has four shots of espresso in a medium cup with ice. Now, you want those same shots but in a large cup which is four ounces bigger, hence four more ounces of ice and water. So

hence, more water. So hence, that would make it watery. I'm trying to explain this to you but you don't seem to get it, but come back almost every time and complain and we try to re-explain it. So yeah, you are dumb. The bigger question is how do you get up in the morning, get yourself together, pay your bills, drive, function in normal society when you are such a fucking dumb ass? God smiled upon you and you should be ridiculously grateful!

Dear customer who points to the exact piece of bakery they want,
That's annoying. Even more annoying then when you say you want something from the bakery and stare at the case while the line backs up.

Dear customer who enters in a cloud of weed smoke,
You are my favorite person to upsell bakery to! Cookies, brownies, muffins... I sell out the bakery because of you.

Dear creepy guy who insists on putting a shot of the "good stuff" in his coffee, and insists we have a bottle back there, so do it,
I don't have a bottle of Baileys. You might think you're being folksy or cute or part of the gang, part of the workaday life of the common man who needs alcohol to get through the day. You're creepy.

Dear customer who acts like they are in a terrible hurry when I offer bakery and then eats the fucking entire sample of Lemon Poppyseed Bread while my back is turned,
Your mother did a great job raising you.

Dear customer who orders Mango Iced Tea with hot skim milk,
Are you trying to make everyone throw up?

Dear customer who gets a Northern Light (less calories in the Caribou world) Vanilla Latte with six sugars,
Are you fucking high? You are adding sugar to skim milk and sugar free flavoring. Who puts your pants on in the morning? Who keeps the toaster away from your bathtub? Where is Darwinism when you need it?

Dear customer who angles for me to say I hate President Obama,
Yeah, yeah, yeah I hate Obama. Would you like a blueberry muffin with your coffee today?

Dear customer who angles for me to say I hate Governor Mitt Romney,
Yeah, yeah, yeah I hate Romney. Would you like a blueberry muffin with your coffee today?

Dear customer who angles for me to say I hate Hillary Clinton,
 Yeah, yeah, yeah I hate Hillary Clinton. Would you like a blueberry muffin with your coffee today?

Dear customer who angles for me to say I hate Sarah Palin,
 Actually, yeah she's a nut! Now how about that blueberry muffin?

Dear half cafe, cubano, iced latte, whole milk, and two splenda....and make that decaf,
 There is a lot wrong with this drink. First you are adding sugar with the Cubano, and then adding whole milk which has a few more calories. Then adding splenda?? That doesn't make any sense. Then now decaf? You are a waste of a human being!

Dear customer who complains we throw away the brewed coffee grounds instead of using them for gardening,
 How much do you want? Oh none? Oh so everyone else should make the effort except for you? Are you embarrassed for trying to embarrass us with your sustainable rant and then has your bluff called?

Dear customer who says I am the big man he is the small man I am the road warrior he is the man I am the true one and he is a small man,
 I appreciate your view, but I'm here to make money for my family. No poetic reason. You make me smile though, but I need your order. You're holding up the line.

Dear customer who complains there is not enough seating,
 Then don't come here. You knew we had five tables the second you walked in, so why are you complaining? Does it look we have room to add more?

Dear customer who complains there is not enough "comfy" seating,
 Then don't come here!

Dear customer who complains we don't have a couch,
 Then don't come here!

Dear tourist that gets dropped off at our area and expects there to be all this shit to do,

Why you came to visit the area is beyond me. This is a local neighborhood not a tourist area. Whoever dropped you off here to hang out for awhile should not be your friend anymore.

Dear customer who reads the newspaper headline and asks me what Obama Care means,
    "News interpretations from your local barista" is quite a headline. How are we on opposite sides of this equation?

Dear customer that complains about the high prices of iced coffee,
    I make the pricing structure so I'm the guy to complain to! You found me!

Dear old woman who waits until after the entire transaction and then asks for your 10-cent sustainability discount,
    It's kind of crazy in here right now at 9 a.m. on a Saturday. I stare at you hoping you will say forget about it. Because it's 10 fucking cents. I want to apologize because I am not a robot. I'm a human and I simply forgot to give your 10-cent discount because you have your own mug. I can't just pop open the register and give you your 10-cents. Do you want me to re-ring it, I ask in a tone that prays you say forget about it because the line is getting longer. You hold up the receipt and say, "you forgot my discount for having my own mug...again." I agree, I say. I'm not arguing. I forgot, I made a mistake. You stand there. I reach into my pocket and take out a dime and hand it to you after what seems like an eternity. You frown and say "it's only a dime." That's right.
    It's only a dime.

Dear customer who reads this book,
Read the book and pass it on.

THE END

ACKNOWLEDGMENTS

First, I want to apologize to my Grandma Jean and my Grandma Carol for swearing so much in the book. Sorry! Thank you to my dear friends Todd and Scott Lotzer (twins!) for valuable feedback and idea bouncing. (Really Todd more than Scott, but still.) Thank you to Erin Langley for hours of editing my shitty writing and excellent notes on when I took "it" too far. A special thank you to Annette Bertelson for being a genius and editing my book. Thanks to Christopher Moyer for making my cover come to life! Thanks Mom for always printing pages for me on such short notice. And thank you to my Grandpa who always encouraged me to "Give'em hell." I think I did on this one.

Coming soon from Sean William Brown...

WAL-MART:
I DON'T BELONG HERE

By

Sean William Brown

Read on for an excerpt from the prologue.

PROLOGUE

Sometime in September...

I get to the store around 7:30 a.m. and I am still sleepy. I'm looking forward to killing some time in the office with a nice lazy morning. I usually zone out until 9 am, when the off duty cop arrives. I walk into the office and Trevor already has something going on. Fuck.

"This guy took an entire peg hook of Boost Mobile phones. They are in his jacket."

This is the absolute last thing I want to deal with at 7:30 in the morning. I didn't put in my contacts yet, I'm wearing my glasses, I'm not really awake. Fuck, fuck, fuck. This is going to be trouble. I wait by the door for the roughly 5'10, wiry, 28 year-old American black male to exit. Some people are afraid of big guys, but not me. It's the small wiry ones that scare me. They will fight all day.

The shoplifter walks into the vestibule and I pop out from behind the doors. I doubt Trevor will help, the Police will not arrive for awhile, and no Wal-Mart employee is allowed to help. It's me against a drug fiending American black man. I hate my job and I really hate my life at this moment. Before I say anything to the guy I regret a lot of decisions in my life.

"Hey dude. I'm with Wal-Mart Security. Lets head back inside, no big deal." He starts veering away from me and I sigh. This is the last fucking thing I want to deal with at any hour of the day. I push him into the wall.

"Come on dude. It's too early for this shit. Cops are on the way, so no big thing."

Trevor arrives as I am tackling the guy into a row of carts. And...watches.

"Are you going to come in?" I growl to the guy. The guy tries to worm away and I again throw him into the carts. "Did you call the police?" I ask Trevor.

"They are on the way." He still is standing watching and not helping.

"Calm down and let's just go to the office!" I try to plead with the guy. "This is not worth fighting." I push him into the carts again. I just want to keep him inside the vestibule so he doesn't run away. We dance the dance of shoplifter and Security, which is not as cool as it looks on TV.

"Ok, Ok." He quits struggling, but I'm ready for anything.

"Go to that brown door." I point.

We head back to the office and I'm behind the guy, waiting for him to run or something. We get to the door and he turns around and puts up his fists like a boxer. He starts bobbing and weaving and I just stand there. I sigh. He punches me right in the face with his right hand! I didn't see stars or blackness, but I was caught off guard. I backed up and took a running start and tackled him into the door. Trevor just watched.

"People Greeter" Jeeka, an African man who I could hardly ever understand, ran over and helped me hold the shoplifter on the ground. Jeeka held his feet, than stood up and stomped on the guy's ankle.

"Jeeka stop that!" Trevor yelled. The shoplifter started screaming he had stomach pains and to leave him alone.

A group of associates and customers were watching, so I dragged the guy into the office. I threw him at the bench.

The Police arrived, of course, seconds after he settled down and we told them he punched me. They discovered the guy had warrants for his arrest and was a Gold Gloves boxer in North Carolina. They were charging him with a felony for hitting me because of his boxing background. Everyone else in the office was excited, but I don't know. The guy obviously has a drug problem and was stealing to get money for his habit.

Trevor pussed out and wouldn't help me. And everyone noticed. It's hard to give him crap thought because he once was stabbed by a shoplifter. He probably shouldn't be in Asset Protection anymore if he will not get involved with fighting and backing up his staff.

"Jeeka kicked that guy." Trevor says as we watch the video.

"He was helping me out."

"He should be coached."

He was helping me when you wouldn't, I wanted to say, but I think Trevor realized it.

I sit in the office after the whole thing. The adrenaline has worn off. After all shoplifter apprehensions I enter a contemplative mood. I looked at my shirt and saw the blood of a black man. I didn't know he was bleeding. Am I bleeding? Is this worth it?

And I decide I am officially done stopping American black people.

This job is not worth getting hurt. The shoplifters can hit and do whatever they want, they might have weapons, or needles, and I am just a person. We have rules telling us if we fight or hit we could be fired. We could lose our lives for shoplifting. I have never felt this way about shoplifters, but black Americans frighten me. Not Africans, not Asians, not Mexicans, not South Americans, and not white people, except for pedophile creepy white males. I feel ashamed for thinking this way. I hate where this has brought me. No one else is looking out for me, but me. I'm sick and tired of being sick and tired. I'm scared.

And so I stop.

CPSIA information can be obtained at www.ICGtesting.com
Printed in the USA
BVOW01s0859030816

457800BV00011B/18/P